INSIDE
NAZI GERMANY

INSIDE NAZI GERMANY

Conformity, Opposition, and Racism in Everyday Life

DETLEV J. K. PEUKERT

translated by Richard Deveson

Yale University Press
New Haven and London

Original German edition:
Volksgenossen und Gemeinschaftsfremde:
Anpassung, Ausmerze und Aufbegehren unter dem
Nationalsozialismus
© 1982 by Bund-Verlag GmbH, Cologne

Translated from the German by Richard Deveson © 1987.

First published in Great Britain 1987 by B. T. Batsford Ltd.
First published in the United States 1987 by Yale University Press.

Typeset by Tameside Filmsetting Ltd and printed in the United States of America.

Library of Congress catalog card number: 86-51431
International standard book number: 0-300-03863-1 (cloth)
0-300-04480-1 (pbk.)

10 9 8 7

Contents

Sources of illustrations

(Numerals refer to pages in the illustrations section)

Cover: *Berliner Illustrirte*, 13th April 1939. Sammlung Alte Synagoge, Essen.

1 Stadtbildstelle Essen.

2 'Resurrection', painting by Elk Eber. Cf. *Der Schulungsbrief*, published by Reichsorganisationsleiter der NSDAP, vol. 6, series 3, 1939.
Sammlung Alte Synagoge, Essen.

3 Staatsarchiv München, Bestand Oberkohle. I am grateful to Klaus Tenfelde for kindly making this picture available.
Stadtbildstelle Essen.

4 *Berliner Illustrirte*, no. 15, 13th April 1939, p. 583. Sammlung Alte Synagoge, Essen.
Stadtbildstelle Essen.
From *Deutschland dankt ihm*, illustrated on the plebiscite, 29th March 1936. Sammlung Schmidt, Essen.

5 From Elly Rosemeyer-Beinhorn, *Mein Mann, der Rennfahrer. Der Lebensweg Bernd Rosemeyers*, Deutscher Verlag, Berlin, 1938, pp. 8of.
Stadtbildstelle Essen.

6 Stadtbildstelle Essen.
Sammlung Alte Synagoge, Essen.
From *Hilf mit!*, schoolchildren's magazine, no. 3, December 1934. Bestand Wördehoff, Sammlung Schmidt, Essen.

7 From hans Roden, "*Polizei greift ein*". *Bilddokumente der Schutzpolizei*, Leipzig, 1934, p. 225. Sammlung Alte Synagoge, Essen.
Essener Allgemeine Zeitung, 1st June 1933. Sammlung Alte Synagoge, Essen.
Hauptstaatsarchiv Düsseldorf, RW 58, Bd. 12111.

8 Hauptstaatsarchiv Düsseldorf, RW 58, Bd. 12111.

(Middle and bottom) From 'Wir wollen eine gesunde Jugend', *Kampf der Gefahr*, vol. 5, no 5, May 1938, p. 19. Bestand Wördehoff, Sammlung Schmidt, Essen.

9 From *125 Krupp*, 20th November 1936, p. 95. Sammlung Schmidt, Essen.

Sammlung Schmidt, Essen.

10 From *Deutsche Jugendburg*, no. 6, March 1939. Bestand Wördehoff, Sammlung Schmidt, Essen.

Bestand Wördehoff, Sammlung Schmidt, Essen.

(Bottom) Stadtbildstelle Essen.

11 From 'Kriminalität und Gefährdung der Jugend. Lagebericht bis zum Stande vom 1. Januar 1941', compiled by Bannführer W. Knopp. Bundesarchiv Koblenz, NSD 43.

12 (Top left) Winter Relief design.

(Top right) From *Monatsblätter für Schadensverhütung*, vol. 5, no. 6, June 1938, p. 25. Bestand Wördehoff, Sammlung Schmidt, Essen.

(Below) From Elly Rosemeyer, op. cit. (note 5 above).

13 *Krupp-Zeitschrift*, vol. 31, no. 10, 15th February 1940. Sammlung Alte Synagoge, Essen.

From an exhibition by Borbeck *Gymnasium* on the history of the school, 1933–45. Sammlung Alte Synagoge, Essen.

14 Stadtbildstelle Essen.

Stadtbildstelle Essen.

15 From *Der Adler*, published in association with the Reich Ministry of Aviation, 26th May 1939. Sammlung Alte Synagoge, Essen.

Supplement to *Filmwelt*, no. 5, 3rd February 1939. Sammlung Alte Synagoge, Essen.

16 *Krupp-Zeitschrift*, vol. 29, no. 18, 15th June 1938.

Essener Allgemeine Zeitung, vol. 63, no. 95, 7th April 1938. Sammlung Alte Synagoge, Essen.

Der deutsche Heimstättensiedler, no. 11, November 1939. Bestand Wördehoff, Sammlung Schmidt, Essen.

17 Sammlung Schmidt, Essen.

Illustrierter Beobachter, supplement to the *Volkischer Beobachter*, 29th July 1944. Sammlung Thorsten Müller, Hamburg.

18 From Otto Helmut, *Volk in Gefahr. Der Geburtenschwund und seine Folgen für Deutschlands Zukunft*, 1934, p. 29. I am grateful to Gisela Bock for this reference: cf. Bock, 'Frauen und ihre Arbeit im Nationalsozialismus', in *Frauen in der Geschichte*, ed. Annette Kuhn and Gerhard Schneider, Düsseldorf, 1979, pp. 113–49.

19 From Dr. Jakob Graf, *Biologie für höhere Schulen*, vol. III for Class 5, 1943. Photo: Sammlung Schmidt, Essen.
Hif mit!, no. 5, February 1935. Bestand Wördehoff, Sammlung Schmidt, Essen.

20 From *Ewiges Deutschland. Monatsschrift für den deutschen Volksgenossen*, March 1937, p. 31. Bestand Wördehoff, Sammlung Schmidt, Essen. Stadtbildstelle Essen.

Abbreviations

ADGB	Allgemeiner Deutscher Gewerkschaftsbund; General German Trade Union Federation (Socialist)
BDM	Bund Deutscher Mädel; League of German Girls
DAF	Deutsche Arbeitsfront; German Labour Front
Gestapo	Geheime Staatspolizei; Secret State Police
HJ	Hitlerjugend; Hitler Youth
KdF	Kraft durch Freude; Strength through Joy
KPD	Kommunistische Partei Deutschlands; Communist Party of Germany
NSBO	Nationalsozialistische Betriebszellenorganisation; National Socialist Works Cells Organisation
NSDAP	Nationalsozialistische Deutsche Arbeiterpartei; National Socialist German Workers' Party (Nazi Party)
NSV	Nationalsozialistiche Volkswohlfahrt; National Socialist Public Welfare
RAD	Reichsarbeitsdienst; Reich Labour Service
RGO	Revolutionäre Gewerkschafts-Opposition; Revolutionary Trade Union Opposition (Communist)
RM	Reichsmark
SA	Sturmabteilungen; lit., Storm Sections, i.e. Storm Troopers
SAP	Sozialistische Arbeiterpartei; Socialist Workers' Party (left-wing splinter group of the Social Democrats).
SD	Sicherheitsdienst; Security Service (of the SS)
Sipo	Sicherheitspolizei; Security Police
SOPADE	Sozialdemokratische Partei Deutschlands im Exil; German Social Democratic Party in Exile
SPD	Sozialdemokratische Partei Deutschlands; Social Democratic Party of Germany
SS	Schutzstaffeln of the NSDAP; lit., Protective Echelons
WHW	Winterhilfswerk; Winter Relief Fund

Preface

This book is an experiment. I have tried to evaluate the wide and uneven range of historiographical information available on everyday life and everyday experience under National Socialism in Germany, and to present the most important findings in the literature. In the process, I also offer an interpretation of National Socialism: I argue that it was a symptom of the crisis of industrial class society in inter-war Germany, and that the pathologies and fractures of modernity were articulated in this crisis with particular force.

The impetus for venturing into two hazardous territories at once, the general survey and the systematic interpretation, was itself twofold. It sprang from the need I had felt, in the course of research and the professional debate within social history, to clarify my own position; and also from the experience of taking part in various projects in non-specialist historical and political education.[1]

It is because professional colleagues, school teachers and non-professionals alike have shown an interest in the problems of drawing general conclusions from the vast, centrifugal mass of information and opinion on everyday life in the Third Reich that I have been encouraged to write this book in contribution to the continuing debate.

The brief Introductory Note on research problems that follows this Preface serves to locate my essay within this wider context. Readers less interested in the specialist debate are advised to omit this section and start with Chapter 1, 'The history of everyday life – a different perspective'. When they have finished the book, they may wish to return to the Introductory Note, armed with more factual information and able to read it with more profit.

This is not a full social history of the Third Reich. The state of current research is not sufficiently advanced to make such a book possible. My purpose has been to provide information, documentation and raw material, and in some places to propose hypotheses, in the hope of contributing towards a better understanding of the era in which my parents and grandparents and their generations lived. I have tried to address myself both to professional colleagues and to teachers in schools and adult education, while also meeting the needs of the interested layman.

I have included a fairly large number of illustrative quotations from contemporary sources and from memoirs of the period. One important reason for this is to convey an impression of the language and styles of thought of the time, which is essential if we are to gain a deeper understanding of as subjective a dimension of history as the quality of personal experience. In addition, the linguistic character of a primary source is often a clearer guide to its real content and slant than the bare information-content alone.

The same criteria have applied to the choice of illustrations, which complement the central points made in the text.[2] The notes[3] and bibliography have deliberately been kept brief, so that they can be of use to the non-specialist. The bibliography is intended primarily as a source of suggestions for further reading.

The present English translation contains certain additions and alterations made by the author. The notes, in particular, have been altered to incorporate information concerning English versions of German publications as well as details of some works published since this book first appeared in German.

I should like to thank all those who have been so patient with me or have gone to such trouble to help me: especially Amir Lewin, who bore with me during the period while the manuscript was in preparation; Michael Winter, who gave me all manner of organisational support; and Frau Feldmann, who converted the manuscript into a legible text. Among the many colleagues whose work and advice have assisted me, I should particularly like to offer my thanks to Dirk Blasius, Ulrich Herbert, Lutz Niethammer, Ernst Schmidt and Michael Zimmermann.

Many of the issues in this book became clarified in the course of discussions surrounding the planning of the Essen research project, 'Lebensgeschichte und Sozialkultur im Ruhrgebiet 1930–1960', and also in joint editorial work with Jürgen Reulecke and Adelheid Gräfin zu Castell Rüdenhausen on our collection, *Die Reihen fast geschlossen. Beiträge zur Geschichte des Alltags unterm Nationalsozialismus*, which was published in 1981. My thanks to them and to the authors concerned.

I am also extremely grateful to all the directors and staffs of archives and owners of private collections who have put textual and pictorial sources at my disposal; to the Stadtbildstelle Essen, which in addition has been most unbureaucratic in helping me with the reproduction of illustrations; and to colleagues at the publishers and printers.

In the course of friendly discussions during the preparation of this English edition, Ian Kershaw of Manchester University and Dick Geary of Lancaster University offered many suggestions and criticisms which enabled me to clarify my position. It is a pleasure to thank them for all their help.

I owe a particular debt of gratitude to Richard Bessel of the Open University. Richard has followed the progress of this book over many years in tireless discussions. The fact that our views have spontaneously coincided on so many points has made me all the more ready to take note of his critical suggestions as well as of his own contributions to the scholarly debate. In addition, Richard has gone to the enormous trouble of closely reading through the present translation in typescript and offering comments on it. His help has extended far beyond what might have been requested even from a good friend. I should like to thank him, above all others, for the fact that this edition has been made possible.

I should also like to offer warm thanks to the translator, Richard Deveson, who, to the best of my foreigner's judgement, has been outstandingly faithful to my German text, and to Tony Seward at Batsford for his help, care and commitment.

I must ask my readers for both forbearance and criticism. I shall welcome comments and suggestions for further collaborative discussion of the hypotheses put forward here. Simply write to me, either via the publisher or via Universität Essen, Fachbereich 1, Geschichte, 4300 Essen, Federal Republic of Germany.

Detlev J. K. Peukert

Translator's acknowledgements

I am greatly indebted to Clare Deveson for all her help; also to Richard Bessel, for answering many queries; and to Tony Seward.

Richard Deveson

Introductory note: research problems

Two decades have passed since the publication of David Schoenbaum's book[1] on the social history of the Third Reich, which followed an approach based on the experiences of everyday life. During this time numerous individual studies have appeared and, concurrently, an intense general debate has taken place as to how the history of National Socialist Germany and European fascism should be assessed and categorized. A new venture at summary and interpretation therefore seems warranted, taking into account the state of research as it has evolved during this period.

In a sense, however, such a project is out of line with current trends in research: the era of grand designs and theoretical debates on the epoch of fascism seems to be past. It is true that disagreements between 'intentionalists' and 'functionalists', or advocates of the 'primacy of economics' and the 'primacy of politics', and debates about the 'mass basis' of fascism or the role of 'monopoly capital', still flare up from time to time,[2] but these debates have become increasingly imprecise and inconclusive as the adherents of the different schools have become more deeply immersed in regional and thematic case studies. The density of material and the complexity of the raw data have led to such an emphasis on qualifications, contradictions and ambiguities that a comprehensive and consistent interpretation has become very difficult to achieve.

This general tendency within research into fascism – the gradual disappearance of the broader outline, as the object itself is approached ever more closely – is most strikingly apparent in studies in the history of everyday life, where the focus is expressly local and specific: namely, 'ordinary people'. Here, not only do theoretical and methodological certainties become blurred as research closes in, but so too, in the process of the interpretative and explanatory reconstruction of the daily experiences and behaviour of individuals, do clear moral criteria. The stereotypes of the utterly evil fascist and the wholly good anti-fascist dissolve. The historian's sense of concern at the fates of individuals deepens his understanding of people's predicaments and his insight into the reasons for cowardice and dubious compromises. Black and white becomes grey on grey. The everyday lives of simple 'ordinary people' turn out to be far from simple and ordinary. If, then, we want to avoid getting lost in pointillism and miniaturism, an approach based on everyday life must have a clear grasp of the complexity of the structures of people's lives; it must be concerned with analytical goals; and it must show an awareness of problems, and a moral outlook, that transcend the concerns of the everyday life from which it itself springs.

Researchers into fascism and National Socialism belonging to the most widely varying schools of thought will, I think, agree with me that at present none of these three basic requirements can be met. This should be no cause for discouragement, however; especially since there are hints from very differing quarters of a convergence towards this view of the problems as I have stated it. But it would be quite presumptuous to claim that the present attempt to summarise and review the research, and to work towards a possible interpretation of the National Socialist experience as a pathology of modernity, can be anything other than an interim assessment.

If, beyond this, I can give some further impetus to the continuing debate, then this book will have fulfilled its purpose.

It seems, as a matter of fact, that there are tendencies within the wider current debate which indicate that the fascist phenomenon should be incorporated within a critical history of modernity. Thus the discussion about a 'special German path of development' ('*Deutscher Sonderweg*'), which supposedly led to the national catastrophes of 1914–18 and 1933–45, has, though inconclusive, sharpened our awareness of the fact that many non-democratic tendencies in Germany did not so much go back to a persisting reactionary tradition as arise quite functionally out of the structures and problems of modern civilisation.[3] This revisionist re-assessment of tradition and modernity in Germany, based on the nineteenth-century past and applied to the first half of the twentieth century, confronts a somewhat older revisionist modernisation theory in which the same period is viewed in terms of the contemporary concerns of the 1950s and 1960s. Schoenbaum and Dahrendorf, in particular,[4] have said that Germany's breakthrough into the manifestly 'modern' era of the *Wirtschaftswunder* must be credited to the intended, and more especially the unintended, radical changes brought about by the Third Reich.

Both approaches, the revision of the '*Sonderweg*' theory and the thesis of the inadvertent push towards modernisation, redeem German history from the peculiar odium that a horrified world has ascribed to it

15

– and which the world has been right to do, morally speaking if not for purposes of analysis. But, by incorporating German history into the 'normal' pattern of development of modern societies, these approaches do not answer the vital question: what were the roots from which the appalling barbarism and mass criminality of National Socialism in fact sprang, if German society was, by assumption, really quite 'normal', either until 1914 (on one theory) or (on the other) after 1945? The dilemma faced by these two conflicting interpretative strategies could be resolved if the implicit coupling, in both theories, of modernity with progress, of social, economic and technological advance with increasing humanisation and emancipation, could be broken or at least critically questioned. If normality and modernity in a society, and fascist barbarism, can be so closely linked in two differing historical accounts, are we not forced to raise questions about the pathologies and seismic fractures within modernity itself, and about the implicit destructive tendencies of industrial class society, which National Socialism made explicit and which it elevated into mass destruction?

This sceptical de-coupling of modernity and progress, given the fact of National Socialism, is supported by a wide variety of debates that have gone on within the social sciences, using such notions as social disciplining (Foucault), the pathological consequences of the civilising process (Elias) or the colonialisation of *Lebenswelten* (Habermas).[5] The debates have not gone nearly far enough towards achieving the sort of theoretical grounding of historical research as historical social science that might provide conclusive support for either of the approaches we have mentioned. In addition, the relationship between the theoretical interpretation and the reconstruction of source-based data is a much more fragile and delicate matter in history than it is in the systematically orientated social sciences. But if historians are not to be led by such reservations to disavow all interpretation and stick unambitiously to non-conceptualised detail, then they should not withdraw from the challenges posed by these debates. And this is especially important since the debates all attempt, within the logic of their own specialist discourse, to examine problems and worries similar to those that confront us as historians when we seek to understand the experience of National Socialism in everyday life[6] in terms of the social experiences, pointing both forwards and backwards in time, of the people involved.

The 'experience of National Socialism', here, involves two dimensions which are distinct but which are linked within historiographical discourse. These are the perceptions and modes of behaviour of contemporaries during the 1930s and 1940s;[7] and our present-day assessment of the results of those people's actions and of the evidence as to how they viewed, and view, those years. These two dimensions must be separated for purposes of scholarly analysis, but not completely so. To separate them completely would be to deny one's own sense of concern and involvement, and would also leave obscure the fact that our questions about Germany's past are prompted by our experience of Germany's present.

Since history in its true sense is a twofold dialogue, a hermeneutic engagement with the testimony of the past and a public discourse in the present, each generation confronts history in a new way and writes history in a new way. For the older generation, all attempts to diminish Germany's specific responsibility for National Socialist barbarism had the unpleasant odour of self-exculpation. For the younger generation, however, undeniably born after it was all over, the position is exactly the reverse: dwelling accusingly on a specifically German set of preconditions for fascism – conditions which have meanwhile reassuringly vanished into the past – appears a particularly easy way of evading the question of the individual's own sense of involvement and concern and of its significance for his own behaviour. Not even the highly committed socio-critical discussions of fascism that arose out of the student movement of the 1960s were without this different whiff of self-exculpation. Arguments raged as to whether the reactionary middle class or reactionary big business was more responsible for National Socialism; it was easy to dissociate oneself from each.

A responsible survey of fascism, therefore, must also acknowledge the confrontations of the present day; it must enquire into the problems which the emergence of our own modernity has opened up, and must be sensitive to the rifts and disquiets within it; and, in the light of the experience of what happened to our parents and grandparents – what need not, though, have happened – it must take account of the moral and political challenges facing us in our own individual lives.

This survey of people's experiences and lives between 1933 and 1945 will, it is hoped, contribute to these ends.

'Everyday life' under a state of emergency

ONE

The history of everyday life – a different perspective

The screening in 1978 of the film *Holocaust*, which showed the National Socialist persecution of the Jews in the personalised form of the history of a family, affected the feelings of large numbers of television viewers in Germany who had been left unmoved by the meticulous historical documentation and analysis that were already available. Since then, however, there has been a growing interest, on the part both of the public and of those engaged in research, in viewing the Third Reich from the perspective of everyday life and everyday experience. The hope is that the reality of Nazi terror, difficult to grasp in terms of abstract statistics, can be felt and understood more immediately by means of concrete description and reconstruction.[1]

But can we, and should we, actually speak about 'everyday life' in an era which, for the victims of persecution and war, meant a perpetual state of emergency? In face of the monstrousness of the crimes of National Socialism, should we not stay silent about the banal everyday routines of the majority who did not feel that they were affected or involved? Does our interest in everyday life not connive with the defence mechanisms operated by so many members of the older generation in Germany, who prefer to remember their schooldays rather than the anti-Jewish pogroms of the *Reichskristallnacht*, prefer indeed to remember soldiering between Norway and Tripoli rather than the cattle trucks which left all the railway stations of the Reich for Theresienstadt and Auschwitz?

There can be no doubt that the term 'everyday life' may seem to be an invitation to obscure what was specific about the exceptional regime of the Nazis, to make the dividing lines between supporters and opponents of the Nazi system harder to draw, and thus to dissolve clear value-judgements into a relativistic 'On the one hand, on the other'. Nevertheless, a history of the Third Reich written from the perspective of everyday life also provides a critical, anti-fascist historiography with opportunities. Such an approach, by concerning itself with the contradictory and complex experiences of 'ordinary people', makes it possible:

1. To understand more precisely how 'Auschwitz' – that is, Nazi racialism and terror – was possible, why it was tolerated and, indeed, in part endorsed.

2. To determine where resistance was actually possible, and where and how it was offered by people who, unlike the military conspirators of 20 July 1944, did not have the advantage of access to the levers of power.

3. To find out what were the sources of the regime's support, and what were the attitudes and expectations in everyday life that fastened on to the Führer's apparent successes.

4. To ascertain how it was that there was a growing readiness to criticise the regime, and in part to engage in conflict with its representatives or with aspects of its policies, and how, although this criticism did not swell into a full-scale opposition movement, it was not suffocated, either, by the Nazis' much-vaunted 'national community' (*Volksgemeinschaft*).

5. To ask to what extent the general lines of development of industrial society that were apparent in everyday life continued during the Third Reich, which of them coincided with the regime's ambitions and which collided with them, and thus to locate the Third Reich more precisely within German social history than can be done following the very generalised explanatory approaches (cf. p. 15 above) of the '*Deutscher Sonderweg*' or the thesis of inadvertent modernisation.

6. To assemble data and contexts of experience in order to understand better a generation which it would be unjust (and unhelpful for learning lessons for the future) to condemn globally – even though this generation was undoubtedly implicated in guilt, either through participation or, at least, through failure to offer resistance.

A final important argument in favour of a history of everyday life in the Third Reich comes from those involved in schooling and political education. It is now more than forty years since the end of the war, and a majority of the population of the Federal Republic of Germany has no direct personal memory of the era before 1945. Indeed, today's schoolchildren have to go to their grandparents if they want to hear first-hand accounts of life in the Third Reich. This lack of personal experience makes for both advantages and disadvantages in the teaching of history. The teacher comes up against fewer defence mechanisms (which for a long time have been a crucial block to the discussion of the Third Reich in Germany); but there is also less sense of concern and involvement, since for contemporary students the Third Reich is almost as remote as the empire of the Kaisers or the French Revolution. If, therefore, education about the Third Reich is to be more than a transmission of mere factual knowledge, and is to awaken a sense of involvement and hence a commitment to democracy, it is necessary to reconstruct the relevant realms of experience historically and to illuminate the experience through teaching.

This kind of search for everyday experience in German contemporary history can make use, first, of the reminiscences of the grandparental generation: through interviews, analysis of already available memoirs, and gathering together photograph albums, letters and diaries. A further procedure is to trace the outlines of the history of National Socialism in one's own area and the attitudes and behaviour of the population as these are reflected in local sources. Such sources include newspapers, documents in town and city archives, personal documents of local citizens, as well as locally relevant documents held in larger regional archive collections. Last but not least, one can ask how the mode of life of the individual was actually moulded by the demands made by the Nazi authorities: what the impact of the Third Reich was on leisure activities such as reading and sport, school and professional careers, means of communication, and so on. In recent years many people in Germany – professional historians, laypeople, schoolchildren and students – have become involved in local research of this sort. There have been large numbers of publications, seminars and exhibitions on everyday life and local history in the 1930s and 1940s.

How, though, does an approach based on everyday life differ from other types of account of the Nazi era? For a long time the dominant approaches to both the theory[2] and the classroom teaching[3] of the history of National Socialism were based either on the theory of fascism or on the theory of totalitarianism.

Although these two approaches differed on matters of interpretation, they none the less had a common subject area: they both dealt with the political system of authority, the wielders of power and the mechanisms of suppression, and they largely ignored the experience of those affected by the system, namely the mass of the population. This was even more true of approaches which concentrated on National Socialist ideology: these were concerned mainly with the mental world of the leading Nazis, especially Hitler, rather than with the question of how far 'ordinary people' were actually influenced by them, merely put up with them or opposed them. Each of these approaches has its merits and gives a partial insight into National Socialism. None of them can therefore be entirely supplanted by an approach based on everyday life. What new and extra contribution, then, can be made by this latter way of looking at the problem? Above all, it provides a different angle of vision. It looks at the Nazi system 'from below' and asks: what was life like in the Third Reich? What were the experiences of the victims, participants and

23

bystanders in face of the National Socialist challenge? What attitudes grew out of these experiences? What forms of behaviour were possible within this framework, and which of these forms of behaviour were actually selected?[4]

Such questions certainly admit of no speedy answers. The history of everyday life is only rarely reflected in the large-scale historical accounts.[5] The social history of the Third Reich was a rank and tangled undergrowth of Nazi projects of reorganisation which never got put into practice, rivalries and jurisdictional wrangles between different state, semi-state and non-state organisations, Schweikian stratagems by the oppressed directed against the overweening demands of the bureaucracy, individual and collective acts of freebooting enterprise and clamours for privileges, if necessary at the expense of others, and deliberate self-sacrificing resistance. The many-faceted nature of everyday life in the Third Reich makes the task of marshalling the data difficult; but it also offers the possibility of a differentiated account, one that records both the huge pressure exerted by the system and the by no means negligible areas in which nonconformist behaviour could and did evolve.

To take an example: all accounts of the Nazi seizure of power include grim pictures of the burnings of books. We learn that libraries were 'purged' of books by Jewish, humanist, Marxist and foreign authors. What we generally do not learn is the effect of these 'purges' on the leisure activity of reading during the subsequent twelve years. A poster from an exhibition by the Essen City Library in 1937, however, helps to illustrate what cultural barbarism meant in daily life (see Plate 1). The document hails the one-third decrease in book borrowings within four years as a 'healthy recovery – decline in indiscriminate reading'. And reasons for the decline in reading are given which depict graphically how the regime's demands narrowed down the individual's area of freedom: the 'return to employment, political activity for nation and state, Labour Service (*Arbeitsdienst*) duty, military service'.

At the same time, however, this example shows that it is off the mark to see the educational basis of the everyday-life approach as akin to that underlying traditional school teaching and local history, i.e. to the commonly-voiced ideas that everyday life and the local region are 'close to hand', appropriate to the 'simpler mind' and immediately 'accessible'. If we want to analyse the causes of the curtailment of reading in the Third Reich, we have to find out all about rearmament and job creation, the obligation to take part in 'voluntary' parades and Party functions, voluntary and compulsory Labour Service duty, and the reintroduction of general military service. Above all, we have to establish how general was the phenomenon sketched out here in terms of a local example from Essen. Merely inspecting everyday life, in other words, does not clarify matters on its own; it leads the historian into the realms of social and economic history, educational history and cultural history.[6] The everyday-life approach does not open up a subject area different from those of the established historical disciplines: it provides a new perspective on existing areas.

A second caveat must also be stated. Not all everyday experience has a bearing on National Socialism. Cooking recipes, tastes in interior decoration, marriage rituals and funeral customs are as a rule longer-lasting than political systems and are subject to different rhythms of change, though they can certainly take on a political colouring in given ways. This is illustrated by obituary announcements. The customary texts of death notices, with their religious references and their formulae for family grief or unexpected blows of fate, remain independent of the prevailing political system. Yet notices for war victims during the Third Reich do give hints concerning attitudes towards the regime: an emphasis on 'a hero's death for Führer, people and fatherland'; a search for consolation couched in religious terms; an unadorned expression of loss and mourning.

The life stories of 'contemporary witnesses' may highlight events and turning-points quite other than the years 1933 or 1945.[7] Given, then, that we cannot deal with everyday life in the broadest possible sense, but only with everyday life with reference to the Third Reich, we must ask: in what ways was everyday life political? What may the very clinging to the non-political aspects of everyday life have had to do with the experience of National Socialism? This way of posing the problem marks out fields of enquiry that include the interaction between the Nazi system and the people, and the shaping of mature life-styles by the demands of the system; but it also involves, operating in the other direction, the impact that was made on the Nazi movement by prevailing attitudes, expectations and forms of behaviour and, especially, the demarcation of the different spheres of the state, organisational machinery, local, religious or social sub-cultures, families and individuals. A perspective centred on everyday life must not get tangled up in all these contrasts and interconnections, but must find clear routes through them. It will then be possible to establish how people lived during the Third Reich, how they evaded or fell in with the regime's demands, and where they positioned themselves along the spectrum between the sidelines and the firing lines.

TWO

The rise of National Socialism and the crisis of industrial class society

Everyday life in the Third Reich was preceded by everyday life during the years of the great crisis that deeply permeated German experience and crucially affected German attitudes and expectations concerning National Socialism. We must therefore deal briefly with these years of crisis before 1933. Although we cannot give even an outline account of the period here,[1] we can highlight some of the aspects of the social, political and economic crisis that were the point of departure for the rise of National Socialism. The crisis was much more than just a particularly deep economic depression. It involved the mutual effects of the collapse of the Weimar political system, already foreshadowed during the economically successful 'Golden Twenties', the second massive economic convulsion within a decade (the first being the inflation that reached its culmination in 1922–23) and an upheaval in traditional social values and attitudes that went back to the fall of the imperial monarchy. Separately, each of these challenges might have been withstood. Indeed, several were dealt with, remarkably effectively, by the governments of the Weimar Republic that were later so often despised. For example, the reparation payments imposed on Germany by the 1919 Versailles Peace Treaty were ended in 1932, even though Hitler was to claim the credit for this himself. The Republic collapsed only when all these crisis phenomena occurred together and gave rise to a widespread sense that an era was at an end. There was a feeling in all political camps and social strata that things could not, and should not, carry on as before; that the meagre prospects for progress, or even simple subsistence, at the level of the individual went hand in hand with an international situation that was intractable, a lacklustre domestic political system that was not worth defending, and a general social decline that was variously interpreted as the break-up of capitalism, the disintegration of traditional values or the 'Decline of the West'.

We should not gloss over the differences in moral and political views which in 1933 were to bring some groups to power and send others into concentration camps; what is relevant, however, is this widespread attitude within everyday life in the early 1930s, over and beyond the political explanations that were offered. Deep though the disagreements about the causes and solutions of the crisis were, there was broad consensus on the level of everyday life that matters could not continue as they had done hitherto.

The debates which the parties of the Republic conducted concerning solutions to the crisis, and the differing views prevalent in Social Democratic, left-wing socialist and Communist circles, cannot be retraced here. But although these debates were overtaken, historically speaking, by the National Socialist seizure of power, they remain significant as an indicator that the barbarism of the Nazis was not an inescapable development. Many members of the labour movement were certain that once the immediate crisis and the intensified political battles were over, a socialist transformation of the Republic would inevitably take place. This view, however, was not capable of attracting a majority of votes (the working class parties remained holed up in their 30 per cent stronghold from 1918 until the last free election in March 1933), nor could the divided labour movement even come close to agreeing to set aside its philosophical and tactical differences for the sake of a common defence against the fascist threat.

The Nazi movement, on the other hand, succeeded in assuming power even though it likewise never obtained a majority in free elections and in no sense offered a seriously worked-out political programme. Hitler, however, was able in 1933 to convert these very weaknesses into strengths. The fact that the National Socialist movement had got bogged down at about 40 per cent of the vote, after making sensational advances between 1930 and the spring of 1932 – and indeed lost votes heavily in the Reichstag elections of November 1932 – ultimately made it seem a respectable alliance partner for the old power elites in business, public administration and the military, which until then had been sceptical about their ability to control the Nazi mass movement.[2]

The fact that the NSDAP had no firm, consistent political programme enabled it all the more easily to entice a wide range of groups in the population with a variety of promises, so long as it could conjure up the prospect that, once armed with the dignity of power and the instruments of propaganda, it would effect a fundamental break with the old Weimar 'system' and a general national 'awakening'.

Pawn of industry or independent movement?

The astonishing fact that the National Socialist dictatorship was established in the space of a few months in 1933, with political institutions being turned upside down, all democratic opposition destroyed, and a labour movement whose supporters numbered millions driven underground, led to the devising of legends even as it happened. While conservatives pointed to the masses who supported the Nazis (thereby neglecting the greater numbers who had not voted National Socialist), many observers on the left concentrated on the villainies of 'capital', which had 'handed over' power to Hitler.

The series of definitions of fascism issued by the Comintern depict the phenomenon as merely a particular form or method of capitalist domination. On its formulation there is both an objective and a subjective correlation between the aims and behaviour of capitalists (in the narrower Leninist theory of imperialism, monopoly capitalists) and the activities of fascist movements and fascist state leaderships.[3] Monopoly capital, on this view, had been deliberately steering, from 1918 onwards, towards dictatorship and revanchist war. It might swap horses now and then, but fascism was where it was always heading. From 1930 at the latest it had cultivated the NSDAP as the instrument of control in a future fascist dictatorship; and with the system of state-monopolistic regulation that was installed in 1933, it got its hands on the levers of power. The relationship between the National Socialist movement and the interests of capital is seen here as a dialectic of 'appearance and reality', of 'class character' versus the 'mass basis', with monopoly-capitalistic class content clearly paramount.

This account cannot give a convincing interpretation of the actual relationship between industry and the NSDAP between 1928 and 1933,[4] nor does it provide a satisfactory definition of the power structure of the Third Reich. The classic Comintern definition is simply tautological. How do we determine which capital groupings are dominant, or 'most imperialistic' – bearing in mind that, at different times within the selfsame fascist system, it may be either coal and steel or (after 1936) chemicals and electricity that are allegedly dominant, on the orthodox Marxist analysis? Answer: by their degree of proximity to fascist state power. Therefore: fascism equals domination by the fascist monopolies; and those monopolies are fascist which are, precisely, dominant. This condensed economistic version of Marxist theory was a source of as much confusion during the Comintern period itself as it is now, since it made it possible before 1933 to underestimate the growing strength of the National Socialist mass movement. The Comintern definition, incidentally, cannot easily be cited as having played a part in the origination of the Communist Popular Front strategy either,[5] since in December 1933 it was invoked by the executive committee of the Comintern to confirm the ultra-left line against the main enemy, 'social fascism', besides being used later by Dimitrov in August 1935 when the

Popular Front was being set up on a 'scientific' basis. The fact is that economism and political eclecticism coexisted within the Comintern.

These contradictions have been pointed out by Marxist theorists of fascism in the tradition of August Thalheimer (the former right-wing leader of the German Communists).[6] These theorists emphasise the relative disjunction between the fascist movement and state institutions and assert that fascism was a genuinely capitalist solution to the crisis, because, whatever the conscious aims of those involved, the objective requirements of the capitalist economy under the conditions of world economic crisis called for a basically fascist outcome. This approach thus offers an interpretative model which, while providing for determination 'in the last analysis' by the socio-economic structure of capitalism, still leaves room for the political dimension to be considered without the constant necessity of delivering proofs of direct personal and institutional interventions by 'capital'.

Such theorists, however, have been notable for contenting themselves with merely calling this political sphere relatively autonomous; they have not put it at the centre of the analysis. They have focused on the economic determinants of a capitalist solution to the crisis and have concluded fairly hastily that these economic requirements necessitated a fascist dictatorship structure. In criticism of such approaches it can be pointed out that scarcely any of the studies which are, by their own account, necessary – of the Nazi movement, of the motives and intentions of the masses who turned to fascism, or of the political system of the Third Reich – have actually been done. More fundamentally, we must question whether the fascist path was necessarily taken for purely economic reasons involving a capitalist solution to the crisis.

There are three usual strands of argument in favour of the thesis that fascism represented a way out of the economic disaster of the thirties. The first is the need for state mechanisms of intervention and regulation in order to refurbish an economy shattered by world economic crisis. The second is the creation of a state of war readiness, both objectively and subjectively speaking, through rearmament and the elimination of internal opposition; rearmament serves in the short term to stimulate production and in the long term to make possible a revanchist war which will put an end to the particular plight of German imperialism on world markets. The third is the need to repress the working class by terror, in order to extract from it the enormous surplus value required by capital if it is to re-emerge from the depths of economic depression.

Certainly, relevant aspects of the Nazi state are described here. But we must also enquire whether these factors, while necessary given German development in the 1930s, are also sufficient to explain the specific phenomenon of National Socialism. To put it another way: could recovery from world economic crisis also have been achieved by non-fascist means, or was the specific form of political control established in the Third Reich simply the 'inevitable' result of such an economic crisis strategy? Neither the war economy of the First World War, nor the economies of the other powers in the Second World War, nor indeed Roosevelt's New Deal involved fascist dictatorship.[7] In times of national emergency a highly efficient apparatus of state control can also evidently obtain the consent of, or at least be tolerated by, socially antagonistic groups. We must therefore ask why it was that the parties, associations and institutions that had previously been the upholders of bourgeois hegemony in Germany were unable to transfer their support to the capitalist reorganisation that was needed in the wake of the world economic crisis. This question involves examining the political context, the particular class pattern and the nature of bourgeois hegemony in the Weimar Republic.

Undoubtedly revenge had been a central element in the long-term strategies of leading forces in both state and society since 1918. In view of the persistence of imperialist thinking after 1918, this was indeed only to be expected – especially since the curtailment of German power by the Versailles treaty led German politicians and leading industrialists to vow territorial revision.[8] But did such a programme necessarily mean a fascist government? At least until 1936, but effectively even until the proclamation of total war in January 1943, Nazi Germany did not rearm to its full capacity, but at most to half strength. This was in contradiction both to its own propaganda and to the warnings of opponents of Hitler. In fact, it was a feature of the years 1933–35 that programmes to stimulate economic activity, on the principle of 'something for everyone', channeled resources to all manner of projects, ones which aided rearmament and ones which did not, ones which generated employment and ones which had no effect on jobs. What typified National Socialism was not the noisily advertised concentration of national effort on a single goal, but the dissipation of resources, losses through disputes, and short-term blitz campaigns.[9] To say this is in no way to deny the war-mongering and criminal activities of the Nazi regime (nor the involvement of business entrepreneurs in responsibility for planning them); it serves to qualify the monocausal and at first sight plausible thesis that fascism is equivalent to arming for war. It is necessary to seek for the specific political conditions in Germany which cast revanchist politics into a fascist state mould. This does not meant that the direct and indirect effects of rearmament on life in the Third Reich were not marked.

The thesis that it was only the Nazi use of terror against the working class that made a new gigantic campaign of exploitation possible also seems plausible at first glance.[10] Unfortunately, however, it is hard to prove empirically that the workers became more impoverished after 1933. On the contrary, wages during 1933–35 remained at about the level of 1932, and rose perceptibly after 1936: at first in terms of weekly real wages, because working hours increased; later in terms of real wages per hour, as labour shortages developed.[11] However this trend may be assessed on points of detail, there is no proof of a reduction in working-class living standards, let alone of a fall to below the deepest recession levels. Nazi labour policy was if anything an anxious attempt to diminish the risks of political disaffection among workers by making social and welfare concessions. The system of terror was counter-balanced by 'buying off' the workers, not by their expropriation. This phenomenon cannot be explained in purely economic terms. Mason[12] has proposed an explanation here which has the merit of being based on internal documentation from National Socialists themselves. On this view, the ambivalent attitude of National Socialism towards the workers (terror directed against all expressions of political opposition; and attempts at social integration, even at the expense of rearmament) was determined first and foremost by its ideological assimilation of the lessons of the revolution of November 1918. The future struggle for hegemony in Europe was not to be hampered by disorder on the home front and the threat of revolutionary upheaval. Nazi labour policy, therefore, can most plausibly be seen as the precautionary pacification of the home front. And for this, carrots were needed as well as sticks.

To summarise the discussion so far: the reason why Germany took the road to the Third Reich was certainly not simply the 'fascist' tendency towards dictatorship inherent in 'monopoly capital'. Even the structural argument that economic contradictions had become so pronounced in Germany as to permit only a fascist outcome, while offering additional necessary explanatory points, is not, in the final analysis, adequate. It is only when we enter the realm of political culture, the field in which the determinants of class structure are translated into actual behaviour, that we find tensions and movements that provide a basis for explaining the particular dynamics of National Socialism, as contrasted with dictatorships by traditional elites.

Why do so many Marxist historians cling stubbornly to one-dimensional explanations of fascism? One undoubted reason is their vested interest in preventing any questioning of the principle that fascism is 'essentially' large-scale-capitalist in origin and that all other determining conditions are derived from this principle or can be subordinated to it. It may be the case, however, that certain other aspects of the 'social basis' of National Socialism played a more significant part in the restructuring of German society in the thirties and forties. This, though, cannot be countenanced by a theory fixated on monopoly capital. Thus writers proposing otherwise more sophisticated arguments[13] still raise the objection against 'modernisation' theory that fascism was not 'progressive'. This is indisputable, if the criterion of 'progress' is taken to be how far a society has advanced towards a humane or indeed socialist future. But 'modernisation' can also mean a reorganisation of society that preserves the old power relationships, i.e. a process that is, in socialist terms, highly 'reactionary'. Schoenbaum, for example, sees the 'Brown revolution'[14] as a process yielding important insights into the social settlement of the post-war *Wirtschaftswunder* era. Such a view ought to be of interest to Marxists too, if they want to go beyond the magical nominalism of the principle that to label a danger is to avert it.

If indeed, unlike the conservative and the orthodox Marxist historians, we are not interested only in great world-shaking events, and if our aim is to explain the everyday experience and behaviour of Germans in the thirties, then we cannot be satisfied merely with snatching a right-wing glimpse into the antechambers of the aged President of the Reich or a left-wing glimpse into the counting-houses of the industrialists of the Ruhr: we must take account of the crisis of the Weimar Republic in all its complexity. At the beginning of the thirties the German political system collapsed for the second time in a dozen years. We may therefore speak with good reason of a deep-seated crisis in the political system which went far beyond elections and parties and which was in many ways a crisis of German industrial class society as a whole.

Whereas the political system under the imperial monarchy relied on giving the middle class preferential treatment, and making the workers' ghettoised existence at best bearable by means of gradual economic improvements, to the rigorous exclusion of all political influence, the Weimar Republic was originally based on the positive inclusion of those sections of the working class represented by Social Democracy and the trade unions. It was the middle classes' loss of their privileged role, but more especially the economic humiliations of the years of inflation, that first impelled them to make moves to detach themselves from the political system. Though the bourgeois bloc governments of the stabilisation period (1924–28) again swung back more strongly towards the socio-political pattern of the monarchy, upgrading the role of the middle classes and reinforcing their anti-working-class prejudices, nevertheless they too were forced to preserve a state of equilibrium vis-à-vis the workers and their Social Democrat representatives. In addition, the deep structural crisis in German agriculture radicalised the traditionally right-wing conservative agrarian leaders and led to a mass recruitment of farmers into the Nazi Party.

With the end of the economic boom, the twin pillars of the political system, the middle classes and the social settlement with labour, began to totter. To the alarm of business, the system of social-welfare concessions to labour, which had been viewed as a temporary and tactical measure, was beginning to be taken as a fixture. (Thus leaders of heavy industry were furious when almost all of the Reichstag parties came out in favour of relief for the metal workers locked out during the Ruhr iron dispute of 1928; fears of a so-called trade-union state were reawakened.)[15] However ready the SPD and ADGB might be to make compromises at their supporters' expense, their mere existence remained a potential obstacle to social-welfare retrenchment during the crisis. The KPD, despite gaining electoral votes, had isolated itself to such an extent through its 'Revolutionary Trade Union Opposition' (RGO) and 'social fascism' tactics that the great menace it seemed to pose was rated as very minor by sober, realistic entrepreneurs. But its potential, too, seemed dangerous enough to many.

The dismantling of the welfare state was being demanded, especially by representatives of heavy industry in the Rhineland and Westphalia, even before the onset of the world economic crisis. After 1929 it became the standard feature of all capitalist strategies for dealing with the crisis. Workers' parties and trade unions would have, at the very least, to be kept in check. Such aims, however, did not necessarily mean that the ultimate goal was terrorist dictatorship on the National Socialist pattern (though even those in big business who had not voted for the NSDAP before 1933 were pleased to note the outlawing and persecution of the KPD, SPD and trade unions). Almost throughout the period of crisis the political options favoured by industrialists oscillated among authoritarian, corporatist solutions, restoration of the monarchy, presidential dictatorship and the like; only a minority backed the NSDAP.[16] By the summer of 1932 the worst point of the crisis had been passed. Welfare retrenchment and the lowering of living standards went ahead within the framework of the Republic up till the end of 1932. After 1933 the National Socialists, though they wiped out the labour movement and certainly sought to preserve the low levels in living standards caused by the crisis, did not carry out the general assault on wages that had been forecast by the left. The Papen government had already met the wishes of business in full.

Panic of the middle strata: the dynamics of the movement

A factor that was more significant in the rise of fascism than the industrialists' strategy of solving the economic crisis on the backs of the workers was the set of processes within the middle and lower-middle social strata which caused broad sections of white-collar employees, public officials, tradesmen and small businessmen and peasant farmers to become detached from their traditional political allegiances and to join the National Socialist movement.[17] They were accompanied by sections of the younger, socially disorientated 'war generation', ex-soldiers who had failed to reintegrate themselves into society, people whose careers had foundered and long-term unemployed who had no links with the labour movement. The ranks of the Nazi movement were also swollen by a large number of groups and individuals 'between the classes', whose lives had been shattered by the social and economic dislocations of the Depression. An advance hint of these processes of radicalisation was given by rumblings within the bourgeois party system even before the onset of the world economic crisis.[18] Millions of people who had previously not voted, or who had supported the bourgeois parties, declined the blandishments of these parties in the Reichstag elections of 1930 and became radicalised into the ranks of the NSDAP. This mass movement occurred before big business came out in favour of the NSDAP on any large scale. If we wish to explain Nazism, then, we must start by explaining the causes of these mass shifts of alignment.[19]

In addition to the sociological account of the causes of the splitting of the middle social strata away from the party system, there is an explanatory approach which lays stress on the psychological causes and dispositions underlying the fascist resort to violence.[20] Its focus is the interconnections between form of life, experience and the articulation of self in those members of the middle classes who became fascists. Klaus Theweleit, basing himself on the work of Reich and Fromm, sees 'fascist' dispositions towards violence and in favour of totalitarian mass movements as rooted in the authoritarian socialisation of the middle class. Theweleit supports this view primarily by tracing the prehistory of the NSDAP in the Freikorps, the irregular troops who took part in the civil-war fighting in post-war Germany, and in the literary testimony of its members. His extension of Reich's thesis is that the alternating rewards and punishments of middle-class early childhood socialisation made it impossible for a child to be 'fully born' and achieve a stable identity. Only the discipline of punitive institutions like the military gave the child a 'body armour' that could hold the chaotic ego tightly under wraps, while also determining the manner of its outbursts into violence. The Freikorps member, according to Theweleit, can find release from this inner pressure only within three characteristic situations or fantasy situations (which also constantly recur as images in fascist aesthetics): the 'bleeding pulp', to which he reduces the disturbing counter-images of women and the proletarian rebel; the 'empty space', where the curbing of the masses (and of the self's inner chaos) is carried out through violent disciplining or annihilation; and the 'blackout' of exhaustion, which is a reward for the ultimate masochistic spending of energy in the service of the leader. (See also p. 205 below.)

Although Theweleit succeeds in making very graphic the connections between psychological dispositions, ideologies and mechanisms of behaviour in the fascist movement, there must nevertheless be reservations as to the degree of general validity of his claims. But there is a whole body of studies of the mentality and behaviour of active members of the so-called 'old guard' (*alte Kämpfer*) in the NSDAP and the SA which, while not making for interpretations as ambitious as that proposed by Theweleit, do contain autobiographical testimony that offers some insight into everyday life in the 'movement'.[21]

Who actually were the active Nazis? The Party's statistical data for 1935, on which most historical investigations are based, are fairly general. They indicate that the lower-middle classes were over-represented and workers under-represented, though the latter still constituted between one-fifth and one-quarter of the total membership. But whether or not some social groups were over- or under-represented in Nazi ranks, we must appreciate that significant proportions of all social groups were involved. Although numerically dominated by the middle strata, the movement in fact had an inter-class character. In any case, the life-stories, experiences and attitudes that lie concealed behind these abstract social categories can be reconstructed only from autobiographical documents. Despite all provisos as to the extent to which information obtained from individuals can be generalised to cover a movement of millions, such reports give a pretty clear idea of the range and nature of the experience of the 'old guard'. Many of them were people whose lives and careers were unstable or indeed shattered. These early NSDAP members had often abandoned their businesses for economic reasons, or had failed to settle back into civilian life after the lost world war, or had undergone frequent changes of job or profession, or had experienced frequent or long-term unemployment. What made the situation more acute was the fact that the majority of them were members of a 'shattered intermediate generation' (Bracher's term) whose whole sense of purpose in life had been overshadowed by the uncertainties of post-war crisis and world recession. Not all National Socialists had first-hand experience of this insecurity and loss of status. But some had, and the others saw it as a constant potential threat – a sign that 'order' had begun to waver and that there could be no prospect of a return to normality unless there was a radical break with the past. For the unemployed worker, the failed small businessman, the young man who saw no hope of better training or social advancement – and, at the same time, for those members of the upper-middle class who saw their life-style and social values threatened – the loss of perspective and meaning in everyday life caused by the crisis could not, objectively speaking, be abolished by active participation in the National Socialist movement; but it could be made easier to bear. A never-ending succession of Party 'missions' and campaigns filled up the empty hours; members could prove their usefulness as small cogs in the larger machine; and even guard-of-honour duty at parades and office work for the Party could take on higher significance as self-sacrifice for the Führer and a contribution to the eventual victory of the 'movement'. After the victory, it was hoped, these efforts would be rewarded by public recognition and a paying job.

> We were kept constantly in motion, taking part in parades and propaganda trips, handing out leaflets and spreading the Führer's message.[22]

The Party also provided the social contacts that the unemployed and *déclassés* were failing to get from professional life. Links and fellowship grew naturally in the course of hectic work for the movement.

If the appeal of the NSDAP was more a matter of the movement's form than of its political content – most members knew only a few slogans, though this was almost all that Hitler had to offer by way of a programme anyway – then it is hardly surprising that the decision to join the Party was not usually the result of careful pondering and political debate but sprang from casual encounters with the NSDAP in its role as a means of social contact, as a stirring 'movement' or as a bearer of meaning cast in a demagogic posture. This mechanism, incidentally, was quite apparent to the more intellectual Nazis, as is shown, for instance, by Schenzinger's novel *Hitlerjunge Quex*. The hero of the novel, later to become the Hitler Youth member Quex of the title, first makes contact with the Nazi movement when, roaming through the forest at night, he comes upon a Hitler Youth camp fire around which a ritual ceremony is just taking place:

> The further he went from the camp, the more quickly he walked, straight through the forest towards the glow of the fire. Not for a moment did he consider what he was doing there. It was good to march through the night towards the brightness, and march he did.
>
> The glow became brighter and brighter. The sound of singing floated across to him again, quite distinctly now; it must be very near. He could already pick out the tune: he had heard it before somewhere, but could not call to mind where that had been.

It was a marching song; it took hold of his legs. He ran up the hill, hitting roots, catching himself in undergrowth [. . .] Reaching the top, he found himself staring in terror at a dazzling flame. He was blinded by the sudden light; he was completely out of breath. He dared not move from the spot. He stood and looked. Gradually his eyes became used to the brightness. At least a thousand youths were standing around a burning pile of wood; or perhaps it was only a hundred. But it was as though this circle of young people stretched to the very edges of the world. Just in front of him, marshalled in lines, stood youths like himself. Each held a long pole with a pennant, rising vertically to the sky, black pennants and brilliant red, with jagged symbols on the field of the cloth. Each of the youths looked like all the others, with shorts, bare knees, brown shirt, a kerchief around the neck. If only they would sing! This, for the moment, was all he could think. His heart was pounding.

But they were not singing! They were all looking in silence towards the fire. A tall young man had taken his stand beside it and was speaking to them. He was delivering a real speech. Heini could make out only a few phrases: he heard the words 'movement' and 'leader', he heard part of a sentence – 'each giving his life for the others'. As he listened, wondering whether he might not creep a little closer to hear better, a great thrill of fear went through him. '*Deutschland, Deutschland über alles*' swept over him, from a thousand voices, like a scalding wave. I too am a German, he thought; and he was filled with profound knowledge, stronger and more unexpected than anything he had felt in his life before – more than at school, at home, more even than when he had watched the army present arms in front of the Reichstag. He wanted to sing with the others, but his voice failed him. This was German soil, German forest, these were German youths; and he saw that he stood apart, alone, with no one to help him; and he did not know what to make of this great and sudden feeling.[23]

The same themes pervade the accounts given by the 'old guard' of the big propaganda rituals of the Nazi Party, especially the national Party congresses in Nuremberg, where the massed discipline of the SA and Party members as they marched in and lined up was felt to be an uplifting experience, a proof both of the 'significance' of the 'movement' and of the individual as an integral part of the movement. The climax of such events, and of the accounts of them, was indisputably the 'thrill' of encountering the 'Führer': this is always portrayed as an intense, wholly personal event, even though it was a fleeting one and generally took place at a distance. These accounts show, indeed, that it is impossible to make sense of the phenomenon of the Führer cult by focusing only on the personal magnetism of Hitler himself. What was important was the fact that Nazi Party supporters had a pressing need to experience a sense of 'heightened' significance, which stood 'in contrast to the *Lebenswelt* [life-world] of a generation bereft of an outlook and opportunities',[24] and that they met this need in the hectic campaigns of the Nazi movement and in the Party ceremonies with their quasi-religious ritual.

In addition, in the street battles before 1933 NSDAP supporters could give aggressive vent to the inner injuries and frustrations they had sustained in their lives. The very style of the subsequent descriptions of these battles with the Communist *Rotfront* clearly shows the mechanism of projection, channelling and discharge of aggression: it is always the others who are the first to use violence; it is therefore 'just' – i.e. legitimised by this violence – to fight back even more brutally.[25]

Admittedly, only the relatively small group of 'old guard' Nazis was fired by such experiences and clusters of motives in concentrated form. But similar situations and frameworks of expectation can also be found among the wider membership of the NSDAP, those who voted for the Party and those non-Nazi Germans who, after Hitler was appointed Chancellor of the Reich, were carried away by the stage-managed excitements of the national 'awakening'.[26]

To the middle class and to a growing number of people between the social classes, bourgeois society in the Weimar Republic offered no outlook or prospects. Traditional loyalties broke down under the pressure of anxieties about loss of status. But the radicalising of the middle classes did not lead towards forms of interest-group trade unionism (though after the November revolution there had been first moves in this direction among white-collar employees), nor towards a strengthening of the democratic left on the lines of Roosevelt's New Deal in America.[27] It led to a mass movement, highly modern in its structures, which had borrowed its ideological precepts from the chauvinistic, anti-modern, anti-Marxist, anti-Semitic and anti-democratic pseudo-theories of the closing years of the nineteenth century. Its hatred was directed against 'modernity' itself, the Weimar 'system' *tout court*; and against its two representatives, capital as well as the proletariat. Yet it would be incorrect to write off fascism as simply an ideological regression into medieval darkness. Its sources were very contemporary ones; although it sometimes employed empty, outdated rhetoric and ritual, its dynamics sprang from the contradictions of the inter-war years.

The fascist ideological mix[28]

Older interpretations of the 'panic of the middle classes' concentrated on the problems of the old middle-class social strata, peasant farmers, tradespeople and craftsmen. Since these categories of employment were becoming increasingly fossilised in industrial society, and since the share in the labour market they represented was declining, a link with the fossilised anti-modern ideology of fascism readily suggested itself. But such a line of argument scarcely works for the modern middle class: the expanding groups, growing in long-term importance, which consisted of white-collar employees in commerce, social and public service and technological jobs. Not only did these groups, like the old middle classes, have privileges to defend against the remorseless march of socio-economic change; they might also, counting on change, either demand a betterment in their position or view a temporary lowering in their status, given the particular weakness of Weimar society with its burdens of reparations and the Versailles sanctions, as a highly outrageous and 'unjust' result of the 'system'. In other words, the social basis of National Socialism also encompasses the new, rising middle class, bewildered at living through exceptional times.

But why, in that case, a backward-looking ideology? On the one hand, it offered the prospect of uniting the old and new middle classes, which had been held together under the monarchy on the basis of nationalistic and authoritarian formulae. On the other hand, though, we must not underestimate the 'modern' elements in National Socialist ideology either: its choreographing of the masses, its glorification of technology, its defence of the 'dignity of labour'. With these, after 1933, went the razzmatazz about the Autobahn and the Volkswagen, architectural gigantism in factories and public buildings, public-relations boasts about achievements in technological and military hardware, and rationalisation in industrial relations and new regulations affecting work and training.

Although the archaic myths and anti-modern slogans of National Socialism can hardly be ignored,[29] they do not amount to the whole of Nazi ideology. Manifestly, this ideology was far from unambiguous; and it was not committed to an unambiguous emotive anti-modernism. Hitler's ragbag of ideas comprised not only his overriding notion of a racial war for *Lebensraum* but also views about modern military technology and a concept of a military tradition that would supplant the Prussian ethos he derided. This applied particularly to the tank corps and air force, but also involved an almost 'American' model of the achievement-orientated worker, the applied engineer and 'inventor' and the personally committed entrepreneur in the armaments industries.

The role of such models within ideology and propaganda was central, and much more effective with the masses than idyllic agrarian romanticism, and it therefore cannot be discounted. Nazi ideology was not nearly coherent enough to offer even a clear-cut distinction between, say, archaic 'ends' and modern 'means'. Rather, it must be

39

analysed on the principle that ideas and measures were important if they worked. This means, though, that modern models and images were of absolutely central significance for the practical, efficient side of Nazi ideology. Furthermore, we should not take all references to Teutonism literally, when they were often only ways of describing in mythic terms an 'aggressive' type of desired behaviour. (Incidentally, this sort of metaphorical reference to remote times in order to reinforce thoroughly modern behavioural norms can also be found in quite different political cultures. For instance, the standing references by Protestants to Old Testament models and exemplars tallied neatly with the pioneering role of Protestants in the development of modern capitalism.)

The triad of factors traditionally cited as giving rise to National Socialism – hostility to progressive politics, the glorification of pseudo-medieval ideology, and a social basis in a moribund middle class – makes it easy to lose sight of the fact that the Nazis' perverted version of modern society not only displayed features of fossilisation but also had roots in wholly modern social groups and their associated ideologies. This mixed social basis, consisting of the old and the modern middle class, young people without a clear outlook or prospects in life,[30] long-term unemployed and *déclassés*, must be borne in mind if we are to explain the strange combination of archaic and brand-new elements within Nazi politics and ideology.

These groups, with goals in life that were uncertain or quite vague, experienced particularly acutely the upheavals caused by the modernisation process of the 1920s – which the whole of society went through – while remaining particularly in the dark about their causes. Here we can give only an incomplete list of these upheavals: the rationalisation of production, with the growth of assembly-line work and the introduction of ingeniously segmented work processes; associated job insecurity, even during periods of boom,[31] along with changes in job descriptions and alterations in gender-specific divisions of labour;[32] seismic upheavals in traditional social stratification, particularly in status hierarchies, which meant a relative decline by the old middle-class groups and a rise in status (albeit viewed as the opposite) by the new middle-class groups; the introduction of a new model in social policy, combining state intervention and corporatism (viz. large unions and big business), which was still going through its birth traumas when it was first hit by crisis and breakdown and had no protective backing of economic prosperity;[33] longer-term changes in processes of socialisation and in relationships between generations, expressed particularly in the upsurge of youth movements and in the general youth cult of the twenties;[34] changes in cultural life, shown in the highly visible breakthrough of modernism in art, architecture and design and in formal and political experimentation in literature, theatre and film;[35] changes, too, in socio-cultural styles, encapsulated in the term 'the Roaring Twenties', with new forms of sexual self-expression, new dances, new fashions, 'sinful' big-city life (much deplored by conservative cultural critics; eyed from the provinces with both mistrust and fascination), a new consumer culture (offering thrills for those with money and disappointments for those with none), and the 'loss of values' that was widely bemoaned at the time;[36] and, last but not least, changes in the system of authority and in political culture, which even the Republic's half-hearted attempts at democratisation had helped bring about.

All of these changes were concentrated into a very short time, leaving no scope for quiet evolution or a period of 'peaceful coexistence' with traditional values and attitudes; there was provocation from all quarters. And given the precarious economic situation and the burdens created by the lost war, such phenomena seemed, to those who were already suffering enough from the upheavals in their own lives and from their generation's bleak prospects for the future, virtually to be symptoms and causes of general decay and imminent collapse.[37] The whole intertwined complexity of crisis and change remained uncomprehended and was commonly reduced to a few easy catch-phrases. It was the whole 'system' that was evil, purely and simply. This umbrella term summed up all the discomforts of modernity and the upheavals produced by the crisis. The causes, since in reality they were obscure and genuinely hard to separate out, were personalised and mythologised. There had to be a 'conspiracy'. Traditional enemy figures were invoked as agents of the 'world conspiracy': 'the Jew', 'the Bolshevist', 'the capitalist'. It is a characteristic feature of Nazi ideology that the notions of anti-Semitism, anti-Bolshevism and anti-capitalism were interchangeable. In the free-associative thinking of its adherents, these notions did not contradict one another.

It was thus easy to conclude that the only way out of the catastrophe of the present was a 'violent blow' dealt by a 'movement' of struggle and self-sacrifice. Notions that could not be made precise on the plane of ideology were made visible and real in the 'movement's' practice, where sensual satisfaction, certainty of aims, security and the chance to vent one's aggression were on offer. The 'ultimate goal' of the movement remained vague, and for that very reason was immune from doubt. The need was to restore the disrupted 'normality' of life, a utopian normality, to be sure, with a social hierarchy which was somehow 'just' and in which everyone had a niche where he could feel secure and respected: in short, a true 'national community' (*Volksgemeinschaft*) from which all sources of friction and unease had been removed, all reminders of 'conspiracy', all abnormality, all that could jeopardise the ultimate 'ideal order'.[38] At the same time, the 'movement' allowed scope for undirected 'action' and hankerings for non-quotidian adventure.

The diagnosis of the crisis was vague; the goals were obscure. The actual practice of the 'movement', and its extreme dynamism, were therefore all the more important. The charismatic movement that was the National Socialist Party was the combined outcome of the experience of crisis, the yearning for security and the desire for aggression, all merged into a breathless dynamism that latched on to whatever was the next immediate event: the next election campaign, the next mass demonstration, the next public brawl. The more distant future could look after itself.

The labour movement was a helpless bystander at these developments; the crisis in the political system could not be exploited to help form an alternative bloc on the left. When the National Socialist movement took shape out of the radicalised middle classes, the prospect of an escape from the crisis was offered which did not tamper with the structures of society. The NSDAP was at once a symptom, and a solution, of the crisis.

Along with the break-up of the bourgeois centre and the exclusion of Social Democracy from political influence after 1930 went a further aspect of the crisis: the loss of function on the part of the state institutions, which thereafter were without their political driving force and were left without financial room for manoeuvre (thanks to deflationary budgetary policies and falling tax revenues).[39] The Presidential cabinets of 1930–33 (Brüning, Papen and Schleicher) cannot be labelled 'proto-fascist', if by that term is meant a deliberate move towards the complete discarding of the Weimar system and the establishment of overt fascist dictatorship. They were, rather, stopgap solutions thrown up by a system of authority that had partially lost its bearings and its political effectiveness. Bracher's notion of a 'power vacuum' is valid here: governments were authoritarian out of weakness.

National Socialism in power: permanent crisis

It is only against this background of the collapse of the political system that the appeal of the Nazi movement to the old political and economic elites becomes clear.[40] The movement had shown that it was strong and that it could count on considerable mass support. It was no accident that the misgivings many businessmen felt about Hitler fell away only when he proved to be the tamer, rather than the tribune, of the fascist masses. The Nazi movement not only brought together the despairing middle classes and other non-integrated groups, constituting a civil-war army to deal with the Communist Party in case it should proceed beyond verbal radicalism into active insurrection: it proved during the first half of 1933 that it was capable of taking over the apparatus of the state in rapid, uncompromising fashion. (These months must be counted as a transitional stage *en route* to the Third Reich, at least in the sense that it was only in the spring that the conservative attempt to 'hem in' Hitler was abandoned.) It could not then be foreseen that the dynamics of the 'national revolution' would soon succumb to jungle warfare over powers and responsibilities on the part of the various Nazi factions. Not the least of the NSDAP's merits was that within a few weeks, between 27th February and 2nd May 1933, it apparently 'solved', through terror, the problem of the organised labour movement that had been vexing capital for the past hundred years.[41]

The crisis of hegemony, then, prompted the old elites to seek an alliance with the National Socialist movement on two counts. They needed new, dictatorial mechanisms to secure their power; and they needed new institutions of hegemony in order to guarantee the consent of the lower orders to the system of authority. The political structure of the Third Reich established in 1933 was an alliance of entrepreneurs and sections of the old political elite (particularly in the army) with the Nazi leaders. With modifications, this remained the key structure on the political level. It was shaped in addition by the economic framework of the capitalist mode of production.[42] The so-called 'national revolution' replaced a pluralistic system, which had been based on the consent of divergent social and political forces, with a new system of hegemony that rested on the exclusion from immediate political influence of all socially subordinate groups and that incorporated the ideological machinery of the state (schools, surrogate *Deutsche Arbeitsfront* 'trade unions', mass organisations and means of communication) directly into the Nazi system of direction and control, so robbing those institutions of such independence as they had. National Socialism led to a reorganisation of the system of hegemony that preserved the capitalist structure. In the process, however, the contradictions which had been the undoing of the previous system of hegemony were transferred to the new state institutions. Where there had previously been pluralistic competitive struggles among clearly demarcated interest groups, there was now permanent confused petty warfare among rival power groups.[43] Each of these groups (party administration, SS and police, business, armed forces) had its vassals and a relatively secure power base, but each tended to interfere with the areas of responsibility of the others.

Following the pattern of large-scale capitalist concerns (i.e. not merely horizontal and vertical expansion, but the maximum agglomeration of unrelated lines of business), the Nazi system of control dissolved into a polycracy of competing domains. By revoking the separation of society and bureaucratic, rational state machinery that had evolved during the nineteenth century, it also destroyed the basis for a unified machinery of state and the state monopoly of violence, in favour of competing wielders of authority and users of force. The attempt to 'nationalise' society led to the atomisation of the power structure. In this sense fascism was basically, to use Franz Neumann's formulation, a 'behemoth' or non-state.[44] To see fascism as an effective answer to the weakness of the bourgeois democratic state, i.e. as a functional solution to the crisis in the interests of capital, is to be taken in by the self-image of National Socialism created by its own propaganda. The Nazi 'solution' to the crisis was headed for disintegration from the start.

The National Socialist dictatorship certainly changed the political complexion of society and brought in a new way of waging economic class conflict. The elimination of the organised representation of labour interests, for example, led to passive resistance (below the threshold that would have triggered police intervention) and to the insertion of workers' demands into the competition between different power groups, e.g. between the Labour Front and industry. But since the basic economic structure – namely, capitalist property – was not affected, fascist 'nationalisation' remained incomplete. The equipping of state bodies with economic functions, and of business enterprises with quasi-state powers, led not to a more effective and rationally functioning 'state monopoly capitalism', but to a welter of jurisdictions and responsibilities that could be kept in check only by short-term projects and campaigns. The splintered state and semi-state managerial bodies adopted the principle of competition. The 'nationalisation' of society by Nazism was followed by the 'privatisation' of the state. This paradox meant that, on the one hand, there were huge concentrations of power as a result of internal and external Blitzkrieg campaigns, while, on the other hand, inefficiency, lack of planning, falling productivity and general decline prevailed. This structural contradiction was also the basic reason why the fascist potential for violence was vented simultaneously in strategies of control that were, technically speaking, rational and in frenzies of destruction that were quite irrational. Both, of course, were inhuman, chauvinistic and dictatorial.

The Nazi movement and the Nazi state alike preserved a detachment from 'the capitalist' that derived from their origins; but they were not detached from capitalism. The political alliance between the old upper social strata and the National Socialist movement was mirrored, after 1933, by the continuation of the capitalist mode of production. Fascism occurred as one outcome of the social crisis of the capitalist system. It took its specific form in the era between the two world wars when the Weimar political system, weakened by defeat in war and by the crisis of the 1920s, began to break down and when the labour movement was unable to muster enough strength to provide an alternative solution capable of winning majority support.

An explanation of the rise of National Socialism which particularly stresses the densely interwoven crises of the post-war period will still retain many references to strands of older traditions in society. The need, however, to posit a long-standing 'special German path of development' disappears.[45] Rather, the various anti-democratic, anti-humanitarian and anti-modern features of Wilhelminian society before 1914 may be seen as a comparatively normal mix for the industrial class societies of the time. The fact that such a radical shift towards barbarism and anti-liberalism could occur during the 1920s and 1930s can be understood only on the basis that, under specific crisis conditions, the normal safety valves within modern industrial society can suddenly and alarmingly fail to operate and that the pressure of crisis can build up (to borrow a term from nuclear power) into the 'worst possible case' – i.e. into devastating catastrophe. Such an explanation may seem trivialising and banal when set against the millions who fell victim to National Socialism. But were the organisers of mass murder not banal personalities themselves?[46] Were not Eichmann and Höss, Himmler and Ohlendorf more like bookkeepers and technocrats than 'daemoniacs'? In Nazism, attitudes and behaviour that were common in 'normal' European warfare, and especially in colonial wars, moved from the periphery to the centre. The brutalities of world war were now directed on to society itself, in the 'operations to restore public order' first of the Freikorps and later of the SA. Social restrictions of the sort to which 'outsiders' had always been subject became so severe as to threaten their very lives. With the world economic crisis, the key question became: what groups should be sacrificed so that the 'healthy' part of the nation might prosper? And the stresses and discomforts caused by the upheaval in values could become exacerbated to the point of violence and destruction if it seemed that the individual's goals in life, or his life itself, were at risk. Once the fascist 'solution' to the crisis had become a general movement, the movement's own dynamics and its tendency to 'conquer the only remaining unsolved problem' by creating a new and bigger problem were sufficient to ensure that relatively harmless acts of slander and persecution became more and more radical. One by one, remaining inhibitions were dismantled; the destructiveness spread, the numbers of victims increased, and the restraints as to methods fell away. Eventually the 'national community' that had once been promised developed into a cartel of active or – in most cases –

passive accomplices, and the much-heralded 'New Order in Europe' ended in the destruction of the continent and the murder of millions of its citizens.

National Socialism had awakened hopes that it could not in actuality fulfil. In place of economic consolidation it provided rearmament financed through inflation. In place of the promised 'just' national community and a government of 'order', it provided an economy of privilege, boss rule and chaotically conflicting spheres of jurisdiction. In place of the unifying national 'awakening' it sought out more and more new groups to persecute and established a system of thought control and surveillance that penetrated right into the family.

All of these disillusioning developments were noted by the 'national comrades' (*Volksgenossen*), and were indeed criticised. Yet opposition and resistance remained fragmented and powerless to the end. It is this remarkable paradox that will be analysed in what follows.

'National community' and 'popular opposition'

THREE

Contradictions in the mood of the 'little man'

Joachim Fest's recent film *Hitler – A Career*, like so many films before it, shows never-ending columns of enthusiastic Germans, boys and girls, men and women. The film critic or historian quickly notes that many of these shots are posed or owe their effect to sophisticated editing, censorship or, not least, the pressure of the system of terror which made it dangerous for people not to look fired with enthusiasm. None the less, National Socialism's highly stylised portrait of itself as a society borne forward by enthusiastic mass consent has persisted in many publications until the present day, including writings by serious domestic and foreign authors. This intellectual construct, however, of a German 'national community', or *Volksgemeinschaft*, totally mobilised save for a few fragments at the margin, is contradicted by the memories of many members of the older generation. There were numerous expressions of dissatisfaction and instances of nonconformist behaviour, ranging from the deliberate refusal to cook an officially prescribed Sunday stew (*Eintopf*)* to the giving of shelter and support to victims of persecution. The intelligence networks of the German workers' parties that had been driven underground and abroad also furnished considerable contemporary evidence of dissent from the regime. Probably the most careful documentation of this mood in the other Germany – or of this other mood in Germany – was in the so-called 'green' reports: the 'Reports on Germany', reproduced on green paper, that were compiled by the exiled Social Democratic Party leadership.[1]

---

*'National comrades' were urged, through propaganda, to eat a cheap 'one-pot' Sunday meal once a month and to donate the money thereby saved to social-welfare purposes. Collectors for the Winter Relief Fund went from door to door putting pressure on people to make their 'donations'.

Outwardly, to be sure, National Socialist society preferred to portray itself as a closed, harmonious national community. In fact, however, the internal situation reports and reports on morale drawn up by Nazi Party and police departments, which remained secret and were used only to brief selected groups in the leadership, documented very deep dissatisfaction among the population. People chafed particularly at failings in the economy and at the manifold intrusions by the Nazis into private life and long-standing customs.[2] This can be illustrated by some examples from the monthly situation reports compiled by the Gestapo's Düsseldorf headquarters, which controlled the western Ruhr and the northern Lower Rhine.[3] In contrast to later analyses which have viewed Hitler's successes in work-creation, particularly, as responsible for winning broader popular support, the Gestapo was still being forced to record in September 1934 that 'the belief [among the jobless] that unemployment can be completely conquered is fading'. In places where the onset of rearmament had created new jobs, the fear of war became more widespread:

> Nearly everywhere there is secret talk about the possibility of a war. Reliable reports therefore almost make it possible to speak of the first stages of a war psychosis,

the Düsseldorf Gestapo noted in October of the same year. Food shortages (meagre supplies of fats, for example) and price rises in basic foodstuffs such as meat, fats and potatoes led during 1934–35 to a growing wave of irritation that took the shape not only of overt expressions of discontent but also of a greater willingness on the part of the 'grumblers' to take risks: semi-public 'grumbling' (*Meckerei*) became widespread.

> Clumps of people at street corners on the lookout for trouble are becoming increasingly common,

the Gestapo reported in July 1935. And in November 1935 they were driven to add:

> [The general situation] is discussed daily in critical, disparaging or malicious terms – in places of work, in the shops, in public houses and on the trains and trams.

There are similar secret reports on popular morale, free of all propagandist gloss, covering the whole period of the Third Reich.

Two examples, from the early and final phases of the National Socialist regime respectively, can serve by way of illustration.

A plebiscite was held on 19th August 1934 on the question of the merging of the office of Chancellor of the Reich with that of President

(Hindenburg, the previous President, had just died) – to secure, in other words, the acclamation of the 'Führer'. In September 1934 Gestapo stations in the Prussian *Regierungsbezirke* (regional administrative districts) were forced to admit, in their reports on the month of August, that one-quarter or more of the voters, especially in Catholic areas and in working-class districts, had not voted 'Yes' but had either returned 'No' votes, spoiled their ballot papers or abstained. (In later 'elections' the regime's control mechanisms were much better-oiled; correspondingly, there was more widespread recognition that nothing could be achieved by casting a 'No' vote which would in any case not be recorded in the final results.)

On 6th May 1943 the Security Service (*Sicherheitsdienst*, SD) of the SS noted, in its secret 'Reports from the Reich', which were intended only for the eyes of the top state and Party leaders:[4]

[. . .] the mood of the national comrades (*Volksgenossen*) is at present calm. There is not, however, the necessary conviction and belief in final victory [. . .]

This lack of faith is captured in a rhyme that was circulating in the Ruhr. It referred to the rally held in the Berlin Sports Palace on 18th February 1943 (and broadcast on the radio), where a specially selected audience, in response to Goebbels's repeated question, 'Do you want total war?', had fanatically roared back 'Yes'. The rhyme was addressed to the English bomber pilots (the so-called 'Tommies'):

Lieber Tommy, fliege weiter,	Tommy, please don't drop that bomb:
wir sind alle Bergarbeiter,	All we are is miners, Tom.
fliege weiter nach Berlin,	Berlin's where you want to drop it,
die haben alle 'Ja' geschrien.	They said 'Yes', so let them cop it.

These examples shed a lot of light on the problem of dissident opinion within the Third Reich. In the first place, they show what the secret reporting on popular morale in Germany was like. Many Nazi and state agencies reported regularly to their superiors on events and views in their regions. Even though a great number of these documents have not survived, extensive supplies of source material remain which have only recently begun to be properly exploited by researchers. For the 1930s the monthly reports of the Gestapo and, in parts, those of the Presidents of *Regierungsbezirke* are particularly important. The late 1930s and the early 1940s are well documented in various areas: for example, by reports by the Trustees of Labour (*Treuhänder der Arbeit* – see p. 107 below) on the economic situation, working conditions and workers' behaviour, and reports of the Prosecutors-General (*Generalstaatsanwälte*) of the Higher Regional Courts (*Oberlandesgerichte*). The period from the start of the war until 1944 is dealt with exhaustively by the SD reports of the type quoted above.

Secondly, our two examples reveal an important characteristic of the majority of these secret reports: namely, that they avoided the usual cosmetics of public propaganda and reported in detail on criticism and discontent. Sometimes one even has the impression that the popular mood is being painted too sombrely, either in order to give body to the demands of the authors (e.g. the Gestapo) or because the agents and informers at the grass roots were particularly prone to peddle rumours about spectacular instances of criticism. The material in the reports, however, is so varied and so consistent as between different regions and different periods (especially in Bavaria, where the sources are exceptionally rich) that it is possible, using the customary procedures for assessing sources, to form a very precise picture of everyday popular feeling and opinion. This picture can be filled out by using judicial and Gestapo documents on legal cases involving so-called 'popular opposition' (*Volksopposition*) and 'malicious offences' (*Heimtückedelikte*): the latter a type of charge which could be brought even for making a joke at the regime's expense.

Thirdly, we have the 'Reports on Germany' produced by the SOPADE (*Sozialdemokratische Partei Deutschlands im Exil*), the German Social Democratic Party in exile. These documents, compiled by the Party executive committee on the basis of reports by Party representatives within the Reich, constitute a source of material for the years 1934–40 that is quite independent of the National Socialist sources and thus provides the researcher with a control. They contain an almost inexhaustible wealth of information about everyday life and the behaviour and views of ordinary people, and critical analyses that are to a large extent free of any anti-fascist wishful thinking.

Fourthly, our two examples mark off, as it were, the two ends of the spectrum of possible expressions of opposition, leaving aside outright resistance of the sort represented by, say, the underground activity of Communist and Social Democratic groups. In the 1934 plebiscite a not inconsiderable portion of the population declared its opposition quite openly at the ballot box. These voters rejected the conferment of the office of Führer on Hitler and in this sense came out against the political system as a whole. This inference cannot be drawn equally unequivocally from the many expressions of criticism and discontent in daily life recorded in later years, as is borne out by the earlier-quoted SD report from 1943, with its stress on the 'calm' mood of the people despite their lack of conviction. In other words, these later manifestations of criticism apply first and foremost only to specific cases: to the partial aspect of social reality to which they directly refer.

Fifthly, however, the satirical rhyme from the Ruhr reveals some recurring basic features of everyday criticism, or 'grumbling', as Goebbels tried to denigrate it in a campaign as early as 1934. We shall try to describe and classify these features now. The expressions of popular criticism and discontent recorded in the reports on morale show similarities and differences as regards causes, subject-matter and forms of behaviour.

Frequently, satirical verses, rumours and catchphrases gave voice to what people felt to be a genuine split between themselves 'down below' (in our example, the miners) and the bigwigs 'on top' (the yea-sayers in the capital); or, to put it another way, between those who had to endure total war and those who had brought it about.

In the joke or the rumour a complicated political process, or the analysis of an entire social structure, could be reduced to a significant concrete detail that stood symbolically for the whole. This symbolic function of the anecdote was the basis of the 'truth value' even of many fairly far-fetched rumours, which circulated more widely as people became less able to believe in Goebbels's propaganda. The ironic tension between explicitly stating the detail and symbolically implying the whole likewise applied to a joke that was going the rounds in 1943: that there would soon be more butter again, because the pictures of Hitler were going to be 'creamed off' *[5] This was a pointed symbolic linking of the problem of food shortages with the decline of the Führer myth.

Criticism of police-state controls was expressed predominantly in small-scale ways (through rumours, jokes, unofficial whispering campaigns, news from abroad passed on in confidence), and it made use of the manifold informal channels of everyday communication: chats during working breaks, when shopping or in the pub; conversations with neighbours, friends and relatives. As early as October 1934 the Cologne Gestapo had ascertained that popular discontent was

> in no sense an assumption, but an indubitable and established fact. The latter point must be emphasised, because this mood of depresssion about the economy cannot readily be detected in a public, outward sense. The relevant elements of the population lack the courage to mount public demonstrations or other such forms of action; they dare not engage in public criticism for fear of denunciation and the informer system. In view of its breadth and depth, we must not be indifferent as regards this discontent. The danger that the dissatisfaction may ultimately develop into opposition to the state

---

*[A pun on *entrahmt*, which means 'taken from their frames' as well as 'creamed off' or 'skimmed'. (Transl.)]

and the movement is a real one. Propaganda deployed by Communist elements at this juncture will increase the danger.[6]

An important contributory factor in fostering this 'second public opinion', as a Gestapo official termed it in 1934,[7] was the opportunity of picking up foreign news broadcasts, thanks to improvements in radio sets. Here the principal tool of Goebbels's propaganda, which had actually been systematically promoted, produced highly unwelcome side-effects. Despite harsh penalties (during the war a so-called 'broadcasting crime' could be a capital offence), this consequence could not really be prevented. Although we should not overestimate the immediate political and ideological influence of Radio Moscow, the BBC and other stations, their news broadcasts (and deliberately disseminated rumours) at least undermined confidence in the German news media, especially as military reports in the second half of the war became increasingly misleading.

The Security Service (SD) of the SS reported on 22nd January 1943, for example:[8]

> It is clear from a wealth of general and detailed reports that the effectiveness of the public media of guidance and control is at present very seriously impaired. Among many reasons, the principal one that may be suggested is as follows:
>
> The national comrades have the feeling that when events take a negative course the public media of guidance and control always put an 'official face' on them. A condition has thus developed whereby, under such circumstances, considerable sections of the nation no longer regard the press as the best source of instruction, but assemble 'their own picture' from rumours, stories told by soldiers and people with 'political connections', letters from the front and the like. Hence often the most nonsensical rumours are accepted with an astonishing lack of criticism.

Compared with the dissemination of news from foreign radio broadcasts and the spread of indigenous rumours and jokes, the influence of information documents produced by the political resistance was depressingly small.[9] In any case, such documents circulated in larger numbers only in the years 1933–35 (though then often in tens of thousands). Distributing them was a much riskier business than listening to the radio within the secrecy of one's own four walls. Production, which meant getting hold of paper, stencils, typewriters and duplicating machines, became more and more difficult; and the disparity between the risks to life and liberty involved in distributing the documents and the tiny effect they were likely to have on their diminishing numbers of readers became steadily more demoralising with the years. To this extent the decline in the number of resistance documents should not be seen as implying a general forswearing of opposition and resistance, although there certainly were such causal links in specific cases. Opposition within the toalitarian state, in fact, found its best expression in informal activities which were hard for the Gestapo and the law to get to grips with.

Even though we may be convinced, in the light of the documents mentioned, that there was far more criticism and disaffection during the Third Reich than the unitary facade of propaganda might lead one to expect, there are still plenty of questions concerning the historical significance of this body of data:

– Which social groups did the critical voices actually come from? Were critical attitudes concentrated in certain groups, while other groups remained predominantly loyal?

– Was the criticism that found expression directed against the regime as such, or against particular measures? How can we establish a correct weighting of the occurrence of criticism, on the one hand, and approval of the regime, on the other?

– Is it possible to trace definite shifts in public opinion over the twelve years of Nazi rule?

– What exactly is the relationship between the relatively frequent occurrence of critical, oppositional *opinions* and the manifestly less frequent occurrence of oppositional *activity*?

To answer these questions, let us first see what are the main themes that keep cropping up in the reports on public opinion.

First and foremost are constant variations on the theme of dissatisfaction with oppressive living conditions and poor material provision. Children in Schwelm in Westphalia sang in public a dialect rhyme that their parents had composed in secret:

Wir hant jetzt einen Führer.	We've got a Leader now, they say,
Et wird ok alles dürer.	Bread's gone up, but not your pay.
Bald gift et groten Krach.	Soon the lot'll blow sky-high,
Dann sagt wi widder goden Tag.	Then once more we'll say 'Goodbye'*.[10]

This was a commentary on the catastrophic price rises in basic foodstuffs during 1934–35. Even the Dortmund Gestapo, which was responsible for southern Westphalia, was driven to comment in August 1934:

> The broad masses in the industrial district live for the most part on bread and potatoes. Such price rises must therefore be simply catastrophic for morale.[11]

---

*Instead of 'Heil Hitler!'

In fact, prices of meat, butter, fats and oils in this region had risen between 50 and 100 per cent, locally, above 1933 levels by December 1935; potatoes cost between 50 and 70 per cent more in 1935 than they had the year before. On top of this there were considerable fluctuations in supply and periodic shortages of essential goods.

Although shortages eased somewhat in the following years, bottlenecks were a constant source of criticism. It is evident, indeed, that the Nazi leadership had learned from the hunger unrest of the First World War and accordingly tried deliberately to keep supplies at acceptable levels. To this end it even used up foreign exchange during the pre-war period that had really been earmarked for rearmament, and from 1939–40 onwards it attempted to keep German rations as high as possible by plundering the occupied territories. Nevertheless, daily provisions for the mass of the population were tight in the Third Reich, were repeatedly disrupted and were therefore a frequent cause for the voicing of discontent. This fact must be borne particularly in mind, since in the memories of many contemporaries the pre-war National Socialist years have been retouched to seem an epoch of recovery and prosperity. This perception owes most to a retrospective comparison with the lean years of the Depression and the war (and immediate post-war period). At the time, the thirties were viewed in a far less optimistic light. The fact that there was a *tendency* in the direction of economic improvement was welcomed, and hopes of recovery were pinned on it, but criticism of crucial and persisting shortages was sustained.

The second recurrent legend, that Hitler rapidly succeeded in generating employment, is a reflection more of Nazi propaganda than of the reality of the Third Reich. Many people were impressed for a time in 1933 by the barrage of propaganda to the effect that the nation was now engaged in the decisive 'battle for work', but the elimination of unemployment in fact proceeded at a sluggish pace. The publicly celebrated fall in the number of unemployed for 1933–34 was caused by a mild upturn in economic activity that had already become apparent in 1932, as well as by the 'voluntary' detailing of unemployed workers into Labour Service (*Arbeitsdienst*) camps and so-called emergency labour camps, where they were drafted to work mainly on public prestige projects for minimal wages. In any case, the statistics were extensively manipulated. The sobering reality was becoming increasingly recognised by 1934, and matters remained thus until the inauguration of the big rearmament projects of 1936–37, which did indeed generate full employment: a critical juncture, noted in many morale reports.

In addition, even enthusiastic supporters of National Socialism realised in the course of the year 1934 that many of the promises made in the NSDAP programme and repeated by Party speakers were not being honoured. Certainly, many National Socialists had been able to exploit the upheavals caused by the seizure of power and wangle jobs for themselves, thereby satisfying their own personal ambitions or at any rate securing steady employment and providing for their material needs. But many NSDAP members, and especially members of the SA, were disappointed too: either because the intertwined apparatuses of Party and state still preserved jobs for enough representatives of the bureaucracy and the old elites to provoke the hatred and envy of the lower-level Nazis who were done out of them; or because everyday routine even under totalitarian rule gave the Brownshirt rebels of the street battles of 1932 relatively little scope for action;[12] or even because not a few of the Nazi leaders who had attained the dignity of office now turned their powers and privileges as fully to account as the 'bigwigs' had standardly been accused of doing under the Weimar Republic. Rumours about careerism, special privileges, extravagance and corruption among the 'Brownshirt bigwigs' became regular topics of popular grievance.

On the other hand, records of public opinion concerning the Nazis' use of terror against political dissidents were astonishingly infrequent, even though in 1933, at least, the press carried very detailed reports of persecutory measures taken against Communists, Social Democrats and trade unionists.[13] There are two possible explanations of this silence in face of the terror against the left. First, many supporters of former centre and right-wing parties welcomed the fact that the National Socialists were cleaning out the 'Reds', and they were prepared to put up with or sanction terrorist 'excesses' in the process. Secondly, however, open discussion of anti-left terror measures was far riskier, in view of its clear political subject-matter, than talking about, say, scarcities of food. Many people who did not condone the terror against the left kept silent for fear of being persecuted themselves.

Public opinion as regards the campaign against the churches was another matter. Critical comments about restrictions on church institutions and activities, about the persecution of priests and active parishioners and about the anti-church stand taken by Nazi leaders make up a large part of the morale reports, especially in regions where Catholicism was still deeply rooted in people's daily lives or in the strongholds of the Protestant 'Bekennende Kirche' (Confessional Church), which was opposed to the regime on religious issues.[14] That the anti-church campaign caused so much stronger a reaction within public opinion than the incomparably more brutal attacks on the left is mainly due to the fact that there was less of a taboo against talking about the former area of conflict: church activities that were still permitted overlapped in various ways with activities that were forbidden or persecuted In addition, impeding a Corpus Christi procession, say, was a real incursion into the lives of practically all the inhabitants of a strongly Catholic area, whatever the inhabitants' individual political beliefs. Dismay was correspondingly more general, and people made no bones about their criticism.

Popular attitudes towards the persecution of the Jews were inconsistent.[15] In places where National Socialism was able to attach itself to deeply rooted anti-Semitic traditions (often with a religious foundation), the racially-based anti-Semitism of the Nazis also found receptive audiences, though on a much lesser scale than might have been expected in view of the central role played by hatred of the Jews in Nazi ideology. The mass of the population, however, was not induced into actively supporting the persecution of the Jews; nor, on the other hand, was it moved to criticise it on grounds of principle or indeed to show solidarity with those who were being persecuted and defamed. Hence anti-Semitism was in no sense, as some historians and journalists have supposed, an essential instrument in integrating and mobilising the population in a National Socialist direction. Yet the persecution of the Jews provoked wide-scale popular criticism (i.e. something more than the few acts of solidarity performed by individuals) only when the material interests of the majority group within the population seemed to be adversely affected. The Nazis' exclusion of Jewish cattle dealers from doing business, for example, was effected only with difficulty, since many farmers clung obstinately to their traditional and financially rewarding business contacts.

Only one event really exposed the anti-Semitism of the National Socialists to almost unanimous public obloquy and indignation: the *Reichskristallnacht* pogrom of 10th November 1938.[16] This is shown, at any rate, both by secret opinion reports compiled by police and government agencies and by information smuggled abroad by socialist informants for the 'Reports on Germany' of the Social Democrats in exile (SOPADE).

From the Reports on Germany, SOPADE, November 1938[17]
The brutal measures against the Jews have caused great indignation among the population. People spoke their minds quite openly, and many Aryans were arrested as a result. When it became known that a Jewish woman had been taken from childbed, even a police official said that this was too much: 'Where is Germany heading, if these methods are being used?' As a result, he was arrested too. [. . .] After the Jews, who are going to be the next victims? That is what people are asking. Will it be the Catholics? Or will an emergency general capital levy by imposed? [. . .] In the whole [. . .] region there is great anger at this vandalism. One clear example of this was when the SA smashed up a shop after dark and were pelted with stones from an

orchard opposite, under cover of the darkness [. . .] Many people are looking after the Jewish women and children and have put them up in their homes. Housewives are shopping for the Jewish women, because it is now forbidden to sell food to them. It has also been established that the violence of the measures taken varied considerably from place to place. [. . .] But among the people the action was certainly a cause of great intimidation. [. . .] People no longer dared to speak so openly. Everyone realised that the Nazis have got the power to do whatever they want. [. . .] The protests by the people of Berlin against the robberies and arson and the evil deeds done to Jewish men, women and children of all ages were plain. They ranged from looks of contempt and gestures of disgust to overt words of revulsion and harsh abuse.

From the Reports on Germany, SOPADE, December 1938[18]
The broad mass of the people has not condoned the destruction, but we should nevertheless not overlook the fact that there are people among the working class who do not defend the Jews. There are certain circles where you are not very popular if you speak disparagingly about the recent incidents. The anger was not, therefore, as unanimous as all that. Berlin: the population's attitude was not fully unanimous. When the Jewish synagogue was burning [. . .] a large number of women could be heard saying, 'That's the right way to do it – it's a pity there aren't any more Jews inside, that would be the best way to smoke out the whole lousy lot of them.' – No one dared to take a stand against these sentiments. [. . .] If there has been any speaking out in the Reich against the Jewish pogroms, the excesses of arson and looting, it has been in Hamburg and the neighbouring Elbe district. People from Hamburg are not generally anti-Semitic, and the Hamburg Jews have been assimilated far more than the Jews in other parts of the Reich. They have intermarried with Christians up to the highest levels of officialdom and the wholesale and shipping trades.

From a report by the Heilbrunn Gendarmerie station, 26th November 1938[19]
Some have welcomed the actions taken against the Jews; others watched them calmly; others again are sorry for the Jews, though they do not necessarily express this openly.

From the monthly report of the Regierungspräsident of Lower Bavaria and the Upper Palatinate, 8th December 1938[20]
The Jewish assassination of the German Embassy counsellor in Paris gave rise to sheer anger in all sections of the population. There was a general expectation that the national government would intervene. The legal measures directed against the Jews were therefore fully understood. What was correspondingly much less well understood, by the bulk of the population, was the reason for the manner in which the spontaneous actions against the Jews were carried out; indeed, these were condemned, including widely within the Party. The damage to shop-windows, merchandise and furniture was seen as an unnecessary destruction of valuable items which in

the last analysis were part of the national wealth of Germany, and it was viewed as a flagrant contradiction of the goals of the Four-Year Plan, especially the salvage campaigns that are being conducted at this very time. Fears were also voiced that the destructive urges of the masses might be reawakened by these means. In addition, the incidents enabled unnecessary sympathy for the Jews to come to the surface, in both town and countryside.

From the monthly report of the Regierungspräsident of Lower Franconia, 9th December 1938[21]

[. . .] The punitive measures, particularly the imposition of a financial penalty, have been generally approved. A majority, especially among the rural population, regrets that the actions have caused valuable items to be destroyed which, in view of our raw-material position, could more appropriately have benefited the community as a whole. A further complaint was that the action was continued even after the decree by the Reich Propaganda Minister ordering its immediate cessation and, in particular, that foodstuffs were deliberately destroyed. In Oberelsbach, *Bezirksamt* Bad Neustadt an der Saale, $3\frac{1}{2}$ cwt. of flour were thrown on to a manure heap and a crate of eggs from storage was thrown on to the road. According to one *Bezirksamt* report, during the subsequent *Eintopf* collection many national comrades declared that since so much property had been destroyed, they felt unable to contribute to the collection.

By contrast, the public labelling of the Jews with the yellow star, the deportations to the east and the exterminations in the gas chambers left no great mark in the public-opinion reports. Part of the explanation for this is the fact that information about the mass exterminations in the east was made available only very circumspectly (and hence was not easily understood, even by the SD's and Gestapo's informants). Nevertheless, it was possible – except for those who preferred to keep their ears and eyes shut – to learn at least the fact of mass murder, even if not all the details, from foreign radio broadcasts and from rumours that percolated through.[22] There seem to be several reasons why public concern and dismay had significantly diminished, in comparison with reaction to the *Kristallnacht* pogroms. The atrocities of the concentration camps did not take place in Germans' immediate sphere of experience; people preferred not to believe such grim reports until their truth had been clearly confirmed; and, not least, the growing everyday distress caused by bombing and by fears for relatives at the front had anaesthetised people to the sufferings of the Jews, who as a population group had long since been displaced from the immediate field of vision of the Germans in any case.

Foreign policy was for a long time one of the regime's particular assets in the balance-sheet of public opinion. The step-by-step dismantling of the provisions of the Versailles Treaty was felt by a wide majority to be a reparation for the injustice that the victorious First World War powers had inflicted on the Germans. Even the SOPADE reports, whose contributors came from within anti-fascist (and mainly working-class) circles, repeatedly confirmed the widespread prevalence of nationalistic thinking. The SOPADE report for January 1935 concerned the plebiscite in the Saar. Since Versailles, the Saar had been administered by the League of Nations. In 1935 the population was able to vote, in a free election, for retention of the *status quo* or for union with either Germany or France. The SPD and KPD jointly urged the former. Over 90 per cent, however, freely voted for '*Heim ins Reich*' ('Back to the Reich').[23]

> In western Germany the National Socialists have played the plebiscite result up into a big national celebration. The great mass of industrial workers let themselves be swept along on the tide of national triumph.

Reaction to the German march into Austria in March 1938 was described by a Breslau Social Democrat:

> On Friday, as I followed the decisive blow-by-blow story on the radio, I thought: 'This means war. In a few hours enemy planes will probably be flying over Breslau.' I couldn't bear to stay in my flat any more. The scene on the streets had completely changed. SA, SS, HJ, BdM were on the streets in large numbers. Although people didn't yet know how it had all happened, they were shouting in a sort of frenzy, 'Heil Hitler! Austria is ours! Sieg Heil to our brave soldiers,' and so on. The atmosphere was similar to that on 30th January 1933, when Hitler became Reich Chancellor. Everyone was carried away by this atmosphere. Only gradually did groups form here and there, and people began to discuss what had happened. You could hear people saying that war was now on the way and that they were going to go home and pack and move out to the villages. But these were isolated voices. The general opinion in the groups was: 'Let's face it, Hitler is a great man, he knows what he wants and the world is scared of him.'
>
> Conversations the next day followed the same trains of thought. Hitler's prestige has risen enormously again and he is now practically idolised. The objection that the western powers might still intervene and issue Germany with an ultimatum was laughed out of court. The western powers simply daren't do anything against Germany, and even if they do, Germany is strong enough to get its own way.
>
> I have discovered one thing about the attitude of the population: if Germany were to become embroiled in a war today, the whole nation would march. And it would probably be a long time before the country began to have second thoughts about the war.

The general approval accorded to the reintroduction of conscription, the remilitarisation of the Rhineland, the Austrian *Anschluss* and the later annexation of the Sudetenland marked the closest convergence between the hopes and expectations of the population and the self-portrayal of the regime and of its 'Leader', Adolf Hitler. The summing-up of the popular mood made by the Dortmund Gestapo in July 1935 is quite fair:

> Thus recognition of the great achievements of the Führer in the sphere of foreign policy [. . .] is coupled with a widespread and unmistakable lack of enthusiasm as regards economic matters.[24]

But a closer analysis of public opinion also shows that the population followed Hitler's revisionist foreign-policy line less unhesitatingly and unreservedly than the enthusiastic acclamation of National Socialist successes may perhaps imply. On the people's part there was always the unvoiced doubt whether it was possible to fulfil these various demands without provoking the danger of world war. During the crisis over the proposed annexation of the Sudetenland in September 1938, misgivings and deep-seated fears of war were even articulated relatively openly in the street, on public transport and in pubs and factories. The National Socialists' reaction to these amazingly plain manifestations of disfavour was to swivel their propaganda round through 180 degrees. Whereas Hitler had hitherto been acclaimed as the statesman of peace who sought only to restore Germany to equality of status, there was now a switch to accustoming the population to the idea that war was an acceptable ('ultimate') means of attaining a position of Pan-German dominance. None the less, popular response to the outbreak of war on 1st September 1939 was muted. In particular, there was none of the uncontrolled enthusiasm that had marked August 1914.

This unenthusiastic mood picked up from time to time as German troops made successful advances in the so-called 'Blitzkrieg' campaigns. The high point of morale was reached after the occupation of Paris and the news of the conclusion of an armistice. Longings for peace were combined with feelings of triumph over the 'ancestral enemy' who had remained undefeated through the four years of the First World War.

> *From a report on morale, Security Service (SD) of the SS, 24th June 1940*[25]
> Reports from all areas of the Reich concur in yielding the following picture on this matter at the present time. Under the impact of the great political events, and enthralled by the military successes, the entire German people now has an inner unanimity as never before, and there is a deep sense of unity between the military and home fronts. Opposition groups have had the ground knocked completely from under their feet. Everyone is looking with gratitude and confidence to the Führer and to his armed forces as they speed from victory to victory. Opposition activity is met by fierce condemnation on all hands. The population's healthy will to resist is in the ascendancy and

is effective proof against inflammatory and defeatist influences. These are either completely ignored or are angrily condemned.

From a report on morale, SD, 27th June 1940
The tumultuous excitement of previous weeks has changed, following the armistice negotiations and the subsequent cessation of hostilities, into a mood of celebration marked by quiet, joyful pride and gratitude to the Führer and the armed forces.

This deep joy found particular expression with the announcement of the news of the implementation of the armistice agreement. Flags were hoisted everywhere, even during the night, and many national comrades hurried out on to the streets and squares to take part in various demonstrations of thanksgiving. Some had to return home disappointed, since no appropriate arrangements had been made, although they had in fact been expected. Only a few failed to seize the opportunity of the night-time celebration. The broadcast was even heard in air-raid shelters, since, much to the people's annoyance, there were attacks by English aircraft at the very time of the announcement.

The secret reports by the SD continued to record upswings of morale following the various German victories, but they also regularly noted unease, as hopes for peace were shattered, and a basic sense of uncertainty as to the ultimate outcome of the war.[26] The invasion of the Soviet Union on 22nd June 1941 and, especially, the defeats at Moscow and Stalingrad in the two following winters increased the numbers of those who felt that the war was lost and wanted it to end. Disapproval remained primarily passive, however; little trace of determined resistance, not to mention revolt, could be detected. Three reasons for this can be cited. First, the Nazi apparatus of terror remained intact until the final days of the war and stifled at birth all forms of individual, let alone collective, rebellion. Secondly, the strains and burdens of the war – the fatigue of industrial workers, in particular, employed on 10- or 12-hour shifts, and of the population in general, subjected to night-time bombing – created a climate of resignation that led people, not to rebel, as British strategy had calculated, but merely to wait passively for the war to be over. Thirdly, long years of experience of living under the Third Reich had given rise in any case to a drastic atomisation of social relations and this now impeded the communal effort that would have been needed for resistance.

The passivitiy of the German people in the latter stages of the war thus points up again the basically limited character of the so-called 'popular opposition'. Most of the 'grumbling' remained fruitless and failed to lead to active opposition. Taken together, the targets of all the adverse expressions of opinion did indeed cover virtually all aspects of life, but as a rule each criticism related only to a clearly defined

63

individual case and did not vitiate a person's assent to other policies of the regime. Likewise, the critics themselves came from virtually all groups within the population, but they did not manage to achieve a true collective identity as an opposition; they remained isolated from one another, held back by passivity or preoccupied by special interests.

The SOPADE reports on Germany had tried several times to assess the extent of the 'grumbling', the degree of serious opposition and the level of support for the regime. The report for November 1935 noted:[27]

> Discontent has increased again and is more extensive than last year's grumbling ['*Meckerei*'], but it is no stronger than before. It is expressed more openly, but it has just as little political content. People say, 'Things can't go on like this' and they also say, 'Things can't be worse after Hitler', but behind these phrases there is neither the will to overturn the system nor any conception of what should take its place.
>
> This being so, and given past experience, when waves of grumbling have always been followed by periods of general disappointment and disillusionment, we must again face the possibility that the present very widespread grumbling may switch round into very general indifference and resignation. After 'Things really can't go on like this' there is: 'What's the point, the Nazis are dug in much too tightly'. These extraordinary swings of mood, which are typical of Hitler's Germany, place great strain on the mental strength and resilience of everyone involved in illegal opposition.

From SOPADE report for February 1938[28]

> To the extent that the attitude of a whole nation can ever be reduced to a formula, we can assert roughly the following three points:
>
> 1 Hitler has got the approval of a majority of the nation on two vital questions: he has created work and he has made Germany strong.
>
> 2 There is widespread dissatisfaction with prevailing conditions, but it affects only the worries of daily life and has not so far led to fundamental hostility to the regime as far as most people are concerned.
>
> 3 Doubts about the continued survival of the regime are widespread, but so is the sense of helplessness as to what might replace it.
>
> The third point seems to us to be the most significant, as far as the present situation in Germany is concerned. Despite the regime's enlargement of its political and economic power, and despite the far-reaching approval this has gained for it among wide sections of the nation, there is a feeling of uncertainty about the future. Whether this feeling springs from worries about a war, or is a result of shortages, the regime has not so far succeeded in eradicating the idea that its rule may only mark a period of transition. This point is more important, as far as the regime's inner strength is concerned, than the recording of temporary oscillations between satisfaction and dissatisfaction. Nor does it contradict our observations that the political indifference of the masses is on the increase.

If we complement our use of these morale reports by examining the vast number of documents covering police and judicial proceedings relating to anti-state offences, then it becomes clear that the picture of a harmonious 'national community cannot be sustained.[29]

This wealth of evidence of the negative underlying attitude of a large section of the population – indeed, a majority of the population, if all separate aspects are added together – must not be built up to look like a secret national resistance. Diverse forms of criticism and 'grumbling' were quite capable of existing side by side with partial recognition of the regime or at least with passive acceptance of authority. What the secret public-opinion reports document is not that there was a broad and pervasive 'popular opposition' but, above all, that the propaganda image of widespread radiant enthusiasm was mere window-dressing. In actuality, after the seizure of power the dynamism of the National Socialist movement petered out in rows about jobs and influence and ritualistic parades and rallies devoid of real emotional participation. The mass of non-Nazis fell back into passive discontent, querulous resignation and privacy-seeking accommodation with the regime.

'Grumbling' and the rumour system were thus indicators, not of an extensive 'popular opposition', but of the deep fragmentation of public opinion into distinct spheres: the controlled (and increasingly discredited) sphere of the Reich Ministry of Public Information and Propaganda; citizens' outward attestations of loyalty within the public domain; the internal opinion-gathering processes of the authorities and Nazi organisations; and uncensored private conversations. Since these different spheres of communication had little to do with one another, and indeed were often in direct conflict, the competition between them reduced the likelihood that realistic views of the situation would be formed or that any rational opinions might emerge at all. Criteria for the truth of statements and for the veracity and credibility of opinions became unclear. It was hence inevitable that the ability of the population to assess the true position – and, ultimately, to act – should suffer. As in other social spheres, the effect of National Socialism on public and private communication was ultimately destructive.

When analysing the reports on public opinion and morale during the Third Reich, we should pay serious attention not only to indicators of discontent but also to instances of clear-cut approval of particular actions of the regime.[30] So far we have dealt especially with public and semi-private expressions of popular opinion, as documented by a vast range of morale reports. We have seen that the political effectiveness of the relatively large potential for discontent and criticism was restricted in double fashion: on the one hand, because people expressing critical views were isolated from one another and were preoccupied with separate individual interests, and on the other because partial criticisms arising on an everyday basis were often tempered by varieties of approval of what the regime was doing. In order, then, to assess the relative significance of criticism and consent, we must examine the life-situations and everyday experience of 'ordinary people' more closely. In doing so, however, we immediately confront a major problem. As mentioned, we possess essentially two large bodies of source material on public opinion: the secret morale reports, and the documents of court cases and police investigations involving oppositional activities and opinions (the so-called 'malicious offences').[31] The former kinds of source are concerned with more generalised analyses of the public mood, but in the process tend to leave obscure the specific, tangible individuals involved and the critics' social backgrounds. The documents of the cases of 'malicious offences', on the other hand, while yielding personal information about the accused, their origins and the social situations within which their acts of criticism arose, relate only to isolated cases coming to the attention of the courts and leave open the question how far they truly reflect overall opinion and mood: in the village concerned, on the worker's housing estate, among the small artisans, and so on. We can attempt to escape this difficulty by suggesting comparative analyses of the two categories of source – that is, making a closer approximation to the complex historical reality by viewing it from both directions at once.

Nevertheless, it must still be stressed that reconstructions of forms of social perception and behaviour can only ever be approximations: they are no substitute for the direct encounter with the individual case, with the unique experiences of flesh-and-blood individuals living their daily lives during the Third Reich. Such individual experiences have to some degree been documented in autobiographical interviews; some people have come forward with their own written sketches and accounts. Police and court documents can help to fill out these kinds of case history.

Both types of access to historical data, the generalising approach centred on social and political structures and the individualised approach tracing people's everyday experiences in all their complexity and inconsistency, are indispensable in the formation of a full and impartial judgement.

FOUR

The Führer myth and consent in everyday life

After the Second World War was over, and Germany underwent Allied occupation, it was regularly asked why there had been no repetition of the revolutionary events of November 1918. The uniform readiness of the Germans – apart from some numerically small resistance groups – to keep doing their 'duty' to the end, as soldiers or as workers on the 'home front', was generally explained by historians in one of two ways: in terms of a seduction theory, or of a supervision theory.

The seduction theory emphasised the active, or at best passive, assent accorded by the overwhelming majority of the population to the National Socialist regime, this assent being generated by the sophisticated techniques of fascist mass organisation and the supposed irresistibility of Goebbels's propaganda. The supervision theory, on the other hand, asserted that the systems of control, internal espionage and policing in the Third Reich were so efficient that even the faintest attempt at opposition was sure to lead to the concentration camp.

Both theories highlight phenomena which were indubitably present in the Third Reich and which hampered the formation of an effective resistance movement. But, as all-or-nothing accounts, they are distortions of the historical reality. There were in fact many kinds of criticism of the regime's social and political measures, as we have seen in the previous chapter. These criticisms of shortcomings in everyday life were voiced despite the stage-managed public appearances of the 'Leader' and the mass rituals at Party congresses which undoubtedly impressed many people, and despite widespread enthusiasm, or at least satisfaction, over Hitler's foreign-policy successes. The fear of war which Germans clearly felt in 1938–39 also shows that even Goebbels's sophisticated propaganda met with disbelief when it flew in the face of the basic everyday needs and experiences of the population, such as the longing for peace and the memory of the horrors of the First World War.

Similarly with the supervision theory. Although the apparatus of control and terror was more elaborate than in any previous political system, there were pockets within which nonconformist behaviour could and did develop, albeit under conditions of constant danger.

A deeper historical analysis of the Third Reich must therefore go beyond emphasising its supposedly unchallengeable techniques of manipulation and surveillance – techniques which in any case always provided an easy excuse for those who persistently shrank from any form of resistance. Rather, we must explain what were the fundamental needs and activities in which the population's active consent, or passive participation, took root, enabling the trains to Auschwitz to continue, metaphorically as well as literally, to leave on time till the bitter end.

The selfsame morale reports by the Nazi agencies and the exiled Social Democrats which recorded a wide variety of critical opinions also noted – simultaneously and, of course, with reference to the same groups of people – a wide range of favourable responses to the actions and characteristics of the Nazi regime.[1]

First and foremost were the regime's successes in foreign policy, which won considerable approval even among members of the erstwhile labour movement, as the SOPADE reports repeatedly and despondently noted. Approval was centred, in the first place, on the fact that Hitler had succeeded in short order in undoing discriminatory provisions of the Versailles treaty ('bringing home' the Saar, remilitarising the Rhineland, reintroducing general conscription) and in achieving long-standing national goals, such as uniting all Germans within one 'Greater Germany'. But the tangible gains in foreign policy were not the only thing that counted with public opinion: the methods did too. The population responded positively to the fact that after a decade of timorous, compromise-minded and inconsistent foreign policy, Hitler seemed to have pulled off his successes despite – or perhaps precisely by – his risk-taking, his radicalism, his refusal to compromise and his unswerving purposefulness. (In reality, Hitler's successes were due more to the incomprehension and disunity of his opponents.) As important as the successes themselves, then, was the posture of the 'Leader', conjuring up, after a decade of uncertainty, a strength of leadership and a desire for success in which it seemed possible to have faith. Popular approval clustered round motifs such as success, strength, recovery and security; national advance was the collective transfiguration of individual yearnings. Daydreams of glory and grandeur seemed to be being fulfilled.

The SOPADE reports on the German entries into the Rhineland in 1936 and Austria in 1938 similarly noted three aspects of popular approval of the new direction in foreign policy: satisfaction that Germany was playing a world role again; acceptance of the principle that violent methods were justified by 'tremendous' successes; and personalisation of the successes through the Führer cult:

> The Führer's foreign-policy statements strike a chord with many workers too; especially with young people. The firm stand the Führer has taken over the occupation of the Rhineland has been universally impressive. Many people are convinced that Germany's foreign-policy demands are justified and cannot be passed over. The last few days have been marked by big fresh advances in the Führer's personal reputation, including among workers.[2]

> There is no mistaking the enormous personal gains in credibility and prestige that Hitler has made, mainly perhaps among workers. The fact that Austria was subjugated by force has had little or no effect so far on the way the event is being judged here. The crucial point is that Austria has been annexed; not how. On the contrary, it is being taken for granted that the annexation was carried out with violence, since almost all the major successes of the system have been achieved with the use of violent methods.[3]

It is a similar story with the economic and social policies of the regime. Here above all there were enough everyday problems and inconveniences to provoke repeated criticism. Yet the overall balance of achievement was positive: in contrast with the depression of 1932, there was a brilliant 'economic miracle' which at the minimum guaranteed the basic needs of 'work and bread' for everyone from 1936–37 onwards and was also beginning to meet the demand for higher-quality goods. Germany's gross national product rose from 58 thousand million Reichsmarks in 1932 to 93 thousand million RM in 1937, overtaking the record level of the 'golden twenties', 89 thousand million RM in 1929.[4]

Admittedly, the share taken by armament production rose enormously (from 1 per cent in 1932 to 13 per cent in 1937). But even though there was a fall in the share taken by consumer-goods production relative to the rapidly growing GNP (81 per cent in 1932 to 64 per cent in 1937), this in no way meant that consumers were deprived, since there was a considerable increase in the disposable volume of consumer goods: whereas the 1932 figures came to only two-thirds of the 1928 volume, by the end of 1936 they had already surpassed this record level of the twenties. Since the number of those in work rose correspondingly (from 12.9 million in 1932 to 18.9 million in 1937, a slightly higher level than in the pre-crisis year 1929) and the length of the average working week settled again at its pre-crisis level (from 41.47 hours in 1932 to 46.07 hours in 1937), total wages and salaries also increased (from 27.4 thousand million RM in 1932 to 41.5 thousand million RM in 1937, just below the 1929 level of 44.9 thousand million). Although the price of the upturn had been the inflationary financing of rearmament, which gave an ominous undertone to Germans' hopes for the future, people had work again, they were earning money and they could avail themselves of the growing number of consumer goods on the market. In order to sustain the feeling of success and the hopes of recovery the National Socialists were even prepared, despite shortages of foreign exchange and strict trade controls, to import materials for consumer-goods production as well as products and raw materials needed for rearmament. Despite their candid plea for 'guns, not butter', the Nazis knew, so to speak, which side their bread was really buttered.

The contradiction between the need to rearm for war and the need to satisfy the consumer demands of the population could certainly not have been kept concealed for long. In fact, the economic situation in Germany became considerably more acute in 1939. It was only Hitler's unleashing of world war that enabled the contradiction to be displaced externally. Half of Europe was plundered so that the Germans could be kept supplied to a relatively high standard. Germany lived on credit: first its own, and then that of other countries.

None of this was apparent to the man in the street in the 1930s. He regarded the 'economic miracle' as a positive achievement of Hitler's, although there was, admittedly, a wide discrepancy between the propaganda images and the Third Reich's actual achievements in social policy. For example, *Kraft durch Freude* ('Strength through Joy', an arm of the official pseudo-trade-union organisation, the German Labour Front)[5] organised holiday trips ranging from weekend excursions to health-cure visits to the Harz and the Black Forest, and Norwegian cruises. In reality, however, long-distance travel was restricted to a hand-picked minority, and most Germans spent their vacations at home or in the immediate vicinity. Similarly, a couple getting married – provided that they were 'genetically healthy', in the sense laid down by the 'racial biologists', and that the wife surrendered her office or factory job – could receive a marriage loan which could be partly 'repaid' by the production of children. (In sarcastic parlance, the loan was '*abgekindert*', i.e., literally, 'childed off'.) The long-term effect, however, was neither to raise the birth-rate nor to reduce women's work. Again, although the construction of the *Autobahnen* and the establishment of a large car factory to build the so-called 'KdF car' (the later '*Volkswagen*' or 'People's Car') led to an eventual modernisation of private transport, the immediate result was that these facilities, and the money which many Germans had saved towards the 'KdF car', were diverted to the rearmament programme. The same was true of the DAF's campaigns that were designed to give a 'social welfare' tinge to industrial relations: annual national job competitions; competitions for the 'model National Socialist firm'; *Schönheit der Arbeit* ('Beauty of

Work') etc.[6] Nevertheless, what was achieved was enough to give the population a foretaste of the better future of their dreams. Since the upward *trend* was maintained, the regime's promises were taken as guarantees that the economic miracle would continue, and the manifest signs that the boom was inflation-based and dependent on the build-up of military weaponry were suppressed from consciousness. Even in 1943, when a majority of Germans, according to the SD reports, had stopped expecting a German victory, the Wüstenrot building society announced new business worth 201 million RM; and as late as February 1945 the Ludwigsburg building society was advertising in the magazine *Das Reich* under the slogan, 'Save in Wartime – Build Later'.[7]

National Socialist domestic policy also met with approval for its promise to create 'order'. Even acts of terror, detentions in concentration camps, the banning of Communists and Jews from public employment, bannings of political parties and the firing-squad executions following the Röhm putsch of 30th June 1934 were awarded positive verdicts, on the grounds that they showed that order would be enforced with a 'firm hand', that there would be a 'clean sweep', and so forth. Attitudes of servility that had been robbed of an outlet ever since the end of the Wilhelminian empire now had something to fasten on again, thanks to the Nazi state and its 'Leader'. But non-monarchist and non-militaristic Germans were won over too: people who had seen the Weimar period primarily as one of political confusion and personal insecurity. The call for order did not balk at terror when it was initiated from above.

The widespread approval of Hitler on the 'law and order' issue, and the wholesale acceptance of the 'Leader's acts of illegality and murder, is documented unambiguously in the SOPADE 'reports on Germany' following the 30 June 1934:[8]

> The immediate result of the murders was great confusion, both as regards the way they were viewed and as regards their future political consequences. On the whole, Hitler's courage in taking decisive action was stressed the most. He was regarded practically as a hero. Hitler's slandering of the victims, their homosexuality and their 30,000 Mark meals, was at first also adjudged heroic. As to what the repercussions of the events of 30th June and their aftermath will be, an agreed and definitive answer cannot yet be given. Our comrades report that Hitler has won strong approval and sympathy from that part of the population which still places its hopes in him. To these people his action is proof that he wants order and decency. Other sections of the population have been given cause for thought.
>
> East Saxony: A small businessman told me that he and his colleagues had known for a long time that Hitler was going to strike at Röhm and his associates. He still sees Hitler, even now, as an utterly honourable man who

wants the best for the German people. It is only Hitler's hangers-on who have been preventing him from working for the people, and now he has got rid of them. When I tried to explain to him that Hitler alone bore the responsibility for all the murders, these and earlier ones, he said: 'Still, the main thing is, he's got rid of the Marxists.' He also said that Hitler undoubtedly still had as much support among the majority of the people as he did before, especially as he was now cleaning out the dreadful SA, who had done Germany great damage. Wages would definitely be cut now, and industry would be able to get back to work and start earning money. He still swears by Hitler as a superhuman being, even if he is a murderer many times over.

Bavaria: 1st report. By slaughtering his 'best friends', Hitler has forfeited none of his mass support as yet; rather, he has gained. Reports from different parts of Bavaria are unanimous that people are expressing satisfaction that Hitler has acted so decisively. He has produced fresh proof that he will not settle for second-best and that he wants decency in public life.

Not the least of the achievements of the National Socialist mass organisations was that despite objections on the scores of bossism, bureaucracy and empty rituals, they provided a considerable number of people with tasks and jobs which boosted their sense of self-esteem and even offered real if limited opportunities for promotion. Even during the earlier so-called period of 'struggle' before 1933 the NSDAP and the SA had held on to their members primarily by promoting an empty but permanent activism which seemed, to people with shattered social or working lives, to offer a way of escape from resignation and despair. National Socialist ritual and staged mass events, particularly the appearances of the Führer, enabled the followers to feel reassured of their own significance. This mechanism explains the effectiveness – though also the limitations – of Nazi propaganda. It fastened on everyday needs for security, sensual satisfaction and social aspiration which the crisis-torn Weimar republic had been unable to meet. But it was also required, after the National Socialist seizure of power, to regenerate the charismatic excitement that otherwise threatened to drain away in the face of an everyday routine of economic difficulties and political disappointments.

This was the very role that the Führer myth performed: it bridged the gap between, on the one hand, the need for uplift, security and a positive outlook on the future and, on the other, the disillusionments of everyday Third Reich life.[9] All the morale reports are agreed that the 'Leader', Adolf Hitler, was popular among all social classes, including sections of the working class. He was expressly and personally exempted from the numerous criticisms of the regime's actions that were voiced. The standard phrase, 'If the Führer knew about it . . .', was used to imply that he would be as 'tough' with the shortcomings and improbities of the lower-level leaders as he was with the political opposition. In this sense Adolf Hitler's popularity articulated a certain basic consent to the system on the part of the majority of the population, a consent that remained unaffected by outspoken expressions of criticism on points of detail.

It emerges, accordingly, that the targets of criticism were generally lower- and middle-rank Party functionaries, officials and subordinate representatives of authority; support was centred round the figure of Adolf Hitler. Plainly, the Führer myth was not merely a product of extravagant National Socialist propaganda but was the focal point of popular consent vis-à-vis the regime. We can help to explain this 'schizoid' attitude by applying to fascism Max Weber's explanatory model of 'charismatic authority'. It was only to be expected that the enthusiasm of the pre-1933 'movement' phase would wear off in the course of everyday life; in order that the swell of approval should not run completely dry as daily concerns reasserted themselves, a highly visible identification-figure was needed who could represent the system as a whole. This was the 'Leader'. The Führer myth made it possible for people to give voice to everyday 'grumbles' and yet consent to the overall dispensation. This basic consent, articulated primarily in the Führer myth, comprised approval of personal, authoritarian control, enthusiastic support for the posture of 'decisive action' and the imposition of order through terror, and uncritical applause for both the real and the specious propaganda achievements of the system.

These elements of basic consent to the regime were also necessary to ensure that the system itself functioned on a day-to-day basis. A system that was unconditionally rejected by most of the people would hardly have been able to call on them to carry out the daily tasks necessary to sustain routine work and public discipline, or to accept National Socialist propaganda and the decrees and regulations issued by the authorities. But there was not only the experience of unavoidable participation in the system on a daily basis, as a small cog in the large machine: there was also, specifically, the mobilisation of a fair-sized section of the population through the National Socialist mass organisations. The mass organisations themselves were a combination of enforced participation, motivated support and purely nominal membership. The virtually inexhaustible supply of insignia, functions and sub-functions, ranging from the *Blockwartsystem* of neighbourhood spying to the *Luftschutzbund* (the air-raid protection association), again made no genuine alteration to the often depressed social position of the office-holders, but they had a symbolic effect. Life was a state of subservience sweetened by privileges.

73

The evidence of Hitler's popularity to be found in both the SOPADE and the police and governmental morale reports is too plentiful and convincing to be overlooked. Approval of, not to say enthusiasm for, Hitler as an individual was indeed a feature of everyday life in the Third Reich. Two extracts from a great range of sources can serve to illustrate this.

A SOPADE report compiled as early as April/May 1934 noted:[10]

A general phenomenon that has been noticeable for some time is still evident: Hitler is generally exempted from criticism.

A report from Bavaria says, 'One cannot ignore the fact that many of those who grumble and complain still have faith in Adolf Hitler's strength and his honourable intentions, but believe that even he cannot prevail single-handed.'

A correspondent from Berlin puts the point in more detail: 'In general we can say that Adolf Hitler is exempted from criticism, his aims are conceded as honourable and people think that he cannot be blamed for the mismanagement of his subordinates. This is partly the result of the systematic Führer propaganda, but it is also undoubtedly the effect of his personality. His personality impresses simple people, and Hitler still has a lot of personal support among the workers.'

It was particularly the Führer's public appearnaces, covered nationwide on the radio, that won approval. The approval began to crumble only when Hitler's optimistic forecasts were all too clearly given the lie by wartime realities. This oscillation between belief and scepticism emerges forcibly from an SD report on popular reaction to Hitler's speech on Heroes' Memorial Day (*Heldengedenktag*) in 1942, following the winter of 1941–42 when German troops outside Moscow had suffered their first defeat:[11]

On the basis of reports now available from all parts of the Reich on the Führer's speech on Heroes' Memorial Day, it can be said that the Führer's words have found a powerful echo among the population.

The sentence in the Führer's speech which left the strongest and assuredly most lasting impression was: 'But we can already be certain of one thing today: the Bolshevist hordes which failed to conquer the German soldiers and their allies this winter will be beaten by us next summer and will be destroyed!' The Führer's words have enormously strengthened the hopes entertained by the greater part of the people that Bolshevism will be destroyed this year. In this connection, numerous national comrades expressed views to the effect that the Führer would never have spoken in these terms if he himself had not had the utmost conviction and certainty that his forecast would be borne out. Only a few individual comrades voiced doubts – in view of the imponderable size of potential Soviet strength and in view of similar forecasts made by the German military command last year –

whether it would in fact be possible to bring the eastern campaign to a victorious and definitive conclusion during the coming year.

The Führer's statement that 'the eventual frontiers of the Bolshevist colossus will prove to be far removed from the sacred fields of Europe' also attracted considerable notice. Many detected a certain contradiction between these words and the Führer's statement closely preceding it, that the 'Bolshevist hordes will be beaten by us next summer and will be destroyed'; and a few even felt that they implied the view that it would never be possible to smash Bolshevism entirely.

The intensity and the wide currency of the Führer myth can scarcely be explained, however, if it is seen simply as the result of National Socialist propaganda or as the product of mass yearnings and wishful thinking. So artificial a construct would inevitably have shattered on making impact with real experiences and real disappointments. For the Führer myth to be effective, two conditions were indispensable.

First, the 'Leader' had to remain well distanced from sources of criticism and discontent in everyday life. Hitler's reluctance to get mixed up in disputes involving rival state and Party authorities contributed to the image of the 'Leader' as the disinterested final source of authority and court of appeal. So did the role he was supposed – quite wrongly – to have played in the so-called Röhm putsch of 30 June 1934. Hitler's intervention was perceived as securing 'order' in response to the threat of SA terror; in the process, the population accepted the unlawful killings of SA leaders as well as the accompanying murders of several other politicians (for example, the former Reich Chancellor Schleicher).

Secondly, the personal charisma of the 'leader' had to be held up as responsible for all the domestic and foreign-policy achievements which promised to fulfil people's yearnings for security, progress and national greatness. This mechanism is much in evidence in the morale reports. Goebbels's propaganda fell on fertile ground here; this indeed was the basis of its effectiveness. The propaganda was believed as long as Hitler could point to a string of successes and soothe any discontent by prophesying new ones. Correspondingly, the ending of military success caused the Führer myth to fade. It is true that the SD reports indicated that even after the turning-point of the war there was still a widespread desire for a while to hear the Führer speak over the radio again. But the enthusiasm became progressively more short-lived after each radio address, and Hitler held back more and more from making personal public appearances, correctly gauging the decline in his powers of persuasion. For most Germans, the Führer myth was dead before Hitler physically took his own life.

Active consent – popular approval of Nazi policies – was conditional upon the regime's ability, by invoking a constant fresh supply of genuine or ostensible achievements, to meet people's basic everyday needs for security, progress and a sense of meaning and purpose in life. Its initial asset was the fact that the Weimar Republic, by virtue of defeat in world war, inflation and world economic crisis, had created a deep-seated feeling of insecurity and made many Germans grasp thankfully even at pseudo-solutions. It was only through the ever more hectic pursuit of real or spurious successes that the charismatic Führer myth was able to withstand the disillusioning impact of ordinary everyday actuality.

The mechanism whereby contrary but genuine experiences were repeatedly repressed called for the construction of adversarial images and scapegoats. The 'forging' (a popular fascist term) of the 'national community' or *Volksgemeinschaft* required, as a complement, the strict marginalising of 'community aliens' or *Gemeinschaftsfremde* – not only Jews, but gypsies and the so-called 'asocial'. The beliefs that Hitler's draconian measures really put a firm curb on crime, that he educated the 'work-shy' into doing productive work in camps (in the Reich Labour Service, in the police Work Education camps and in the concentration camps) and that he saw to it that women could walk unmolested through the streets at night, are among the hardiest popular myths about Hitler. The approval of the manifest use of force against outsiders also revealed a readiness to countenance latent force within the ostensible 'national community' itself, if this was in the interests of 'order'. Putting it perhaps over-forcefully, we can say that an aspect of consent to the Nazi regime was not so much the often-cited fear of terror as the emotional approval of terror when it was directed against 'community aliens' and hence served the supposed restoration of 'order'.

Here we plumb the most deep-lying reason for the consent given by the majority of the population to the Nazi regime. The real appeal of the Führer myth was to the longing for normality felt by a population which had been shaken by crisis and whose social reference-points had been thrown into disarray.[12] The recognition that National Socialism was constitutionally quite incapable of restoring normality could be kept repressed as long as new campaigns and partial successes preserved expectations and a sense of promise; and as long as the regime's 'restoration of order' conveyed an impression, however spurious, of efficiency and strength of will. Within the 'national community', 'order' was upheld by appeals for discipline, by ranking the people into hierarchies and by obtaining self-imposed participation; at the margins, 'community aliens' faced outright violence. The 'normality' that people craved thus embraced both regimentation and subservience, and was underpinned by the overt use of force.

Active consent and sympathy with the goals and actions of the regime, however, are not sufficient on their own to explain why National Socialism remained politically unchallenged within Germany, even after the turning-point of the war. Here we must ask why it was that those who had not subscribed to the promise of National Socialism were not roused into positive acts of opposition. This widespread *passive* consent – accepting the regime as a given, and being prepared to do one's day-to-day 'duty' – rested on a process which the Nazi regime simultaneously combated and fostered: a retreat from the public sphere into the private.[13]

As National Socialism penetrated traditional social milieux and institutional structures, partly breaking them up, partly taking them over, so it drove their former members into the private domain. Views that had become politically taboo or criminal could be maintained only within the family circle or among close friends, if at all. Even politically-minded people withdrew into privacy in face of the constant pressure to conform, the perpetual need to demonstrate loyalty, the thought control and the bureaucratic routine that marked public life under National Socialism. But the withdrawal into the private sphere was not only a mass retreat from the Nazi pressure to conform: it was also the product of long-term socio-cultural trends. The development of German industrial society into a modern mass consumer society on the American model, which had first come to expression in the 'golden twenties', was reactivated by the economic recovery of the 1930s, after the hiatus caused by the world recession. Although the manifestations of modernity had provoked the censure of the fascist 'blood and soil' Romantics, the Nazi regime was only selectively hostile to these developments. 'Degenerate art' disappeared from the galleries; but the modern designs of countless consumer goods remained. 'Judaised' and 'nigger-ised' jazz was officially combated; but up to the outbreak of war jazz records not only remained on sale in Germany but were actually produced in large quantities. Even during the war, watered-down versions of modern dance, spectacular revues and lavish film musicals were among the forms of entertainment expressly promoted by Goebbels. The Third Reich was actually the great age of the 'unpolitical' films of the UFA (the biggest German film production company).

Even Coca-Cola consumption rose significantly in Germany in the thirties. Agrarian romanticism notwithstanding, the Nazi regime fostered enthusiasm for modern technology, not only because it needed it as part of its armoury for conquering *Lebensraum*, but also because the toughness, frictionless functionality and efficiency of the machine matched the ideal of the fighter and the soldier, the man 'hard as Krupp

77

steel' The mass adulation and star treatment accorded to German racing drivers in the thirties is a case in point.

Especially important was the growth of broadcasting, which achieved a breakthrough with the cheap mass production of the 'People's Wireless Set' (*Volksempfänger*). Leaving aside the question of political propaganda, the result was a pronounced shift whereby people found their daily (or rather, evening) leisure entertainment within the family. Radio, and particularly television – the development of which was accelerated during the Third Reich, both technically and as regards programme-making, though the decision to go ahead with mass production of sets was blocked by the outbreak of war – were media which in fact positively emphasised the individualised private sphere.

In addition, until the outbreak of war it was not illegal to listen to foreign broadcasts, apart from Radio Moscow. German radio magazines published the details of programmes from neighbouring countries. Even during the war, when listening to so-called enemy stations carried the risk of severe penalties (including death), radio remained a much-used medium, and people could check improbable German military reports against, say, the BBC within their own homes.

These examples also show, not just that there was an increased desire during the Third Reich to withdraw into the private sphere, but that the demand for non-political entertainment was met by plentiful offerings from the repertoire of modern leisure culture and mass consumption. The Reich Propaganda Minister Goebbels, in particular, made it quite clear that he assumed that a broadcasting policy based on 'non-political' relaxation would have a more positive effect on the population, given the likely demoralising realities of the war, than programmes filled with dogmatic Nazi ideology and diehard slogans. In his inaugural speech at the 16th Broadcasting Exhibition in Berlin – held from 28th July to 6th August 1939, when preparations for the invasion of Poland were in full swing – he declared:[14]

> Broadcasting has certain quite definite tasks to perform, particularly in view of the times in which we are living at this moment. What is needed is not heavy, serious programmes which, after all, only a fraction of the people can grasp; we must provide the broad masses and millions of our people, engaged as they are in a struggle for existence, with as much relaxation and entertainment, edification and improvement, as possible.

By contrast, National Socialist dogmatists were certainly zealous in recommending a return to old 'German values'. But their practical efforts to stem the flow of 'Americanised' modernity had patchy results. Even the massive wartime police operations directed against jazz and swing, which culminated in young swing fans from Hamburg being sent to the youth concentration camp at Moringen, were not strikingly successful.

The 'double life' that was led by a large section of the population – in the public domain, delivering the required pledges of loyalty and quotas of economic output; in private, pursuing non-political spare-time pleasures with minimal possible interference – certainly ran contrary to National Socialist mass mobilisation, but it can in no sense generally be reckoned as opposition or resistance (although the dividing lines between these notions were fluid, as the case of the young swing fans shows. See Chapters 8, 10 and 11.) The very retreat into privacy crippled possible resistance and weakened people's sense of concern at the excesses of the regime. It led to self-absorption and self-sufficiency, to the mixture of 'apathy and pleasure-seeking'[15] described by one wartime diarist:[16]

> And the world? The best thing is to shut your eyes to it and to stop hearing and seeing all the dreadful fuss and bother that is getting more and more confusing and difficult to sort out. No one has any idea where it is all going. Most people have completely stopped even asking, and are just sticking to the tiring daily business of shopping and thinking about food. The emptiness inside one is getting more and more noticeable . . .

Paradoxically, then, even the population's counter-reaction to the National Socialist pressure of mobilisation served to stabilise the system.

It is clear, if we follow the everyday-life approach, that the experiences of separate individuals cannot be neatly and mechanically categorised under labels of 'dissent', 'passive consent' and 'active participation'. This very fact, however, seems to me to be a vitally important result of the everyday-life approach, since it shows that the Third Reich cannot have failed to leave its mark on all members of society: on the common people, who some would allege to have been basically in opposition; on the middle class, alleged to have been basically non-political. It serves as a warning against a facile recourse to percentages: what proportion of Nazis in the population was opposed by what proportion of nonconformists and what proportion of people prepared to resist? It is heartening in a socio-political sense because it demonstrates that even fascist fellow-travellers or active participants could undergo liberating experiences from which a democratic outlook was capable of emerging. It is dispiriting, on the other hand, to those who would like to think that 'another Germany' remained intact through twelve years of fascism: a Germany not integrated into the system, not caught up in the system's functioning – maybe only a minority of the regime's political opponents, but in its essence undamaged. Even the resistance fighters who did not conform were weighed down by the experience of persecution, by the sense of their own impotence and of the petty compromises that were imperative for survival. The system did its work on the anti-fascists too; and often enough it worked despite the shortcomings of the fascists themselves.

FIVE

Areas of conflict in the Third Reich

Unlike the simple version of totalitarianism that is nowadays mainly confined to German school history textbooks, where it is graphically represented by pyramid-shaped diagrams with Hitler at the top, the Third Reich was very far from being a monolith. To say that it was riven by internal conflicts, however, does not mean that it was a chaotic phenomenon without a specific mode of development, a fascist logic of progressive radicalisation,[1] nor does it mean that all, or even a majority, of the conflicts that occurred should be set down as resistance. In schematic terms, we can sketch three differing types of conflict within the Third Reich.[2]

1 *External conflicts* between the National Socialist system and its opponents, and/or between the system and the groups which it combated in the course of its history. Opponents of both foreign and domestic policy are included here, especially the labour movement and, to some degree, the Christian churches.[3] The characteristic feature of this type of conflict was that the opponent groups all possessed their own distinctive identities and traditions which enabled them to offer differing patterns of behaviour in response to National Socialism and its demands. They might yield to the pressure to conform, or form temporary coalitions, or persist in outright rejection. In all cases they opted for those forms of behaviour which most allowed them to maintain their identities and traditions.

2 *Internal conflicts* occurring horizontally, so to speak, among different factions within the ruling National Socialist system. Researchers into fascism are nowadays agreed that National Socialism was not a monolithic system free of contradictions, but that it broke down into a 'polycracy' of competing power blocs. These blocs (additional personal fiefdoms, satellites and offshoots can also be identified) were in a state of permanent and raging conflict with one another that was very costly in material resources and, in the long run, was damaging to the system's ability to function. This type of conflict is

fundamentally different from the first type, since the parties involved were concerned to improve their standing within the system and to mobilise the resources of the Nazi regime to their own advantage. Nevertheless, under certain conditions such conflicts could also lead to a rejection of the Nazi system as a whole, as was shown by the path taken by the military, which proceeded from internal opposition within the system to the conspiracy of 20th July 1944.[4]

3 Another type of conflict, again involving fissures within the National Socialist system but this time ones running *vertically*: conflicts between the Nazi elites and the masses, or between the elites and individual groups within the population under Nazi rule.[5] This may seem to be the same as the first type, but the parallel is misleading. In the first place, these groups by no means necessarily possessed the firm, traditionally-rooted identities characteristic of the clearly-defined opponent groups; secondly, these conflicts did not arise out of a confrontation between the Nazi regime and the world outside it, but sprang from the inner dynamics of the Nazi regime itself – for example, from the contradictions created by rearmament. Rearmament generated a demand for labour which in practice led automatically to wage increases in armaments firms; these increases in turn caused financial and material resources to be diverted from rearmament. A similar conflict arose from the mobilisation of young people into the Hitler Youth: successful mobilisation inevitably permitted the youth organisation areas of autonomy, that led to clashes with the original goal of training young people for membership in a dictatorial and authoritarian society and establishing the discipline necessary for war.

Conflicts between elites and ruled need not destroy the very framework of the system. They can also merge with the other forms of conflict: for example, rival leadership groups can play off the demands of different sections of the population against one another; or bodies expressly devoted to resistance can fasten on the day-to-day conflicts between the population and the elites.

The Nazi regime did not resolve the social contradictions that were inherent in a modern industrial society; it disguised them, and offered no distinctive functional model of conflict resolution. The much-heralded unifying 'new order' had little real substance. Agrarian romanticism and racialist ideological indoctrination were at odds with the demands posed by modern technological armaments and warfare. Policing and surveillance systems became so ramified that they got in one another's way; in many areas of society, improvisation replaced plans for reorganisation which in any case had been badly thought out. The unresolved contradictions piled up, driving the National Socialist leadership into trying increasingly reckless and under-funded solutions, until the regime perished amidst the chaos of war and mass destruction.

These internal contradictions created a wide variety of situations in which people were faced with the choice either of complying with National Socialist orders or of resisting them.[6] Decisions of this kind often faced people who were not even conscious and persistent opponents of the regime. Ought you to contribute to the Sunday *Eintopf* collection? Ought you to send your son to join the Hitler Youth, even though you were afraid of the 'bad influence' it might have on him? Ought you to ignore the possible penalties and listen to foreign radio broadcasts, even if you only wanted to find out how the war was really going? In all cases the specific nature of the situation determined whether the individual was aware of the import of the decision or whether he simply acted spontaneously and unreflectingly in the way his social background and everyday experience indicated.

No system is capable of punishing all infringements of its norms; any attempts to do so would make the system itself seize up. Accordingly, within each system, including National Socialism, there are whole areas of behaviour that normally lie below the threshold of police intervention. It was in these areas – usually private ones – that most acts of *nonconformist behaviour* vis-à-vis the Nazi regime were clustered (see diagram). As a rule these were separate individual acts of infringement of the norms and did not call into question the system as a whole.

Forms of dissident behaviour in the Third Reich

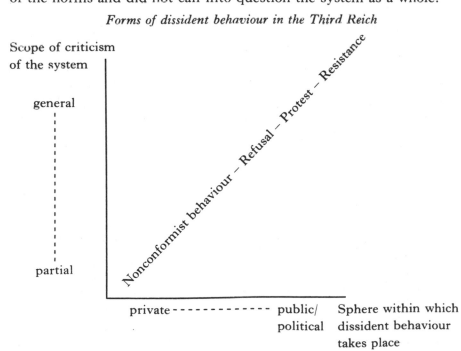

83

Acts of nonconformist behaviour became one degree more general, and hence directed politically against the regime, if they were more than just breaches of particular norms of the system but were undertaken in opposition, say, to orders issued by the authorities. *Refusals* of this sort could, for example, include not sending one's son or daughter to the Hitler Youth or the League of German Girls (BDM, *Bund Deutscher Mädel*) in contravention of repeated official injunctions, or failing to increase one's personal work output despite recurrent calls by management.

More far-reaching again, because one stage further in the direction of wholesale rejection of the regime, was *protest*, though this might still be a matter of single-issue action, such as the churches' campaign against euthanasia (that is, the murder of disabled people).

On the gamut of dissident behaviour, *resistance* can be taken to denote those forms of behaviour which were rejections of the Nazi regime as a whole and were attempts, varying with the opportunities available to the individuals concerned, to help bring about the regime's overthrow.

Of course, many of these forms of everyday behaviour are, in the customary sense of the term, non-political. In most other societies they are permissible, or are at least put up with as long as they take place in the private sphere. The all-pervasive interventionism of the Nazi regime brought about an objective change in their significance. Whereas it is a fundamental assumption of a liberal social order that the domains of the private (and/or social) and the political coexist side by side, National Socialism politicised society by importing political claims into domains that had previously been private. At the same time it broke up the separate sphere of politics, characterised in liberal society by the rule of law and the rational organisation of administration, and gave the vacuum over to the competing claims of different bureaucratic groups. One possible reaction to this enforced politicisation – and one that was, in actual practice, widespread – was to retreat into what was held to be non-political privacy: to keep an uneasy distance from all semblance of public and politically accountable behaviour. Yet even if people subjectively viewed their behaviour as non-political, and sought to justify it in these terms when faced by National Socialist sanctions, their behaviour nevertheless often fell, as a matter of objective fact, within the area of jurisdiction claimed by the regime. Deciding precisely where a particular act or form of activity should be located on the scale of dissident behaviour must depend on the individual case, but in practice National Socialism commonly gave people no choice, if they did not succumb, other than to progress from nonconformity to refusal to resistance. It was, indeed, their experience of the regime's encroachments on their lives that often drove people who had merely given cautious voice to dissident attitudes into espousing more decisive opposition.

As we try to understand the motives and preconditions underlying the various forms of nonconformity and resistance, the question arises: where were oppositionally-minded people able to take refuge? Were there areas from which they were able to draw strength and encouragement for oppositional activity? It is not for nothing that reference has been made to the fact that the National Socialists were at pains to smash traditional socio-cultural structures of solidarity. These indeed proved to be particularly stubborn sanctuaries of opposition and became bases for unexpected counter-attacks into the National Socialists' own territory. Particularly significant here were sub-cultural structures of solidarity within Catholicism, solidarity among friends, neighbours and colleagues in workers' housing estates, and comradeship in the workplace itself.

Yet even though these traditional social environments became sanctuaries of dissident behaviour, they were by no means left untouched by the social and political changes that took place during the Third Reich. The dynamic effects of economic boom based on rearmament not only altered the social position of the working class but affected the middle classes too. Life in the provinces was changed both by the process of migration from the countryside to the cities with their better-paying industrial jobs and by the National Socialists' attempts to penetrate all the traditional structures of political life. Changes in the position and conduct of young people were particularly noticeable; young people, after all, had not undergone the sorts of experience which adults had under the Weimar republic.

Some of these changes in social status and social environment worked in the Nazis' favour; in other cases, different tendencies cut across one another; in yet other cases, changes went contrary to the Nazi social design, vague though this was. In the following chapters we shall try to weigh up these different processes, from the point of view of their effect on the National Socialist system of authority.

SIX

The middle classes and the Nazi state

We shall now try to see whether the conflicting evidence of criticism and consent can be more readily assessed if it is set against 'ordinary people's' actual social situations. This chapter will begin by taking the case of the middle classes; the two subsequent chapters will examine the situation and behaviour of workers and young people. (Comments on the history of women under National Socialism will be found in Chapters 9 and 12.) The reason for choosing these three major social groups will be readily apparent. In so far as it is possible to generalise about such large-scale and complex groups, we can say that they differed considerably in their relationship to National Socialism and in the general outlook on life which they brought to bear on the years 1933–45.

The middle social strata provided a disproportionately large number of recruits to the NSDAP before 1933, as all analyses of elections and studies of Party membership structure show. The working class, by contrast, represented the electoral force which, in spite of Nazi attempts to woo it, remained loyal as a majority to the two workers' parties, the SPD and the KPD, and to the Christian Labour Movement that was closely linked to the Catholic Centre Party. Young people, the group we shall turn to last, did not come into conflict with the Hitler Youth (and later the Gestapo) until the late 1930s and early 1940s, following years of exposure to primarily National Socialist educational influences both inside and outside school.

These, then, are our three 'strategic' groups, representing different social environments and different responses to National Socialism. First, the middle classes.

Allegiance and disenchantment[1]

Electoral studies and surveys of Party membership show that the NSDAP drew particularly on the middle social strata for its intake during the Weimar Republic. The traditional bourgeois parties were squeezed into insignificance as the NSDAP expanded; in middle-class neighbourhoods the NSDAP obtained greater-than-average numbers of votes, as it did in rural areas not influenced by political Catholicism; there were disproportionately more teachers, small traders and craftsmen (*Handwerker*) in the Party than in the population generally; and, not least, even before 1933 the National Socialists had captured key posts in middle-class trade associations and representative bodies. Even members of the middle class who had not voted for Hitler shed no tears for the Weimar Republic he destroyed.

The revolution of 1918 and the inflation of 1923 had brought about a marked deterioration in the political and economic position of the 'old' middle class or *Mittelstand*, in comparison with the Imperial period. Before 1914–18 the Social Democratic labour movement was politically excluded from the authoritarian state, and the middle classes enjoyed special favour as a bulwark against revolution. With Weimar, established as it was on the social compromise between organised 'big' labour and big capital, the middle classes found themselves squeezed out by these twin fundamental classes of industrial society. Weakened in any case by the effects of war and inflation, they were hard put to it to hold their own amidst the competition for spoils between the two major organised groups; certainly, they no longer had the protected and crucial role they had enjoyed under the Empire.

The NSDAP held out to the middle classes the promise that it would lead them out of their no-man's-land in modern industrial society, where they were seemingly being trampled and buried by the big social blocs and the dynamism of mass society. National Socialism would restore them to their position of privilege. The influence of big capital would be generally curbed; 'rapacious' Jewish capital in banking and department stores, for example, would be expropriated; 'Marxism' would be smashed, and with it not only the Social Democratic and Communist parties but also the trade-union organisations whose concerted influence had kept up the wage-rates of journeymen, apprentices and skilled workers in small businesses and workshops; the malaise induced by a modern pluralistic mass society would be cured by a reassertion of traditional values of authority and obedience. In other words, the intermediate social strata of an industrial society dominated by big capital and big labour would once more become the respected and authoritative centre-ground of a hierarchical, corporatist society.

Analysing this 'check-list' of Nazi propaganda directed at the middle classes, we can distinguish three areas of concern: general unease at the marginalisation of the *Mittelstand* in industrial class society; demands for an authoritarian political and social system of values; and interests of a more immediate current or local nature, affecting particular sub-groups within the *Mittelstand*, e.g. traders, craftsmen and farmers, and formulated in greater detail.

Until the Nazis seized power, their catalogue of promises remained at once nebulously general and extravagantly specific. Vague plans for a general new corporatist order went side by side with unambiguous pledges to write off agricultural debts or to close down department stores. After 1933, however, there could no longer be any concealment of the extent to which the National Socialist leadership was prepared to honour its promises and comply with the wishes of its grass-roots supporters. The proponents of a middle-class offensive soon experienced a three-fold disappointment.

First, since the Nazi seizure of power led to the amalgamation of traditional state, economic and military leadership groups with the NSDAP leadership and the formation of a new cartel of elites, the most the *Mittelstand* could hope for was the role of junior partner. The state was not radically transformed along corporatist lines; Nazi politicians who backed the idea were thrust aside. Secondly, the banning of all forms of political opposition and the huge-scale persecution of the labour movement made a revival of the middle class's Imperial role as a bulwark against 'revolution' redundant. Thirdly, as the economic policy of the Third Reich increasingly gravitated around the needs of rearmament based on heavy industry, so the financial and economic resources for stimulating areas such as small-scale craft production or small business were inevitably restricted. The dreams of a new flowering of the 'productive classes' (*schaffende Stände*), which many a *Mittelstand* Nazi politician had cherished, were shattered by the harsh realities of an industrial economy: realities which even the Nazis had to accept, at least for the sake of their overriding aim of achieving war-readiness.

With the recovery from depression and the rearmament-led boom, Germany in the 1930s resumed its longer-term development as a capitalist industrialised society. The 'old' middle class of craftsmen, traders and peasant farmers lost ground. This is demonstrated by data on social structure as well as on production.[2] Despite the 'blood and soil' propaganda, the proportion of those earning their living from agriculture and forestry declined, from 30.5 per cent in 1925 to 28.9 per cent in 1933 and 25.9 per cent in 1939. In the same period the number of self-employed fell from 5.013 million in 1925 (15.6 per cent of the workforce) to 4.816 million in 1939 (13.9 per cent), whereas the number of industrial workers rose from 16.024 million in 1925 (50.1 per cent) to 17.577 million in 1938 (50.8 per cent). Thus the old middle class was continuing to shrink.

These various negative factors have suggested the thesis that the original mass of Nazi supporters, having become excluded from politics, was forced in its disillusion to recognise that it had become a 'redundant class' within the Third Reich too.[3] This view has been advanced by historians fairly often, in certain contexts quite legitimately. More recent research, however – in particular, more detailed studies of public opinion and of regional units small enough to be surveyed in detail – has shown that the *Mittelstand*, for all its criticism of the Third Reich, nevertheless continued to show it an especially high degree of loyalty. This paradox suggests that it is worth examining more closely how the policies of the Nazi regime affected the middle class's position, and which of the regime's measures were viewed as achievements and which as deserving of criticism.

It is also necessary to clarify which concrete hopes and expectations entertained by *Mittelstand* supporters of National Socialism were in fact disappointed by the regime and which were fulfilled. It should not be simply assumed that the non-fulfilment of the pie-in-the-sky programme which the middle-class Nazi politicians promised their supporters before 1933 inevitably meant a massive withdrawal of support from the Nazi regime. These overblown plans were undoubtedly important only to highly committed Party functionaries. And even in their case we should ask whether their commitment to the NSDAP was based primarily on policies and programmes, or whether it was not equally, or more, a matter of the outward forms of the fascist movement, its symbols, its rankings, its myths and its charismatic methods of mobilisation. Testimony by the 'old guard' suggests the latter. As far as our question is concerned, however, this implies that we should take note of the extent to which the *Mittelstand* representatives received special symbolic recognition in the movement and by the state, and how far their standing and professional status were enhanced even if their economic position was not fundamentally improved.

Of course, a decisive factor in the everyday relationship beween National Socialist policies for the *Mittelstand* and the targets of those policies still remains the extent to which the immediate social and economic demands of craftsmen, tradesmen and peasants, to single out the three major *Mittelstand* groups, were actually fulfilled.

The three areas of demands and perceptions distinguished above (the maximum programme; non-material expectations; and instant socio-economic measures) cannot be entirely separated from one another in practice. Nevertheless, let us begin with the third set of problems, those which came 'closest to the bone'.

The most important economic and social demands emanating from *Handwerk*, or the *craft trades*, were directed against competition from large-scale industry, which could produce goods more cheaply or could control raw-material markets, against state fiscal policy and the banks' credit policies; against the wage protection enjoyed by employees; and, not least, against competition within the fold, particularly from unskilled 'intruders' who had entered the craft trades. Craft-trade officials accordingly called for the establishment of something amounting to a special protection zone that would allay the impact of capitalist competition and give small firms a chance to recover from the effects of the world economic crisis.

Several of these demands for immediate action were met after 1933, at least in part. In 1934 compulsory guilds and corporate disciplinary procedures were introduced, barring craft professions to outsiders and establishing a rigid hierarchical organisation. This was hailed as a great success, although occasional complaints that the craft trades were now 'over-organised' came to the surface. In 1935 the entitlement to conduct a *Handwerk* business was made conditional on the acquisition of a 'major certificate of qualification' granted by the corporate craft organisation: usually the master craftsman's certificate. These measures enabled competition within the trades to be regulated.

The ban on trade unions, the establishment of the 'works leader' (*Betriebsführer*) as a key figure of authority within the firm (with the 'Law for the Regulation of National Labour' of 1934) and the official freeze on wage-rates also served to strengthen the position of craft bosses vis-à-vis their workers. Subsequently, however, this victory was to prove less satisfying, since the compulsory National Socialist employees' organisation, the German Labour Front (*Deutsche Arbeitsfront*, DAF), attempted (albeit with mixed success) to extend its influence from industrial firms into the craft trades. Here, contrary to design, the competition over spheres of influence that was typical of the Nazi regime picked up where the tension between the trade unions and the craft trades had left off. In addition, the character of the labour market changed. The attainment of full employment meant that the expanding industrial armaments firms could attract new workers only at the price of offering wages at higher than standard rates. Craft firms were faced with the choice either of seeing their employees drift away or of raising their own wages too. This dilemma is a graphic instance of the conflicts over goals in Third Reich society. Quite contrary to the National Socialist programme, the inevitable economic effects of the rearmament boom caused the *Mittelstand* to be caught once again between the pincers of industrial labour and industrial capital. Until 1935–36 the craft trades had relatively few complaints on the score of waged labour; indeed, the absence of such complaints from the bosses' usual litany is a clear indication that the situation was felt to be reasonably satisfactory. Later, however, the grievances began to pile up: about the attrition of the workforce, about demands for higher wages and about workers' renewed refractoriness in face of the threat to their position.

Significant gains in the areas of taxation and credit were beyond the reach of the craft trades. Here they were up against the ultimate sticking-point of National Socialist economic policy, the primary concern of which was to support large-scale capital for the sake of rearmament and the alliance with the old elites. On the other hand, several craft firms, especially in the second half of the 1930s, profited from rearmament either directly or indirectly and hence participated in the economic expansion. There were many firms, in particular, which benefited from redistributive measures within the *Handwerk* sector and in commerce. The elimination of firms with Jewish proprietors, which was completed by the end of 1938, played a part here, as did the 'self-purging' and 'closure' measures, directed particularly against non-viable small and part-time businesses, that were prescribed by the state although implemented by the *Handwerk* corporations. The repercussions of the 1939 closure measures show the equivocal character of documents recording public opinion: the measures were naturally the target of criticism and anger on the part of the small craftsmen who were adversely affected, whereas the tacit approval by those who were thereby relieved of competition came less obviously to the surface in the reports.

By way of summary, we can say that while craftsmen did not obtain the wide-ranging prerogatives which they had hoped for and which would have protected them, as an entire class, from the processes and developments of modern industrial society, nevertheless certain important specific demands were met and some craftsmen at least profited from the economic boom induced by rearmament. The longer-term result of National Socialist policy was to reinforce internal differentiation within the craft trades, rewarding the more efficient firms with an improved livelihood while the less viable went to the wall. There was a corresponding differentiation of everyday mood among the craftsmen themselves, with vehement complaints over specific measures accompanying a certain basic satisfaction with the regime. The mood is seen to shift considerably in the regime's favour if, instead of looking at immediate material demands, we consider expectations on the symbolic level. The high value publicly placed on craft work in National Socialist propaganda did not fail to affect the craftsmen's own sense of their worth, especially as the Nazi and corporate organisations had a wealth of posts at their disposal with which to 'honour' them.

There were similar developments in *trade and commerce*, though here, especially during 1933–35, complaints about National Socialist economic policy were noticeably more widespread. The complaints were, particularly, that the promised break-up of the department stores and co-operatives did not take place; and that the state policy of price control, which was in general fully welcomed, meant in specific cases that profit margins were too tight, squeezed between the prices charged by suppliers such as farmers and the purchasing power of customers, limited as it was by the freeze on wages.

The situation and mood of *farmers*, however, cannot be so straightforwardly summarised. National Socialist agricultural policy oscillated between the ideological promotion of the peasantry and the 'soil', as reflected particularly in the Reich Hereditary Farm Property Law of 1933, and campaigns to increase agricultural output (such as the annual 'battles for production'), which inevitably led to preferential treatment being given to efficient concerns.

Although the Hereditary Farm Property Law met some of the farmers' long-standing basic demands – in particular, the writing off of farm debt, a ban on compulsory auctions and the safeguarding of adequate farm sizes via protection of the right to undivided inheritance – it led in practice to numerous problems which fuelled the farmers' irritation. Those affected included not only the people directly disadvantaged by the new law (e.g. children who forfeited the right to inherit) and the so-called *Landwirte* (owners of smallholdings), who, because they lacked sufficient property or were pursuing agriculture only part-time, were not admitted to the privileged group of 'hereditary farmers' (*Erb-Bauer*); they also included owners of perfectly efficient middle-sized concerns whose needs for credit (to finance the requisite modernisation and mechanisation of production) failed to be covered by the new law's restrictions on borrowing.

There was a similar ambivalence in the way the compulsory organisation of agriculture in the Reich Food Corporation (*Reichsnährstand*) was perceived. In itself, this structure was entirely in keeping with the farmer's long-cherished wishes. But the excessive organisation that resulted gave rise to complaints, particularly about the encroachments of bureaucrats on the autonomy of the producers. Similar criticisms were directed against price regulations, controls over marketing and the controls that were even imposed on output in the 'battles for production' – even though these measures were also welcomed in principle.

In the later 1930s, as labour shortages in the armaments industries drew ever-increasing numbers of country-dwellers into the cities, the flight from the land came under attack from the farmers, not only because it conflicted diametrically with the National Socialists' often-invoked vision of 'blood and soil' but because it meant that the agricultural workforce – employed farm labourers and unpaid family members alike – was becoming ever more depleted.

The ebb and flow of expressions of disapproval among the peasantry is a clear reflection of market changes and variations of economic activity within agriculture. When agriculture picked up, day-to-day criticisms of the socio-economic aspects of National Socialism, at least, became muted.

Altogether, for farmers as for small traders and craftsmen, their perception of everyday life under National Socialism was undoubtedly conditioned in part by the prevailing economic situation, and for this reason became more favourable overall in the course of the thirties; but it was also affected by the more complex processes of political and social life. Thus, despite everyday 'grumbles', the *Mittelstand* became acclimatised to the authoritarian political system; it – or at least its more ambitious and successful members – accepted the regime's challenge of differential rewards for higher efficiency; and it enjoyed the esteem that was accorded to the 'productive classes' in symbolism and propaganda. Hence this 'old' middle class provided a considerable share of the mass basis for National Socialism, or at least of potential passive support, while furnishing only a few individual cases of active resistance.

The rising 'new' middle class[4]

The NSDAP drew particular support not only from the radicalised yet traditionalist small-scale self-employed groups, but from the so-called 'new' intermediate or middle strata (*Mittelschichten*): wage- and salary-earning commercial and technical white-collar employees, foremen, engineers, employees and officials in public authorities and administration, and students and graduates of higher education generally.

In contrast to countries such as the USA and Britain, the division between blue- and white-collar jobs in the German Reich was traditionally very pronounced. White-collar employees (*Angestellte*) claiming admission to the more highly-regarded *Mittelstand* could cite their distinctive system of salaries and insurance and various relics of the pre-industrial 'corporatist' order as criteria determining their social status. For these reasons they also felt adversely affected by the shifts in relative status between middle and working class caused by world war, revolution, inflation and rationalisation. After the world economic crisis they joined the NSDAP in large numbers, since it promised to make good the loss of status that they had experienced, or believed they had experienced, within mass industrial society.

At the same time, however, the non-self-employed intermediate strata realised that they were much more closely tied to modern society than were the small traders, craftsmen and farmers. The absolute numbers of white-collar employees and officials, and the relative proportion of people in employment they represented, were continually on the increase. Even though certain types of work were downgraded by the process of rationalisation, a new demand for office personnel and technical staff was arising. It thus took the particular crisis syndrome of the twenties, and the superimposition of immediate short-term distress on to the white-collar workers' belief in their long-term upward mobility, to persuade them that only a radical and violent new beginning with the impending 'Third Reich' could secure their goals and ambitions.

In any event, we can assume that white-collar workers were attracted less by idylls of craft work and 'blood and soil' romanticism than by the modern aspects of National Socialist ideology and propaganda. Nazi ideologues such as Gottfried Feder, a qualified engineer who had designed a concrete ship towards the end of the First World War (a notable though not economically viable achievement), and Fritz Todt, who had obtained a doctorate for his work on road construction and later played a leading part in building the Autobahn system, sketched a plan for society in which industry and technology, and hence engineers and other technical workers, would play a central role. They would provide the 'inventions' which would be the basis for the 'refortification' of the Reich. (Hitler himself had a lot of time for 'inventors' and self-made industrialists such as Porsche.) Such men also saw themselves as providers of expert technical and specialist knowledge in the service of the 'common good' which they were protecting against the self-centred, profit-seeking depredations of employers. In this sense Feder was even able to say that technology was 'bound to the soil and the nation', always provided it was National Socialist in orientation.

In its accompaniment to the work-creation measures, the Autobahn construction programme and rearmament, Nazi propaganda surpassed itself in its glorification of technology and its designers, producers and operators. (On the other hand, for the bulk of those involved, the scurrilous attacks on Einstein's 'Jewish' theory of relativity in the name of 'German physics' were of little consequence – especially since in this instance a *modus vivendi* was soon reached; experimental research in atomic physics was not forbidden, though it was fortunately not sufficiently encouraged to make possible a German atom bomb.) At the same time, unemployment among technological workers resulting from the world recession, which had lasted till about 1935, disappeared. Indeed, after 1936 a shortage of engineers became apparent. Whereas student numbers at technical institutes had declined to less than half the 1932–33 totals by the winter semester of 1937–38, owing to the long period of poor job prospects, they were now frantically built up again and in just two years, by the start of the 1939 semester, had risen by 25 per cent. These statistics are a good index of the extent to which engineers had come into demand in armament production in the intervening period. The improvement in material and intellectual status weighed more with the individuals concerned than any theoretical realisation they may have had that the National Socialists' policies for technology and research were unresolved and, for the medium term, disastrous: all measures were aimed at the quickest possible results, to the neglect of basic research and basic education and training. The consequences, indeed, soon became apparent, and bottlenecks in war production occurred, though they could be circumvented by *ad hoc* measures in the short run.

Similar contradictions arose with regard to other white-collar categories. Again, the trends which redounded to the regime's credit, the regeneration of employment, the gradual growth of prosperity in the later 1930s and, as a minimum, the safeguarding of legal and material benefits, went hand in hand with countervailing tendencies that served to lessen the gap between white- and blue-collar workers. The 'corporatist' myths which the Nazis were happy to propagate seemed at first sight to clash with the German Labour Front's ambition to win blue-collar workers the same legal status as white-collar workers.

For one thing, however, such aspirations fell foul of the maze of Nazi bureaucracy, and it is doubtful how far they were even noticed by the average white-collar employee. In the second place, the DAF was seeking to annul the white-/blue-collar distinction by raising the status of blue-collar workers, not by the proletarianisation of white-collar workers: by no means an identical threat. Altogether, the *Volksgemeinschaft* propaganda proposed not an egalitarian levelling-away of social differences, but merely a restructuring of the hierarchy on the basis of efficiency and performance. The replacement of the class model by a hierarchical continuum of achievement, with ascent the reward for 'merit', may not have corresponded to the old static ideal of the *Mittelstand*, but it exactly matched the norms and values of wage- and salary-earning members of the new middle class, with their individualistic expectations of upward mobility. If, behind the talk of a 'national community', the blurred outlines of a more open, flexible, achievement-orientated modern 'middle-class society' were discernible, then the 'new' middle-class groups in the Third Reich could indeed see themselves as midway up that social scale. They could make a link between their own group norms and the idealised *Volksge-*

meinschaft vision of the 'German family'.

A full assessment of the position and behaviour of white-collar workers in the Third Reich is still needed. It will have to take particular account of the fact that the processes of 'modernisation' of the white-collar class that were socially and historically more far-reaching took place as a result of the war and the immediate post-war period.

The equally ambivalent situation of public officials and civil servants (*Beamten*) cannot be dealt with in detail here. What can be said is that their actual behaviour in the Third Reich was the product of, on the one hand, continuities deriving from the model of the authoritarian state and, on the other, the progressive breakdown during the Nazi years of rational administrative procedures as a result of competition between institutions and arbitrary interventions by a dictatorial state. Nevertheless, there were also many people, particularly among the younger officials, who happily and unhesitatingly sacrificed the old traditions of state and public service in favour of the 'concept' of a new career-minded and unscrupulous elite. It is not without significance that one in every three members of the leadership corps of the SS had received higher education and, of these, one-third in turn had studied law. As the trials of war criminals were to show, similar numbers of qualified and 'promising' young lawyers were found among the administrators of the SD task forces (*Einsatzgruppen*) and of the 'final solution'.

National Socialism in the provinces[5]

We have said earlier that by no means all of the conflicts between the Nazi state and middle-class social groups can be subsumed under the fascism/anti-fascism schema. The problems often arose from the nature of the development of industrial class society as such, from long-term economic and social tendencies, or from the confrontation between traditional patterns of behaviour with the new forms of orientation offered by a mass society, in the unfamiliar guises created by National Socialism. But these problems were not unaffected by the political scenery set up by the National Socialists; there were varieties of cross-cuttings and interactions. Nazification and social modernisation partly ran on separate but parallel lines; partly obstructed one another; and partly reinforced one another. Within these areas of conflict the middle classes, with their largely traditionalist social and economic orientation, played a key role, albeit less as agents than as patients.

These many-layered processes cannot be condensed into simple formulae. Certain aspects of them can be illustrated by reference to conflicts between members of the middle class and National Socialist authority in small provincial towns and villages.

The Nazi seizure of power in the countryside made use of the local traditional structures in many ways, but it also came up against many stubborn obstacles. (And this is the point at which to mention the caveat that the 'countryside' is not a single unified entity but a collection of communities varying widely as to religious denomination, socio-economic structure and political colouring. Our discussion will hence bear only on certain shared types of problem.)

The seizure of power was made easier by the fact that as a rule the prominent members of provincial communities, and the small-town and rural middle classes on which their positions were mainly based, mistrusted the republican, democratic state, rejected the Weimar 'system' (particularly after the crisis of 1929–33), were favourably disposed towards the model of a strong authoritarian state such as they remembered from the days of the Empire, and, not least, were glad to see the elimination of the left-wing parties, the SPD and KPD.

The selfsame rural tradition of lack of sympathy for democracy, however, and the dominant role played by prominent local citizens, formed a fairly sizeable barrier to the formulation, dissemination and, after 1933, implementation of the NSDAP's aim of a political monopoly. Before 1932–33, especially in places where no key traditional local figures had gone over to the Party, the Nazis with their disproportionate numbers of young people and social outsiders had a hard job making headway against familiar local politicians. This was particularly true in the strongholds of political Catholicism, but it also applied in many conservative middle-class Protestant districts.

Conflicts between the traditional local ruling strata and the 'new men' of the National Socialist movement, who after Hitler's appointment as Chancellor of the Reich in 1933 began the step-by-step process of 'co-ordination' (*Gleichschaltung*) even in communities and districts where they were not in the elected majority, took on different shapes in different areas, depending on the local balance of forces. Certain basic patterns, however, which repeatedly recurred in varying combinations, can be distinguished.

There were communities in which the NSDAP, by dint of violence, prevailed against the ruling middle-class politicians. It was often, however, forced to see its attempts to enforce its leadership from above and from outside worn down by the labyrinthine social relationships of village and small-town life.

In most places, however, elements of compulsion and accommodation existed in tandem. In the *Landkreis* (rural administrative district) of Günzburg in Bavaria, for example, it is reckoned that 80 per cunt of the burgomasters who remained in office after 1933 had not belonged to the NSDAP before that date. Even in 1935 half of these were still not formal NSDAP members. In such communities, then, the new power structure of the Third Reich was a blend of the old elites and the newcomers.[6]

Local conflicts arose and might last for years, both in places where the NSDAP tried to establish itself mainly by force and in cases where there was wrangling over shares of power within the newly-formed cartels of old local elites and new NSDAP representatives. Disputes of this sort cannot usually be regarded as resistance, if resistance is taken to mean deliberately activity aimed directly or indirectly at the overthrow of the regime. Commonly there was a mixture of acts of accommodation, personal conflicts, conflicts over status, refusals to fall in with particular demands by the regime, and simultaneous support for other National Socialist measures. Nevertheless such everyday conflicts over local influence and politics, while falling short of overt resistance, were often factors which significantly hindered the regime's attempts to impose itself and implement its political goals.

Disputes about the 'co-ordination' of clubs and associations followed a similar pattern. Sometimes the independent traditions of particular bodies were stubbornly and shrewdly defended against the Nazis' demands; sometimes there was outward conformity, as when the existing chairman joined the Party or, if this was not possible, a Nazi chairman was elected *pro forma*; sometimes, however, clubs and societies went over intact into the structure and role laid down by the regime.

In the realms of sport, particularly, and of non-political cultural activities (e.g. music societies), the parades, competitions and displays that took place within the framework of the numerous National Socialist campaigns and public holidays certainly gave club members the opportunity to express themselves and gain public recognition. Whether their motives were political or not, such people thus became active contributors to the National Socialist ceremonial rituals that were important landmarks in the rural calendar.

The processes of *Gleichschaltung* and accommodation generated real political conflicts only when they came into collision with the elaborate and ramified structure of Catholic social and cultural life and its associated clubs and organisations. (We shall leave for later consideration the question of potential non-compliance by workers' clubs: the ban on the sports and cultural organisations of the labour movement was enforced with such harshness and rigour that the most their members could do was to keep up semi-illegal links through small circles of friends or to work entirely unpolitically in a 'bourgeois' organisation.) The Catholic organisations, especially the Catholic youth associations, were at first protected by the 1933 concordat between the Vatican and the Reich government.[7] None the less, the scope of their activities was progressively whittled down to 'purely church activities', and then one organisation after another was banned. The result was a whole series of protracted overt and hidden conflicts between the Nazi regime and the Catholic world right until the end of the decade. The National Socialists' attempt to enforce a cultural monopoly provoked a variety of acts of protest, refusals to co-operate on the everyday level, the secret continuation of club activities, and attempts to steer a course between semi-legality and prosecution.

There were particularly explosive disputes over the Nazis' attempt to impose uniformity in education. Guerilla warfare flared up between the Hitler Youth and church youth groups; Catholic parents and teachers battled against the introduction of non-denominational schools and, for instance, the removal of crucifixes from classrooms.[8]

Amidst all these manifestations of conflict between 'authority' and 'society' there were also occasional political quarrels with the National Socialist drive to monopolise political organisation, social life and the dissemination of information. But at the same time other types of dispute which do not easily fit into this interpretative scheme persisted in virulent form.

For example, many parents withheld their children from service in the Hitler Youth primarily because it would have robbed them of their authority over the children (or enabled the children to use their Hitler Youth 'work' as an excuse for getting out of helping at home). At the same time, many Hitler Youth activities were positively calculated to provoke teachers, parents and other 'respectable' people. Although the National Socialists had set out to enforce the restoration of the system of order and authority threatened by modern mass society, the character of their own mass mobilisation itself frequently served to chip away further at the traditional structures of authority and thus had a 'modernising' effect.

The compulsory enrolment of girls into the League of German Girls (BDM) also contributed to this modernisation of rural life-styles, since the education of girls had traditionally been much more definitely a matter of preparing for family life than that of boys. Nazi efforts at setting up womens' organisations in rural areas had a similar effect. Despite the reactionary image of women purveyed in propaganda, the momentum of organisational practice carried women away from the confines of family and home and into the public domain. Similarly, the arrival of modern mass media in rural communities and small towns (e.g. film shows and, especially, the 'People's Wireless Set') in the long run had a revolutionary impact on leisure habits. The tours organised by *Kraft durch Freude* also enlarged provincial horizons, although, as is now known, fewer people actually took part in them than the Nazis' publicity boasted. Yet even those left behind at home were at least offered the possible prospect of greater mobility. People from villages and small towns also became more mobile not only as the rearmament boom triggered off the flight from the land in the later 1930s but, grim though it sounds in view of the wartime sufferings involved, as a result of conscription into the Labour Service and the armed forces; these likewise contributed in the long term to the break-up of traditional structures.

All of these processes were either welcomed or were subjected to severe criticism, as personal interests dictated. Thus it was quite possible, in specific cases of conflict, for the individual National Socialist Party member to be in favour of given Nazi measures because they had served to give him a sense of liberation from confining traditional circumstances, while the opponent of such measures defended the increased weight of authority against 'modernistic' innovations. These sorts of cross-cuttings are also an important reason why people's personal memories of the 1930s are often more favourable than their knowledge of the criminal character of the regime might otherwise permit.

We can say by way of summary that 'ordinary middle-class' people's experiences of the Third Reich cannot be reduced either to the straightforward formula of growing disillusionment and disobedience or to the cliché of docile subordination. Middle-class perceptions and behaviour formed a complex set of layers of criticism and consent. Even the many instances of conflict with local wielders of National Socialist power that arose in the course of *Gleichschaltung* show a split pattern: the defence of traditional beliefs, values and life-styles was cut across by long-term conflicts between tradition and modernity in German society. The outcomes of these varying forms of unease were by no means identical with the professed goals of National Socialism. To this extent social pressure and the refusal to comply were not without effect. They impeded the smooth implementation of the National Socialist programme, they often obliged the regime to retreat or at least to take extra factors into account, and they made manifest a wide range of non-compliant behaviour within daily life from which the minority actually engaged in political resistance could draw support. On the other hand, the day-to-day conflicts between 'authority' and 'society' did not amount to a serious body of resistance against the regime as such.

SEVEN

The working class: everyday life and opposition

In the many elections held before 1933 the traditional core of the working class showed itself to be the social group least susceptible to National Socialism.[1] In 1930 the working-class parties, the SPD and the KPD, together received 37.6 per cent of the unspoiled votes cast (the SPD, 24.5 per cent; the KPD, 13.1 per cent), and in the last free Reichstag elections of November 1932 they still received 36.1 per cent of the votes (the KPD now 16.9 per cent, with the SPD falling to 20.4 per cent). In addition, a considerable portion of the 12 per cent or so of the electorate who voted for the Centre Party were members of the Catholic workers' movement. Evidently, one cannot simply identify the working class *qua* social stratum with voters for working-class parties *qua* political grouping; there were members of the middle class who voted Social Democrat and, of course, workers who voted first for middle-class parties and then for the NSDAP. Despite this methodological proviso, however, the election results certainly serve to indicate that most of the traditional working-class environments were particularly resistant to National Socialism. This is also shown by case studies comparing specific electoral districts with, respectively, particularly high and particularly low proportions of industrial workers. In general, the former show disproportionately low levels of NSDAP votes.

None the less, these facts leave several questions unanswered:
– Why was it that 'left-wing' voters, unlike 'centre' and 'right-wing' voters, did not switch to the NSDAP?
– Did the rejection of Nazism by these workers go beyond mere voting?
– What were the effects of the split in the working-class vote?
– Did the rejection of National Socialism continue after 1933, and to what extent did it lead to active resistance?
– To what extent did workers, no longer able to make their voice heard through politics or trade unions, come to terms with the regime in their everyday behaviour after 1933?

We shall deal somewhat cursorily with these questions in so far as they concern the initial situation in 1933; we shall then look rather more closely at workers' perceptions of the Third Reich, and at their behaviour.

The relative firmness and compactness of the bloc of left-wing votes in all elections in the Weimar Republic is due above all to the extraordinarily close-knit organisational texture of the German working-class movement as it had developed in the course of seventy years or so. The movement ranged all the way from political parties and trade unions to sports clubs, cultural organisations and consumer and housing co-operatives; even to non-religious cremation insurance schemes. The split into the SPD and KPD after the First World War made no fundamental difference to this system. Indeed, by the late 1920s it had led if anything to a sort of duplication: parallel to the Workers' Sports Association, for example, traditionally run by the Social Democrats, there was now 'Red Sport', run by the Communists, as well. But the key fact remained that participation in the workers' movement did not merely amount to casting a vote on election day but affected the whole of everyday life in the working-class social environment (at least within the strongholds of the SPD and KPD). Thus political activity, everyday patterns of living, opinions and values were interwoven, all deriving from the traditions of the movement and from matching experiences of a common class situation.[2]

The NSDAP, with its largely middle-class profile, was unable to penetrate this tight-knit proletarian milieu, at any rate before 1933 (though it did succeed in attracting workers outside it). If the meagre political appeal exerted by the Weimar system and the hardship and mass unemployment of the depression did cause considerable numbers of workers to desert the traditional policies of the Social Democratic Party, then the principal party to profit was its competitor within the working-class camp, the KPD.

The NSDAP's attempts to destroy this dense socio-cultural network centred around the parties of the left were repulsed by the members of the workers' parties before 1933. These defensive actions gradually brought about the realisation that fascism posed a threat to the workers' movement as a whole, although the full extent of the danger was underestimated. The supporters of the workers' parties not only conducted agitation against the NSDAP in elections and demonstrations and through the workers' press, but also defended their own headquarters, party offices, trade-union headquarters, meeting-places, bars, restaurants and housing estates against provocative actions by SA squads.

Yet defensive measures of this sort were generally the furthest they went. The strategic thinking of the leaderships of both the SPD and KPD, and the everyday structures of political perception on the part of the rank-and-file members, were taken up far more with the question of the traditional competition between the two parties than with the struggle against the Nazi common enemy. Although, as said, there was a degree of readiness on the part of Communists and Social Democrats to make common cause against SA provocations that affected them directly, the conflict within the left was stronger than the will to offer joint resistance against the right. This was as true of the grass-roots as of the party leaders, who were committed to mutual confrontation in any case.

The situation and behaviour of the working class

This initial situation also explains the labour movement's immediate reactions to Hitler's seizure of power in 1933, which, apart from some demonstrations (quickly banned) and some purely verbal calls for radical action by the party leaderships, was effectively accepted without resistance. Recognition that the 30th January 1933 had ushered in something more than a mere change of government came only as assaults on the institutions of the labour movement by the SA and the police (steadily coming under the control of the National Socialists) began to build up, as newspapers were banned and buildings taken over, as arrest squads swarmed far and wide in the aftermath of the Reichstag fire and the 'Emergency Decree for the Protection of the People and the State', and as raids by the SA on workers' housing estates and arbitrary imprisonment and torture of workers' officials spread to all cities during March 1933. By now, however, the regime was firmly in the saddle and was able to stifle all open resistance by the combined terror of 'legal' police measures and 'unauthorised' onslaughts from the SA. The *de facto* banning of the Communist Party in March 1933 (with the issuing of warrants for the arrest of its parliamentary deputies) was followed by the smashing of the trade unions on 2nd May and the banning of the SPD on 22nd June. Simultaneously the many workers' clubs and co-operatives were either banned or 'co-ordinated'. Within six months the National Socialists had crushed the largest and best-organised workers' movement in the world.[3] The psychological effect of this catastrophic defeat was all the greater for being unaccompanied even by a symbolic act of resistance. Such action might have been hopeless, but it would at least have enabled the workers to feel that they had not gone down without a struggle.

The Nazis, however, had not only smashed the entire organisational structure of the labour movement but had made huge inroads into the texture of everyday working-class culture: the densely-woven social environments of the workers' housing estates and the workforces in the factories. This was the particular purpose of the 'spontaneous' SA terror of the spring and summer months of 1933, and of the extensive raids in working-class districts. The many-layered popular culture and organisational network of the labour movement had, after all, taken shape primarily in the so-called 'red' housing estates, where people knew one another, were in the same protelarian class situation as their neighbours, had similarly alternated between wage-earning and mass unemployment, and had common living standards, means of communication and general daily rhythms of life.

After the first persecutions and bannings the Communists, in particular, as well as Social Democratic and trade-union groups which wanted to carry on illegally, had hidden their working equipment with trusted neighbours and colleagues, in attics and allotment huts. In the workers' districts they had set up living quarters for officials who had gone underground and illegal print shops and storerooms for anti-fascist documents and leaflets. In doing this they were hoping, partly on the assumption that the situation was analogous to that created by Bismarck's anti-socialist legislation, that they would be able to switch their political work away from the public domain where the police could observe it into the semi-privacy of the working-class social environment where it would be safe. This calculation, on which most schemes for underground resistance in 1933 were explicitly or implicitly based, was frustrated by the National Socialists by the spring of that year, principally thanks to the systematic raids in working-class districts. Units of the SA, the SS, the Gestapo and the police, often assisted by the fire brigade and the Technical Emergency Service (normally involved in dealing with disasters), hermetically sealed off particular housing estates and combed through them house by house. They confiscated everything from socialist and classical literature, sports-club footballs and brass-band instruments to party card-index files and illegal leaflets, and sometimes also weapons belonging to proletarian self-defence groups. These planned raids, together with threats, insults, beatings and arbitrary arrests, and the spontaneous acts of vengeance and terrorist onslaughts carried out by local SA groups which set up their own 'private' concentration camps, created an atmosphere of insecurity and helplessness even in working-class strongholds that had until recently seemed to be so safe.

The terror measures made it clear to all that even the solidarity of the everyday proletarian social environment was no longer an adequate shield against the naked tyranny of the National Socialists. From now on the decision to pick up a leaflet or to shelter the member of an illegal party was not a matter of personal, individual courage: at any time, flats could be searched and other members of the family caught up in the processes of terror. The image of the resistance fighter able to move through his environment like a fish in water is quite inappropriate to the Germany of 1933. The 'water' was being constantly trawled. After the Nazi terror of the spring of 1933, and with the increasingly systematic build-up of the Gestapo's surveillance apparatus, resistance could be pursued only by determined minorities. The structural preconditions for 'mass resistance' did not exist.

Within a few weeks the political side of the *proletarische Öffentlichkeit* – working-class public life – bound up as it was with demonstrations by trade unions, parties and other organisations, lay in ruins. Even where the old ideas still held sway, the external, public face of the working-class districts signalled Nazi victory on a scale that no one had thought possible. From Offenbach, for example, the non-orthodox Communist activist Heinrich Galm reported:[4]

> I could not recognise the town. Offenbach under the swastika! Swastika flags everywhere. The Marktplatz was astonishing. We went down the Biergrund, the Ziegelgasse, into the workers' districts where our votes used to come from, Kantstrasse, Bieberstrasse . . . They were hanging so thick in the narrow Biergrund that it was almost impossible to get through. And that was the main stronghold of the KP and the SAP. The Hasenbachgasse, my mainstay: swastika flags in every window. That was hard to take; it was a deep disappointment. Where on earth had they got all the flags from? Well, we knew, of course, there was a lot of despair involved. Of course there was. But the fact that they had actually done it: I was . . . We simply couldn't understand how this change could have happened.

Declarations of loyalty similar to flag-flying were constantly being demanded of the workers: they were compelled to demonstrate on the first of May, which had been given the counterfeit title of the 'Day of National Labour', or to join the *Ersatz* National Socialist trade-union body, the German Labour Front (DAF), or to take part in the regime's never-ending round of fund-raising collections, inspections and campaigns. Those who did not bow to the pressure and make their peace with fascism still had to split every aspect of their day-to-day behaviour into inner reservation and outward loyalty.

The Nazis' use of terror in the working-class districts and the continuous pressure to conform combined to generate a ubiquitous sense of persecution and insecurity, as in a city occupied by foreign troops. Yet the omnipresence of terror and, of course, the growing riskiness of hitherto safe neighbourly communication because of denunciation and informers could not prevent some measure of everyday solidarity from surviving, along with a basically mistrustful attitude towards Nazism. National Socialism continued to be an institution of the middle classes, part of the apparatus of state, police and administration that was alien to the working-class environment. People who did more than conform out of necessity – who crossed the invisible dividing-line – ceased to count for much in working-class society.

National Socialism, then, shattered the political, formal organisational elements of everyday working-class culture; but the informal elements, rooted in daily social behaviour and not readily susceptible to political pressure, were less affected. Here, basic attitudes, basic experiences arising from class society and traditional forms of leisure activity (such as workers' sport) were preserved, even though no longer within the framework of politically-based organisations. The survival of informal structures of everyday solidarity also nurtured a certain measure of potential resistance and created sanctuaries for opposition. This does not mean, however, that basic political attitudes in these areas went into a kind of hibernation where they remained untouched. That may have been true of the nuclei of the workers' parties and unions – officials and members who had become politicised under Weimar – but not of the working class as a whole. This is an important reason why attempts to re-establish the system of socialist and communist clubs and associations met with failure after 1945; and the same held for the diversity of Catholic cultural and political organisations.

Organised resistance remained the work of minorities. None the less, we can pinpoint a number of ways in which the rejection of National Socialist demands, under the impact of sanctions and threats of sanctions by the regime, turned into more deliberate refusal or even into protest and resistance. We shall illustrate this process below by reference to the cases of workers in the armaments industry and young people who opposed the monopoly on leisure exercised by the Hitler Youth. In both instances people's need to assert themselves in response to the National Socialist challenge meant that conflicts that had originally been containable within the system grew into ones that threatened the system. Admittedly, only a minority took part in the underground organisations (though numbers ran into the thousands), but even the politically passive majority was not readily reconciled to the National Socialist regime. This is made clear by the results of elections to *Vertrauensräte* (see below) in factories in 1934 and 1935 and by the Gestapo morale reports. Passive aversion was not, of course, to the regime's liking. On the other hand, it could put up with it as long as the workers lacked the means of giving effective expression to their opposition in a way that fell short of provoking police intervention.

Of all social groups, the working class was most directly and deeply affected by the National Socialist seizure of power. It was robbed of its political organisation; it lost the rights and institutions, built up over decades, which had enabled it to defend its day-to-day interests in the workplace; and, on top of this, it was now forced into the Nazi mass organisations such as the German Labour Front. Day in and day out the National Socialists proclaimed the end of class struggle and the establishment of a species of 'socialism' that primarily consisted in the individual's self-sacrificing assimilation into the so-called 'national community'.

The law establishing a new 'Regulation of National Labour' was enacted on 20th January 1934.[5] It consolidated the position of the entrepreneur and manager as 'works leader' (*Betriebsführer*) vis-à-vis the *Gefolgschaft* – literally, the 'retinue', or subordinate staff – and it replaced negotiated wage settlements by a system of frozen wages and working terms and conditions, embodied in factory-level regulations (although issued from above); these were to be monitored by so-called 'trustees of labour' (*Treuhänder der Arbeit*), who as a rule were representatives of the employer's side appointed by the state. In place of the disbanded shop stewards' committees were so-called 'councils of trust' or 'consultative' committees (*Vertrauensräte*) having purely advisory functions, which had to meet under the chairmanship of the *Betriebsführer*. They were chosen by the *Gefolgschaft* from a list compiled by the *Betriebsführer*. But even the limited scope available for exercising influence here, through abstention, wholesale 'No' votes or the deletion of particular names, was blocked in 1936 by the 'postponement' of the elections, which subsequently never took place in any case.

The German Labour Front (DAF), set up as the compulsory organisation incorporating all wage-earners, was likewise deprived of all trade-union potential, despite having been formed out of the occupation and enforced takeover of the old trade-union organisations. Admittedly, it soon became clear that the DAF would not get very far with its allotted task of 'educating' the workers along National Socialist lines if it was unable to win a certain degree of respect by notching up social and political achievements, or if it failed, not least in peripheral areas of working life, to establish itself as an advocate of its members' interests. Nevertheless this led the DAF into two areas of conflict where, despite isolated successes at the expense of more powerful and fundamental interests within the power structure, it could not but keep coming off second-best. The fact that its social and political projects made financial demands on the Reich could not be countenanced; and even less welcome was the fact that it disturbed 'industrial peace' and threatened employers' profits. All initiatives to 'improve' working life and leisure time therefore quickly ran up against insurmountable obstacles. This means that it is difficult to assess, from amongst the flood of 'successes' claimed by propaganda, the actual effects of campaigns by the 'improvement' agency 'Beauty of Work' (*Schönheit der Arbeit*), of the travel and leisure opportunities offered by *Kraft durch Freude*, of the so-called 'national job competitions' or of the attempts by the Ergonomic Study Institute of the DAF to reorganise vocational training, improve working conditions, develop job evaluation and reform wage-scale structures.

The campaigns seem to have been most successful when they coincided with reformist efforts in work study that had already been under way in industry under the Weimar Republic. These efforts, copying the American model and based on the philosophy of Henry Ford, envisaged a permanent workforce that was efficient but was correspondingly well paid and furnished with welfare benefits. In this respect the dominant tendency within work study, of both the overtly Nazi and the non-Nazi varieties, was committed to the same goal of the 'works community' that was being pursued by the 'Law for the Regulation of National Labour' and its associated National Socialist policies. There was also widespread agreement that if 'harmony' was to be achieved, the 'trouble-making' influence of the unions and the workers' parties had to be eliminated.

It is doubtful whether these efforts to win over the workers had much chance of succeeding, given workers' actual experiences during the years after 1933. We may venture the hypothesis, however, that a combination of intended political developments and of other factors outside the rulers' awareness may at most have produced some shift in workers' attitudes in favour of individualistic, highly-paid work efficiency inside the workplace and passive integration into leisure activities outside. Certainly, the regime's continuous pressure to induce conformity was immediately and vividly apparent, and the pressure undoubtedly had some effect. Yet it failed to secure its main aim, to win the workers over to the regime. A morale report from Berlin which Social Democrat informants managed to transmit to the exiled members of the party executive committee (published in the SOPADE 'Reports on Germany' for April–May 1934) draws the following distinctions among worker's attitudes:[6]

> 1 *Previously indifferent* These have gone over into the NSBO [National Socialist Works Cells Organisation] because they were told that that is where the fight against the 'red' bosses would be waged. Now they are becoming increasingly disenchanted, because they have to pay more than they did when they were in unions and, instead of 'red' bosses, they have got 'brown' ones.

2 *Our previous people* They are still as solid as ever. The total inability of the new people to run a trade union has seen to this, as well as the fact that the Labour Front subscriptions are higher than the old ones without producing anything to show for it. (Top subscription: 7 Mk a month.)

3 *The old NSBO people* Are angriest, because they are terribly disappointed. Reams of letters of protest are arriving at the NSBO head office demanding information, particularly, about the way subscription money is being used.

An analysis from the SOPADE 'Reports on Germany' for January 1935 fills out the picture:

> It became clear that the effects of the economic crisis on the inward resistance of the workers were more appalling than had previously been thought. We see it time and again: the most courageous illegal fighter, the most relentless antagonist of the regime, is usually the unemployed man who has no more to lose. Whereas if a worker gets a job after years out of work, then – however bad his pay and conditions – he at once becomes apprehensive. Now he does have something to lose, however little, and the fear of the renewed misery of unemployment is worse than the misery itself. The National Socialists have not conquered the factories. The standing of the National Socialist 'shop stewards' has constantly fallen, while that of the old free union works committees has risen in corresponding degree. But the National Socialists have destroyed the workers' self-confidence; they have crushed the forces of solidarity and crippled their will to resist. That is the basic position at the end of the second year of dictatorship. There are isolated first signs of reawakening resistance, but it is too soon to say whether these first signs will lead to a general movement.

The longer the Nazi regime lasted, the less people believed its slogans about the new solidarity of the 'works community' and the 'national community'. Workers' disapproval and criticism related primarily to practical everyday matters, the social achievements and failures of the regime, while the personal figure of Hitler – as even the SOPADE reports confirm – was largely exempt from criticism. This fact suggests that, for all the importance of the working class's spirit of opposition, its will to resist on grounds of principle should not be exaggerated. We have already seen, when analysing the popular mood in general, that the fact that people's high regard for the figure of the 'Leader' was unaffected by the general 'grumbling' can be taken as an indication of a certain basic consent to the regime, or at least of a passive adjustment to a situation which could not be changed in any case.

Let us nevertheless look more closely at criticism from within the working class.[7] In the immediate aftermath of 1933 the gulf between propaganda and reality became particularly apparent on two counts: the ending of unemployment was still not in sight, and conditions in the so-called 'emergency labour camps' and Labour Service camps were harsh. Once the rearmament led boom had brought back full employment (by about 1936–37), workers' initial satisfaction at earning a living wage quickly receded in face of their daily experience of continuing in a subordinate position within the workplace. Arbitrary behaviour by bosses was no longer held in check by trade-union monitoring of wage agreements or elected works committees, as before 1933. The stage-managed pseudo-elections of impotent works *Vertrauensräte* deceived few. In any case, the elections were suspended after 1936, since in the two previous elections the ballots had revealed too much opposition. Workers' standing grievances were accordingly their lack of rights in the workplace, the increasing pressure of work, the incompetence of the self-appointed Nazi workers' representatives, and the high cost of subscriptions and social-welfare contributions, which were assumed, not without reason, to be going to finance top-brass corruption and rearmament.

The less the *Volksgemeinschaft* propaganda matched the everyday reality of workers' lives, the greater became the mockery, and even contempt, directed by workers at the relatively small number of their fellows who paraded their zeal in the Nazi organisations or tried to contrive their own personal advancement at the expense of their class colleagues. Miners in the Ruhr divided the wearers of brown shirts into 'poor sods' and 'brutal sods'.

The writers of the National Socialist reports themselves were struck by the way the working-class environment was shut off from the outside world, so that propaganda messages and calls to join organisations left most workers unmoved. This day-to-day refusal to participate went only rarely as far as open criticism (and then most readily in a familiar atmosphere, amongst work colleagues or neighbours). Strikes and non-co-operation at work were also rare, since they would inevitably lead to intervention by the Gestapo – although the National Socialist agencies were forced to record a whole series of small-scale strikes. Nonconformist behaviour by individuals was more significant.

The workers' attitude of non-compliance during the Third Reich, then, can be summed up as follows: the lack of enthusiasm for the character and policies of the regime, and the lack of zeal in the workplace, went along with a wary retreat into privacy and into the atmosphere of solidarity in small, intimate groups within the working-class social environment.

The regime might have been able to put up with this arrangement – characteristic, of course, of drab everyday reality under charismatic systems of authority generally – had its drive to put the economy on a war footing not caught it ever more tightly between the demands of rearmament and the continuing lack of allegiance by the working class. Whereas the SOPADE reports of January 1935 had pointed out that workers who had found a job after protracted unemployment were anxious not to make themselves conspicuous, workers' self-confidence and readiness to engage in criticism or protest grew considerably once general labour shortages built up from 1936–37 onwards. Armaments firms looking for workers in order to fulfil their production targets were compelled to pay wages above the standard rates and to offer special bonuses; this forced firms in other fields to raise their wages in order to avoid losing their own staff. This new situation is apparent from reports by state agencies:[8]

From monthly report by Defence Industry Inspectorate XIII/Nuremberg, 16th December 1936

In order to retain their trained staff many firms, especially in the metal-working industry, have voluntarily raised the wages of skilled workers. Wage increases in firms supplying the army are particularly noticeable. In part these take the indirect form of special allowances. For example, the firm Aluminiumwerke in Nuremberg is paying its staff a full month's wages as a Christmas bonus. The firm Siemens-Schuckert-Werke in Nuremberg is said to be allocating approx. 3.5 million RM for the same purpose. Export industries in particular cannot keep pace with these wage trends, which lead to migrations by skilled workers into armaments firms and, it is said, create ill-feeling among workers in firms whose commercial position does not allow of wage increases. In the view both of Employment Exchange representatives and of the Chamber of Commerce representative, the restrictions laid down in the Four-Year Plan are not sufficient to stem the outflow of skilled workers to the required extent.

From monthly report by Defence Industry Inspectorate XIII/Nuremberg, 15th June 1939

The effects of the labour shortage are becoming increasingly apparent, and also of deep-seated discontent among workers at excessive working strain in some cases. This has been expressed in open insubordination or in sabotage or attempted sabotage.

At the Siemens-Schuckert-Werke in Nuremberg two workers attempted to put finished transformers out of commission.

At the Nuremberg tank works Busenius und Co. two men were arrested by the Gestapo for incitement, and one man for attempting to put the factory's main fuse out of order. [. . .]

It would seem that workers have been made too many promises of wage increases without sufficient emphasis being placed upon the obvious pre-condition, namely the Führer's call for increased efficiency. Individual representatives of the DAF have made comments that have been positively inflammatory. [. . .]

The labour policy of the Third Reich was an attempt simultaneously to mobilise and straitjacket the workers. It sought to eliminate the social conflicts of a capitalist industrial society by prohibiting the forms of representation of workers' interests that had developed historically, such as strikes, wage negotiations and trade unions. While workers, however, were thus deprived of the ability to defend themselves, the conflicts themselves were not wiped out: they reasserted themselves in new, individual and unprompted ways – in dissatisfaction, go-slows, movement between jobs, and so forth. To the degree that the National Socialists wanted to go beyond politically neutralising the workers, and to win them over to the fascist mass organisations, they were forced to take up many of the workers' demands, albeit in demagogic fashion.

In place of the abolition of class conflict, in the sense of a pre-emptive 'cleaning up' of the home front before the outbreak of war, there was now a pattern of cross-cutting rivalries within the Nazi ruling apparatus accompanied by unadorned social pressure from below. Given this tangle of conflicts, economic trends such as the rise in wages caused by the labour shortage occurred as a sort of spontaneous growth. National Socialism, which had set out to impose a dictatorial order on industrial relations, actually destroyed the rational procedures for resolving conflict in such areas as wage policy. It had thus also become inextricably entangled in its own contradictions in the socio-political sphere even before the war brought about the regime's final downfall. The significance of this for the working class was that despite having lost its rights and becoming bureaucratically regimented, it was nevertheless forced to attempt to defend its interests within the Nazi system itself and, to a degree, to play off the regime's clashing power groups and policy goals against one another.

After 1936–37, then, workers took full advantage of their improved position on the labour market. The numbers of workers giving notice rose considerably, as did general labour turnover; cases of go-slows and absenteeism also increased. The National Socialist authorities attempted to check the labour turnover, like the wage increases, by means of administrative restrictions on mobility and threats of penalties, but, except in isolated cases, these measures were unsuccessful because the armaments firms' unassuaged demand for labour kept asserting itself.

Accordingly, once all trade-union organs representing workers' interests had been eliminated, a sort of 'do-it-yourself' wage system developed. Left to their own resources, workers singly or in small groups obtained some measure of improvement in their material position by exploiting the constraints under which the regime and industrial firms were placed. Since the threat of dismissal no longer cut ice, because of the labour shortage, absences through illness, other forms of absenteeism and cases of time-wasting also became more frequent.

Such everyday refusals to co-operate on the part of workers were roundly deplored by the regime, and indeed, objectively speaking, militated against the aims of National Socialism, particularly rearmament. Yet it is very difficult to establish the concrete motives for workers' behaviour in specific cases.

As far as the National Socialist authorities and agencies were concerned, people primarily voiced complaints about the increasing fatigue caused by mounting pressure at work; it is not clear to what extent such statements were merely prudential. Much of the individualistic 'wage system' was certainly a straightforward matter of exploiting the laws of the market, without any wider political motives coming into play. Yet even such cases indicate that for the people concerned a realistic insight into their own class position counted for more than the Nazis' *Volksgemeinschaft* propaganda. With workers who came from the trade-union movement, traditions of collective trade-union pressure-group activity undoubtedly made themselves felt even if 'only' when questions such as overtime pay or improved working breaks were at stake. Even the National Socialist officials in factory 'councils of trust' and the DAF could not wholly escape the legitimising pressure exerted by workers' expectations and criticism. They would often take up workers' demands, either to avoid completely losing their colleagues' respect or to give themselves weapons in the constant internecine struggles among the National Socialist organisations.

In view of all this, we must ask to what extent this sort of 'do-it-yourself' wage bargaining and makeshift Schweikian individualism, while weakening, objectively speaking, the Nazi drive for rearmament, nevertheless in the long run came to symptomatise a change in workers' attitudes that was more in line with the National Socialists' intentions. It is at least a moot point whether or not individuals' exploitation of the armament boom to step up their wages also gave rise to the feeling among workers that entrepreneurs and employees were, after all, in the same boat and that workers would be better off if the economy were prospering. Not only did the ban on trade-union representation of workers' interests suggest an emphasis on individual initiative for temporary, emergency purposes: the very success of the 'do-it-yourself' wage system may have left in its wake the belief that 'Every man for himself' was a much more realistic tactic than 'Unity is strength'. Thus the very success of the workers' individualist guerilla warfare within the context of the fascist rearmament boom may also have narrowed the basis for trade-union activity and solidarity in the longer run.

The SOPADE reports for November 1935 had already warned that such a gradual shift away from traditional collective solidarity was possible and that solo efforts could lead workers to fall in with the production needs and economic logic of capitalist enterprise:[9]

> The National Socialists are well aware that the sense of solidarity is the source of the working class's strength, and as a result the aim of all of their measures, whether directed for or against the workers, is to stifle the sense that solidarity is essential. The damage they have done to the workers as far as wages, taxes and welfare insurance are concerned has always been so designed as to avoid affecting large groups in equal measure. General damage might possibly provoke general counter-moves. It is debatable how successful this policy of the National Socialists has been, not least because the destruction of the sense of solidarity began earlier, during the economic crisis. The crisis induced the worker to place a low value on negotiated wage agreements – the most precious achievement of collective action – and to seek work at any price. The National Socialists have now reduced the worker to the point that he often goes to the boss on his own to try to avert a deterioration in wages, especially over piece rates, and gets a concession out of the boss on the condition that he tells his workmates nothing about it. One often has the impression, particularly with young workers, that the idea no longer even occurs to them that their demands might carry more weight if backed by collective action – even if only on the smallest scale.

A survey of wage trends in different branches of industry (see tables) backs up the twofold finding that the achievement of full employment led to almost universal wage rises, while wages in the privileged armaments industries nevertheless rose much faster and higher than those in other sectors.[10]

Average gross hourly earnings of workers (male and female) in industry, according to official wage statistics

(a) In Reichspfennig

Industry	Dec. 1935	Dec. 1936	Dec. 1937	Dec. 1938
Building and construction	72.4	72.1	72.3	75.4
Carpentry, joinery and furniture manufacture	68.4	71.3	73.6	78.5
Chemicals	82.0	82.0	84.6	85.3
Iron and steel	—	86.3	93.5	96.1
Fine ceramics	—	—	60.7	61.9
Casting/founding	—	—	88.2	93.3
Glass	—	—	63.6	67.9
Rubber	—	—	—	87.8
Metal-working	83.6	85.7	88.9	91.1

Industry	Dec. 1935	Dec. 1936	Dec. 1937	Dec. 1938
Non-ferrous metals	—	—	—	91.7
Lithographic printing	81.1	81.9	82.7	84.8
Quarrying	—	—	60.1	73.7
Sawmilling	54.2	54.8	57.6	61.6
Letterpress printing	106.5	106.1	106.5	108.5
Clothing	53.8	54.5	55.7	59.6
Textiles	55.0	54.6	55.8	59.1
Paper manufacture	63.0	63.3	64.6	65.6
Boots and shoes	62.3	63.2	64.7	66.5
Baking, confectionery and cereal products	50.1	50.7	51.0	52.1
Brewing	101.2	100.7	101.1	101.2
Paper processing	58.8	58.4	59.2	61.5
All industries	73.6	76.7	78.2	81.0

(b) 1936 = 100

1936 = 100

1928 = 122.9	1932 = 97.6	1936 = 100.0
1929 = 129.5	1933 = 94.6	1937 = 102.1
1930 = 125.8	1934 = 97.0	1938 = 105.6
1931 = 116.3	1935 = 99.4	

Wage trends, 1933–1939–1942

Type of industry	Increases in real national average earnings by 1942			
	per hour, per cent compared with		per week, per cent compared with	
	1933 (= 100)	1939 (= 100)	1933 (= 100)	1939 (= 100)
Mining	+ 18.3	+ 10.4	+ 56.6	+ 18.5
Iron and steel	28.6	6.0	49.8	10.8
Nonferrous metals	—	9.4	—	12.4
Casting/founding	—	10.3	—	14.3
Metal-working	30.3	9.7	56.0	12.5
Chemicals	15.1	5.8	43.4	10.2
Quarrying	35.4	5.2	29.2	2.0
Ceramics	31.0	15.5	54.6	16.8
Glass	44.7	18.3	57.1	21.3
Building and construction	19.4	2.5	20.3	1.0
Sawmilling	34.7	11.0	40.5	13.5
Carpentry, joinery and furniture manufacture	34.2	13.7	52.9	19.3

Paper manufacture	13.0	8.7	38.5	11.8
Paper processing	20.5	11.8	37.8	7.9
Letterpress printing	7.9	6.1	20.8	8.0
Lithographic printing	—	9.0	—	9.5
Textiles	21.3	11.5	31.1	10.2
Clothing	32.6	14.1	25.6	7.1
Boots and shoes	—	14.6	—	13.4
Baking, confectionery and cereal products	—	10.7	—	2.7
Brewing	—	2.2	—	8.1

All types of industry, average:				
nominal	25	10	41	12
in terms of purchasing power	9	0	23	3

Whereas members of the older generation at least took a sceptical view of both the obnoxious and the enticing aspects of National Socialist labour policy in the light of their experience before 1933, this corrective was not available to the younger generation. As will be seen in the next chapter, young people certainly remained cool towards, if not critical of, the Nazis' idyllic images of a harmonious *Volksgemeinschaft*, if only because their own everyday experience as wage-earners – spied on, deprived of political rights and at the mercy of the authority vested in the *Betriebsführer* by the 'Law for the Regulation of National Labour' – was at odds with the slogans of National Socialism. None the less, there were also areas of life in which the younger generation became alienated from the values and social norms of the older workers.[11]

This applied particularly to opportunities for maximising earnings through high individual productivity and transfers to more advantageous jobs. (During the last years of the war, when there was no longer very much for money to buy, the same basic attitude often switched to find expression in go-slows at work.) This purely instrumental sort of attitude to work was foreign to many older members of the labour movement from the skilled ranks, for whom pride in their ability and in the quality of their work remained bound up with feelings and forms of behaviour founded on workers' solidarity and comradeliness.

Younger workers also availed themselves to some extent of the opportunities (greater than in the period before 1933) for gaining further qualifications and professional promotion that had been more deliberately encouraged in National Socialist work study and by employers. They saw the annual 'national job competitions', for example, as offering an opportunity of escaping, at least on an individual basis, from the collective social fate of working-class life.

Hopes of escape and advancement also centred around many of the leisure opportunities offered by National Socialist organisations. For many people, their first holiday trip, even if only to a camping site in the surrounding countryside, dated from the 'good' pre-war years of the regime.

Occasionally, too, the Hitler Youth acted as a focus for such hopes of escape, especially when the uniform could be used to justify rebellion against figures of authority: teachers, priests or, for that matter, fathers.

On the other hand, the seductive force of the sorts of opportunities for establishing their own identity that National Socialism gave to younger workers – whether directly (as in the Hitler Youth) or indirectly (via, for example, the rearmament boom) – was, taken all in all, limited. In part it was countered by other tendencies (such as the bureaucratisation and militarisation of the Hitler Youth); and anyway it lasted only a short time before the young people concerned were conscripted into the Labour Service, the armed forces and war duty. The longer-term impact became evident only after the war, when, although workers' parties and trade unions emerged once again, the old traditional proletarian social environment did not.

All this evidence indicates that the working-class environment – at first, and among older workers – remained relatively intact despite National Socialist harassment, and that its members expressed their mistrust of, and refusal to co-operate with, Nazi demands in ways that remained below the threshold provoking intervention by police and state. While the *Volksgemeinschaft* propaganda, therefore, on the whole had very little effect on workers, it must remain an open question whether or not the very retreat into the private sphere, on the one hand, and, on the other, opportunities for individual advancement created by the rearmament boom had the effect of reducing working-class solidarity in the longer run. The compulsory 'community' of the Nazis was rejected. But did the spontaneous conflicts sparked off by the rearmament boom not teach the new lesson that workers were best off if the economy was thriving, even if rearmament and war were the cause? There is much to be said for the argument that the Nazis' destruction of the old structures of solidarity in the labour movement paved the way for a new, more individualistic, more achievement-orientated, 'sceptical' type of worker, of the sort described by sociologists in the 1950s.

Given this context, two facts are all the more striking. First, tens of thousands of members of the banned workers' parties joined the organised resistance, especially in the early years of the Third Reich (till 1935–36). Secondly, even the broad majority of the working-class population, while remaining politically passive out of necessity, did not make its peace with the regime, but kept up an attitude of sullen refusal which on many occasions led on to positive acts of opposition.

As an illustration that the old solidarity of the working class and the organised labour movement had not been entirely extinguished by Nazi terror, a secret report drafted by a Gestapo agent on 16th January 1936 may be cited, concerning the attitude of the population of Wuppertal during legal proceedings taken against anti-fascist trade unionists:[12]

> At midday on the 14th inst. I conducted a plain-clothes investigation in the company of the *Kreiswalter* [Nazi Party district chief] and confirmed that at this point in time the special court hearing in Hamm is in session in which charges are being brought against the national comrades [*Volksgenossen*] previously arrested at the firm I.P. Bemberg A.G., Barmen, who have been found guilty of illegal activity. The picture we obtained concerning the transportation of the prisoners away from the hearing after its adjournment caused us to inform the local office at once of the necessity of an immediate cessation. The adjoining streets between the court building and the prison are densely thronged by the population, since it has become known in the interim that the detainees are being taken back at the same time every day, between 3 and 3.30 p.m., and will probably continue to be until Saturday. The transportation takes place daily under the close watch of the police, which naturally always attracts considerable attention.
>
> This is the picture which the three Frenchmen have taken back to France with them and which they will portray in a much cruder form. What guarantee is there that unauthorised photographs are not being taken of these transportations? Given all the lying reports from abroad we already have to put up with, one wonders why we ourselves supply the ammunition.
>
> If one mingles with the n.c.'s [Vgg., *Volksgenossen*] watching the transportations as bystanders, one can also hear disquiet and/or critical comments.

Resistance

Despite the disheartening experience of defeat, then, despite persecution and the incursions made by the National Socialists into the working-class environment, organised resistance on the part of workers did take place, as well as stubborn refusals to co-operate on an everyday basis.

Resistance by workers formed the most significant component of the German resistance movement. It is not possible in this book to cover all aspects of the resistance, which embraced the military conspirators of 20th July 1944 and the unpretentious Catholics who circulated Cardinal von Galen's sermon against euthanasia. Given, however, that workers' resistance was the most extensive in scale, it can be used for purposes of a discussion of the relationship between organised illegal work and the everyday lives of a large stratum of German society.

It is now generally accepted by historians that workers – notably, members of trade unions and the parties of the left – represented, in terms of sheer numbers, the major group of those who were politically persecuted.[13] But is it possible to speak in generalised terms of 'workers' resistance', when this phrase implies a particular combination of underground political work, individual protest and collective non-co-operation by an entire social class? In a strict methodological sense we should speak of 'resistance' only where the motives and actions of the people involved were directed towards the overthrow of the Nazi regime as a whole.[14] Activities such as organised underground work, distribution of leaflets, the forming of cells, and sabotage certainly count as resistance in this sense. How, though, are we to classify acts of assistance to individuals, or protests against individual measures of the regime? What of forbidden activities such as listening to foreign radio broadcasts, telling anti-government jokes or keeping up regular conversations with like-minded friends? The regime punished such activities, and, in its attempt to penetrate society totally and to regiment the 'national comrades' within the Nazi organisation, it converted, willy-nilly, even acts of individual deviation from the National Socialist norm that were possibly not meant to be political into opposition to the regime *in toto*.[15]

In the final analysis the basis of the methodological distinction between conscious political activity (resistance in the narrower sense) and nonconformist everyday behaviour (refusal and protest) is the division between state and society, which took shape with the development of bourgeois society during the nineteenth century. Fascism, however, was characterised precisely by its revocation of this division. On the one hand, it politicised everyday life by force; and, on the other, it also destroyed the independence of the traditional bureaucratised state. Hence the National Socialist attempt to totalitarianise society transported a large portion of everyday conflict into the realm of anti-Nazism. In an armament economy, conflicts over wages and work, for example, acquired an anti-war thrust whether they were meant to or not. On the other hand, it is difficult to lay down in any general sense how far these confrontations were reflected in the thinking of the people concerned and can thus be regarded as conscious, deliberate resistance.

Furthermore, while it is possible to demarcate clearly the sphere of activity of a political group, this cannot be done with the behaviour of a whole social class like the working class, differentiated as it was with regard to qualifications, branches of industry (armaments industries boomed while export and consumer-goods industries and agriculture stagnated), sex (women's work expanded during the war) and nationality (up to one-third of all workers were foreigners during wartime). Granted, however, that the labour movement's internal make-up and external boundaries are not precisely definable, it is nevertheless possible to offer some general comments concerning its attitude towards the National Socialist movement and the Nazi state.

The hostility to National Socialism on the part of the members and supporters of the political and trade-union wings of the labour movement was conditioned, both before and after 1933, by the assessments of their adversary that they had already formed under the Weimar Republic, by the basic social and political ideas on which their strategies rested, and by the traditional patterns of behaviour that had evolved within their organisations. After the consolidation of the Nazi dictatorship they further evolved three versions of resistance, distinct yet overlapping in various ways: resistance in order to preserve traditions, opinions and cohesion (informal discussion groups, camouflaged clubs and associations); resistance in order to devise plans for a post-fascist democratic state; and resistance in the sense of immediate action designed to damage the Nazi regime (strikes and sabotage) or to pave the way for its overthrow (underground organisation).

Those who decided to take part in the organised underground struggle waged by the KPD, the SPD or the smaller socialist or trade-union groups did so out of a variety of political motives and general attitudes deriving from their personal situation, the generation to which they belonged and the types of activity in which they had previously been involved. Memoirs by resisters of different political persuasions can serve to illustrate this.

Adam Wolfram,[16] born in 1902, was a miner, a member of the SPD and, in the years before 1933, a full-time official of the free trade union (dominated by the Social Democrats) for the mining industry. During the National Socialists' assault on trade-union offices on 2nd May 1933 he was away from his home town of Halle in Saxony and was hence left unmolested when he returned some days later. Losing his job after the banning of trade unions, and then being served notice to quit his flat, he suffered considerable hardships as a result of the widespread fears about giving refuge to 'outlaws', until he managed to find lodging with a Social Democrat he knew. Like many party and union officials, Wolfram had no choice but to become 'self-employed'. By working as commercial representatives or travelling salesmen, such people were able to seek out old political contacts without arousing suspicion. On their travels they got a sense of who had stayed loyal to the cause and who had become waverers in the aftermath of the political upheaval.

> As a silent witness when men were signing on at the labour exchange, in conversations with workers on the streets and at Nazi public functions, I could not help being repeatedly amazed how the mass of the population exulted in their new masters. The slogans and grand words and promises of the National Socialists found considerable response among these embittered and destitute people. Hopes for security and a new prosperous life drove people to the Nazis. Anyone who had been in a trade union for a long time could see through it all and could recognise the propaganda for the lying it was. But they had to keep silent for fear of endangering themselves and their families. [. . .] If we wanted to have a heart-to-heart talk among old friends we met by the river Saale or in the Dölauer Heide, where we would be unobserved. Here we exchanged information or discussed the chances of obtaining work. We rejoiced for every colleague who found a job. Obviously we encouraged one another and we nurtured the hope that the whole Nazi nightmare would soon be over. The main thing was that we were remaining true to our beliefs and were trying to keep the genuine democrats together. [. . .]
>
> Everyone tried to preserve links with party and union colleagues for the sake of exchanging information. In this way the old solid party and union officials developed into a passive resistance. Side by side with this there were also active resistance groups which, at great risk to themselves, distributed information, leaflets and newspapers among the population. Unfortunately Gestapo spies managed to track down these groups, round up the participants, torture them and send them to prisons and concentration camps. [. . .]

After April 1934 Adam Wolfram built up an underwear sales business, which secured for him both an income and a legal excuse for making contact with trade unionists and Social Democrats:

> Nearly 90 per cent of my clientele was made up of former members of trade unions and the SPD. I travelled the length and breadth of Saxony-Anhalt, covered Lusatia and parts of Thuringia. On these trips I learned what had happened to many colleagues. I was also told about the resistance groups which existed in the different districts, and I was able to pass on to others the knowledge I had acquired.

Wolfram was arrested by the Gestapo several times. But on each occasion they had to release him because nothing could be proved against him. Between 1936 and 1938 he also had links with Berlin, where the illegal national headquarters of the trade unions operated. When war broke out in September 1939 he was arrested once again and this time was not released until much later, even though no charges were brought against him. In 1941 he was drafted into the Wehrmacht.

Jacob Zorn,[17] from Cologne, born in 1907, joined the KPD in 1928.

Like many of his comrades who had been unemployed for several years, he got completely immersed in party work, which was bound up for him with hopes for a fundamental transformation of society:

> At that time, when I had perhaps been a Party member for two years, in 1929–30 – when the effects of the crisis were already being very strongly felt – we were all convinced that this class struggle in Germany would build up into revolution. We were still absolutely certain – I was, at any rate – that we were *the* force in Germany at the time which would be able to carry out the revolution. Of course, on the other side there was the growth of fascism; fascism got stronger in the same measure as we ourselves got stronger. [. . .]

In this state of expectancy and permanent political activism they entered the year 1933 relatively unprepared:

> The setback that happened in 1933 was actually beyond my comprehension. I had never thought that organised labour in Germany, the powerful trade unions – the ADGB [General German Trade Union Federation] – giant unions even in those days – that they would fail at the crucial moment. [. . .] It is quite clear that the blame lies with the Social Democratic leadership, and also the leaders of the ADGB. [. . .] For most of my friends – I had only been in the Party five years – it was astonishing. We were expecting civil war! There would be bitter struggles if the fascists tried to seize power! And then nothing happened. [. . .]

Like tens of thousands of other officials and members of the Communist Party, Zorn felt the effects of arbitrary Nazi terror at first hand. He was arrested and put in one of the early temporary camps that were set up under the control of the SA and SS. After his release he joined the KPD organisation that had been built up illegally:

> At that time the organisation was working really well. All the city wards were intact. In other words, the whole organisation was intact and ready to go, right down to the smallest unit. I am talking about the Communist Party. The Communist Party, if I remember rightly, was really the only party which managed to offer organised resistance – that is, resistance on a broad basis. By 'organised resistance' I mean getting money for the organisation, distributing leaflets, making contacts abroad, all these things. We hardly saw anything of the SPD at this time. [. . .]

The KPD was still living in hopes of a rapid revolutionary upheaval which would vindicate its approach based on the mass circulation of leaflets and self-sacrificing underground activity.

> At first we conducted our resistance relatively openly. We didn't pay proper attention to the rules of conspiracy which you have to follow if you are up against such a brutal enemy. I think that is the main reason why we suffered such heavy losses. Hordes of informers infiltrated the party – waverers,

people who let themselves be bought off, the sort of people you always get. Behind almost every court case in Cologne there was an informer who had belonged to the labour movement. And then the comrades were ill-treated, so chain reactions could happen – arrests, and then waves of arrests. In other words, if a comrade in prison wasn't rock-solid, then it was hard for him to stand up to it all. But really, in my opinion, the secret planning ought to have been much better, from the word go. We shouldn't have set up the old chains of command as they had existed beforehand. We ought to have developed other methods, and the methods we did eventually develop, to ensure security of organisaion, came very late. [. . .]

By 1933–34 many Communists were already beginning to have doubts about the likely success of these 'offensive tactics'. The Düsseldorf Communist Rudi Goguel,[18] who composed the famous 'Moorsoldatenlied' (Song of the Moor Soldiers) in the Börgermoor concentration camp in 1933, recalls the months of illegal Party and union work in the Lower Rhine KPD district in the spring of 1934:

Franz – I learned his real name only some months after his death [Franz = Erich Krause; committed suicide while in custody] was district organiser of the [Communist] trade-union organisation, the RGO. He was a tailor by trade, short, agile, plump-faced, a Berliner, about thirty years old; he was our best instructor. We would meet in the woods or in a comrade's flat and spend hours discussing the rebuilding of our organisation. The Party was in a whirl of optimism at that time, despite its very severe setbacks.

'We've got to be prepared for big trouble in the very near future. Therefore we must set about building up illegal mass organisations and direct them into active struggle, in order to create the preconditions for the overthrow of Hitler.' This was how Oscar expounded the Party's line to me. [Oscar = Adolf Rembte, until spring 1934 KPD district organiser for the Lower Rhine; arrested in March 1936 in Berlin; executed 4th November 1937.] It was shortly before the Röhm revolt. 'What's the good of this pretty picture you're painting, Comrade?' I objected. 'The reality is quite different. Go out into the factories and look around. In Phönix, in Rheinmetall, in Mannesmann, we've got little groups of twenty or thirty activists at the most, and these activists are spread out among all sorts of quite different illegal organisations. So where are the masses you're proposing to lead into the struggle? All I can see is passive, indifferent workers who aren't going to be persuaded to carry out any kind of resistance. Let's build up an organisation instead from a few active cadres and work on a long-term basis. Then we'll actually be *able* to work!'

My objections were fruitless. The thinking of our leading officials was dominated by the fiction of an imminent popular uprising against the National Socialists.

Full of bitterness, I went to Franz and explained my views to him. 'Franz, I'm frightened we're deceiving ourselves. When I suggested to your predecessor Erwin [Erwin = Max Reimann; arrested in 1939; remained imprisoned in Sachsenhausen concentration camp until the end of the war] that I might go into the Labour Front, he rejected the idea, saying that we couldn't waste any time. The decisive moment was sure to be coming very soon!'

[. . .] The organisation remained unwieldy and rigid, officials carried on working according the old routine, the old party machine kept on running mechanically. People talked about fascist terror, and about the work-creation swindle. They declared that not even Hitler could solve the capitalist crisis. They were convinced that the elections were faked and that the majority of the people was really against Hitler. They believed that they were the representatives of a movement of millions – no, of working people as a whole – and they didn't see how our activists were becoming more clearly isolated every day, while every day Hitler's party was becoming more solidly ensconced and making deeper inroads into the working-class masses.

And yet, despite all these mistakes, the Party remained the great driving force. Hosts of new, anonymous heroes kept emerging from its ranks, to fall on the battlefield.

Like Goguel and his comrades in Düsseldorf, Jacob Zorn became the victim of a series of mass arrests in Cologne in 1934, was put on trial and sentenced to several years' imprisonment. When he was released, in 1937, hopes for a rapid end to fascism had vanished, party cadres had been destroyed by waves of arrests, and resistance had been reduced to a matter of keeping political opinions alive and preserving personal cohesion within very small groups.[19]

I was astonished: I came out in 1937, and it was a year before I made contact. So I could see, over that year, how much the resistance had shrunk. The number of victims was enormous. It was not, therefore, the same resistance of 1933–34, which had been huge, massive. The losses which the Party had suffered – which anti-fascism as a whole had suffered – had left the resistance comparatively small. But it had also taken on a new form. [. . .]

It was only after the turning-point of the war, in 1942–43, that these small informal groups linked up more closely again. Zorn himself, who had been called up for military service, took part in the illegal 'Popular Front Committee of Free Germany' in 1944, deserted and went underground in Cologne. At the end of 1944 the Gestapo uncovered the organisation and arrested its leaders, including Jacob Zorn.

Not all officials and members of the labour movement took part in the illegal struggle, even though they remained faithful to their opinions. The prominent Offenbach Communist Heinrich Galm, who had been expelled from the KPD in 1929, saw more clearly the illusions involved in the underground struggle. In his memoirs he emphasises how little could actually be done, and he does not conceal the feelings of isolation and impotence this caused:[20]

We organised no resistance during the entire period. It would have been perilous for everyone concerned. And those who did organise resistance against the Nazis were obsessed with the idea that it would all be over soon, that the Nazis would not last long. It was very clear to me, however, that they would remain in power for many years – and so it proved. I still believe today that this decision was correct. If we had acted differently, we would have sacrificed many people. The National leadership of the SAP [*Sozialistische Arbeiterpartei*, Socialist Workers' Party] went into exile abroad. We had no chance of going abroad. Nor did we maintain any links with the main organisation later. That was the effect of going into our shell. If we had not done it, none of us would still be alive.

Of course, we were still in contact with our friends, purely socially. We met in the evenings to play rummy. On Sundays we often went off somewhere as a group to go swimming, to Kahl . . . Berker, Bröll, Bilz, Hebeisen, Felix Trejtnar, Schleiblinger, Heiner Krüger – they were some of our closest freinds at that time. We had scarcely any contacts with the Communists or the Social Democrats. Everyone was careful – to put it mildly.

The people who now say that they engaged in resistance against the Nazis – they mainly distributed leaflets. Well, we didn't think there was any point in all that leafleting. With people who didn't share your views you were always afraid that they would denounce you. And with other people – well, why try to persuade them, they shared our views anyway . . . I said: 'If you want to stay alive, you'll have to go into your shell.' But even for that to work, you needed plenty of luck. As was proved by the fact that we were often thrown into jail.

These memoirs show how varied were the assumptions, actual experiences and forms of behaviour that made up the reactions of officials of the labour movement to the fascist challenge. The nature of working-class resistance varied from one group to another and according to time and place. These differences, and indeed direct contradictions, must be borne in mind when one examines the principal organisational and ideological strands within the working-class resistance.[21] Organised resistance had been smashed in the waves of arrests of 1934–36, and it was smashed once again when new attempts to rebuild it were made during the war in 1941–44. The nucleus of the labour movement, however, sustained its beliefs and its cohesion in small informal groups, and it was from these that the non-partisan Antifa (anti-fascist) committees and later the re-established parties and trade unions emerged in the years after 1945.

Foreign labour

Our survey of the situation and behaviour of the working class in the Third Reich would be incomplete if it did not make some reference to the millions of foreign workers and prisoners of war who made up, particularly from 1942 onwards, a sizeable proportion of the industrial and agricultural workforce. Their history, and that of the growing army of prisoners in concentration camps who were forced into armament production, cannot be dealt with properly in this study. None the less, we can give at least some indication of the effects on the structure of labour that were brought about by this massive compulsory employment of foreign nationals.[22]

The attitudes of German state and Party leaders to the foreign workers were by no means homogeneous. Tactical considerations of war and occupation policy existed alongside longer-term ideological schemes for the future European hegemony of the 'Greater German Reich'. Himmler's goal was a racial war of annihilation against the peoples of Eastern Europe, and he decreed that their labour effort must be 'exhaustive in the truest sense of the word'. In contrast, the technocrats in the Reich Ministry of Labour and the armaments industries emphasised that a hegemonic Germany would have a long-term need for foreign workers:[23]

> Even after the war it will be impossible to dispense with the employment of foreign workers in Germany. Such employment will [. . .] be necessary in order that the great tasks of peace that lie ahead may be completed. The formation of the extended European economy will aid in this development. In the process, apart from the importation of supplementary labour from the continental states, there will undoubtedly be a considerable growth in the mutual exchange of resources in the form of so-called 'visiting workers' [*Gastarbeiter*].

Wartime policies in the Third Reich gravitated between these two objectives: 'annihilation through labour', and the longer-term re-structuring of the German labour market through the introduction of foreign workers or *Gastarbeiter* into fields of employment below those reserved for Germans. In addition, the most pressing concern became the need to use foreigners to fill the vacancies in agricultural and, increasingly, industrial employment caused by the drafting of German workers into the armed forces. Altogether something like 12 million foreigners were incorporated into the labour force in Germany during the war. About 7.5 million of these were still in the country near the end of the war. In 1944 this new proletariat was composed, roughly, of 2 million Soviet civilian workers, 2.5 million Soviet prisoners of war, 1.7 million Poles, 300,000 Czechs, 200,000 Belgians and 270,000 from the Netherlands, besides nationals of almost all other conquered countries.

The combination of racialist objectives with the aim to integrate western Europeans into an extended German economic region gave rise to a hierarchy of foreign workers and highly differentiated scales of remuneration, accommodation, diet, general treatment and permitted freedom of movement. Relatively best off were the west European workers and Czechs from the so-called Protectorate. Below them came western prisoners of war; then 'eastern workers' (*Ostarbeiter*) viewed as 'capable of Aryanisation', particularly Ukrainians; then the mass of civilian 'eastern workers' and Poles; and below them, in turn, Russian prisoners of war who eked out an existence on, or often below, starvation level. Further down the scale still came the inmates of penal camps, to which foreign workers could be committed for disobedience or 'idling' at work; German 'idlers', however, could also be sent to these 'work education camps'. The lowest position in the hierarchy was held by the inmates of the concentration camps. Production plants had been set up in the immediate vicinity of these camps, but the whole of Germany was also covered by a network of satellite concentration camps, from which workers were directed to local armaments industries. Within the concentration-camp population, in turn, there was the racialist hierarchy headed by 'Aryans' and with those of 'inferior race' at its base.

All told, foreign workers made up about one-third of the workforce of the armaments industries, and in some instances, such as Krupp's tank manufacturing plant in Essen, about 50 per cent.[24]

The living conditions of the foreign workers varied greatly, depending on the workers' place in the hierarchy. The main problems for all of them were inadequate food (even the degree of inadequacy was determined by their position on the scale) and accommodation, which got progressively worse as the war went on. The wages of the 'voluntarily' recruited workers from the west were only a little lower than those of their German counterparts, but deliberate deductions kept the 'eastern workers' permanently down to a level of net earnings at or below one-tenth of German skilled workers' wages. (Prisoners of war were effectively provided with only their wretched food and living quarters.) A typical monthly wage packet was that of the Polish worker Josip Smaczny, who in April 1942 worked 258 hours for Krupp of Essen and earned 172.60 RM gross, very much on a par with a German unskilled worker. Of this, 100.90 RM went on various deductions and a further 49.50 RM on camp accommodation, so that his effective pay was only 22.00 RM.[25]

If we are to understand the role and position of foreign workers in the Third Reich, it is not enough to describe their situation as one of 'slave labour', even though this concept without doubt readily suggests itself in view of the workers' inhumane living conditions. The concept, however, blocks off any deeper insight into the function of 'alien workers' within the special form of modern industrial society that Nazi Germany represented. The use of 'alien labour' (*fremdvölkische Arbeitskräfte*) was the regime's own distinctive contemporary answer to a number of standing structural problems which had become more acute: the tension between skilled and unskilled workers, and between long-term and transient work personnel; the clash between short-term cyclical economic changes and differently-phased long-term demographic trends; and, not least, the twofold suspension of the principles of supply and demand under conditions of war production, where products were needed whatever the cost, and labour to produce them was procured by any means possible. Nazi policies adapted themselves to these problems by creating a bewildering network of pragmatic devices, technocratic schemes and racialist global designs in which the role of 'alien workers' embraced the contradictory poles of the 'normal' use of *Gastarbeiter* and 'annihilation through labour'. Both of these poles must be taken seriously if we are to do equal justice to the day-to-day experience of the well-paid, well-treated Dutch skilled worker in the German armament industry and of the 'eastern worker' who was, literally, worked to the bone.

What, then, was specifically National Socialist in the overall policy towards 'alien workers'? Not merely the inhumane treatment of the one group; and certainly not, of course, the careful treatment of the other. What was characteristic, rather, was the open acknowledgement that Nazi society was in fact, and ought in the future to be, constructed upon this very inequality of treatment, embracing prosperity at one extreme and destitution at the other. The internal hierarchical structure within the 'works community', based on criteria of achievement and efficiency and supposed aptitudes for leadership and subordination, here reappeared writ large: the egalitarianism of 1789 was revoked, and inequality of treatment was proclaimed, which actually arose out of the problems of modern industrial production mentioned above. Hierarchies were not declared to be functional and hence conquerable by means of mobility and changes of roles (this might apply, at most, to 'national comrades'); they were enshrined in perpetuity. The ideal was that of the German worker, with his sense of cardinal, 'essential' superiority to his foreign colleagues: the *Herrenmensch* with a clear conscience.

Very many of the Russian prisoners of war[26] – who were well towards the bottom of the hierarchy – did not even reach the camps in Germany. Of the total of 5.7 million Soviet prisoners of war, about 2 million died in the first year of the war on the eastern front, from hunger and epidemics, in mass camps that had no infrastructure and cannot even be called temporary. (Altogether, 3.3 million Soviet prisoners had died by

1945: 57.8 per cent of the total.) These mass deaths cannot be explained on the ground that the rapidly advancing German army was unable to cope with the organisational difficulties of providing for its vast numbers of captives. They were the result of the deliberate decision by the National Socialist leadership to pursue a policy of genocide. This decision was, unquestionably, transmitted to the military high command even before the invasion of the Soviet Union (and also, incidentally, before the decision to seek the so-called 'final solution of the Jewish problem'). Thus, the Chief of the Army General Staff, Halder, noted in his diary the following key points from a speech by Hitler to 250 senior officers on 30th March 1941:

> Colonial tasks!
> Struggle between the two world-views. Crushing verdict on Bolshevism: akin to asocial gangsterism. Communism an enormous future danger. We must move away from the notion of comradeship among soldiers. The Communist is not a comrade, never has been nor will be. It is a war of annihilation. [. . .]

Similarly, on 2nd May 1941 representatives of different government ministries and the director of the subsequent 'Economic Staff (East)', General Dr Schubert, concluded after a planning conference on the war in the east that

> x million people [will] undoubtedly die of starvation if we extract everything from the land that we need for ourselves.

Fatalities among those exhausted and under-nourished Russians who were put to work in Germany's armaments industries were so high that they too indicate the continuing genocide. In the first six months of 1944 the German coal industry, for example, recorded 32,236 'losses' among a total prisoner workforce of about 160,000.

Despite an expanded system of surveillance and penalties – in Krupp, for instance, 4,000 Germans belonged to the works security force or to emergency squads and similar vigilante bodies in charge of foreign workers: at least one in every 15 members of the workforce[27] – conflicts involving 'alien workers' did not disappear. The latter, weak and exhausted, tried in particular to slow down the pace of work, and this was punished as 'idling', refusal to work or even sabotage. It is impossible to assess the extent to which such conflicts were due, on the one hand, to sheer fatigue and, on the other, to deliberate resistance. Gestapo interrogation documents indicate deliberate resistance in specific cases. In addition, in many camps of 'eastern workers', particularly the Russian prisoner-of-war camps, there were organised resistance groups which committed acts of sabotage, distributed lcaflets, established contacts with other foreigners and with German anti-fascists, and prepared for armed struggle.

The reflection of such day-to-day acts of resistance in the Gestapo's files can be illustrated by a weekly report from the local station in Gummersbach for 27th November 1944:[28]*

Secret State Police   Gummersbach, 27th November 44
State Police Central Station, Cologne
Gummersbach Local Station

Weekly Report

The arrest of the female Eastern Worker
   Ludmilla Ponomariowa
referred to by Crim. Sec. [Kriminalsekretär, approximately Detective Sergeant] Richards in the report for 3.11.44, led to the arrest of additional female Eastern Workers who have either made copies of or distributed the inflammatory document a copy and/or translation of which was attached to the report for 3.11.44. In the course of enquiries it was established that a further inflammatory document was and/or is in circulation, concerned with the lot of female Eastern Workers employed in Germany. (Translation of this document appended.)

Those so far arrested in this connection are:

1 *Klawdia Kostenko*, b. 2.6.22, Schmerowko
2 *Annastasia Piskun*, b. 22.4.25, Poltawa
3 *Domnikia Chodschenko*, b. 7.1.1900, Kiew
4 *Nikolai Lobedew*, b. 25.3.21, Brest-Litowsk
5 *Wasilina Kusiomko*, b. 14.1.23, Wilnia
6 *Annastasia Weklitscheva*, b. 8.11.23, Grabewo

Enquiries have not yet been completed. It would seem likely that the first leaflet originated with a male Eastern Worker, whose name, however, has not yet been ascertained. He was employed in Denkingen in 1943 and is known only by the first name of Stefan. Enquiries proceeding.

The Eastern Worker
   Wasilj Schepeljew
b. 12.2.1908 in Saporoschje, was arrested for activity as a trouble-maker in the Eastern Workers' camp of the firm Karl Rud. Dienes in Overath and for injuring another Eastern Worker in the course of a brawl. File still in preparation.

The Belgian Worker
   Jean Maeschalk
b. 5.8.1899 in Brussels, last resident and employed in Marienheide (hospital), was assigned to this department after repeatedly staying in the

---

*[German spelling of Russian and Polish names has been retained. (Transl.)]

Eastern Workers' camp and uttering threats against the Camp Leader. In view of the insignificant nature of the charges against Maeschalk, viewed in another light, he was assigned to Gummersbach Employment Exchange for re-allocation, since his previous employer no longer wanted him.

The Eastern Worker

Nikolai Kowalenko

b. 20.1.20 in Zhitomir, was arrested. He left the Construction camp in Bielstein without permission and was drifting in the Bergneustadt area at night. Since he was found in possession of a bag containing rabbit fur and droppings, it appeared likely that he was engaged in larceny. Two of his accomplices are still at large. File still in preparation; final report upon completion of enquiries.

Arrests were made of the following married couple of Polish origin:

Civilian Worker

Stanislaus Praski

b. 21.3.1894 in Malpolscha, and

Anna Praska, née Jemarkiewiecz

b. 2.11.1905 in Minsk, both last resident and employed on the farm estate Burghof in Overath. Arrests were made because the husband, Praski, in particular, had ceased to conform to the instructions of the estate manager and was under suspicion of larceny. Both husband and wife have been assigned to Cologne State Police Station for a further ruling, where it is understood further charges have been brought against them.

The following Eastern Workers were arrested at the security gate of the Eastern Workers' Construction camp in Overath, on suspicion of larceny and/or receiving stolen property:

1 *Eugen Leonow*, b. 14.12.1919 in Jennanowskaja
2 *Nikolai Kolodka*, b. 20.8.24 in Saumy

Leonow was found in possession of a drive-belt, and Kolodka in possession of 10 tins of shoe polish. L. alleges that the drive-belt was purchased from a person unknown, while K. alleges that he received the shoe polish from a fugitive Eastern Worker for whom he was keeping it. Both transferred to Cologne State Police Station with files.

Proceedings were instituted against the Householder

Ernst Eggers

resident in Derschlag, for listening to enemy broadcasts for a lengthy period and also indulging in defeatist statements. File still in preparation; additional detail not available at this stage.

The female Polish Worker

Irene Wilesek, née Korepta

b. 26.3.1903 in Sosnowitz, was arrested in Wipperfürth on suspicion of belonging to a Bolsh. resistance organisation and for contravention of Aliens' Regulations. Wilesek was admitted to the police cells in Wipperfürth. Enquiries not yet complete; further detail unavailable at this stage.

Following instructions from Cologne State Police Station, Wipperfürth Station arrested the Polish Worker

Rima Remitschenko

and assigned her to Cologne. She is under suspicion of complicity in the escape of Russian officers.

The Eastern Worker

Nikolaus Alfonin

b. 28.11.1897 in Kasern, was arrested in Wipperfürth, having been found at 24.00 hrs on 23.11.44 on the edge of the forest near Kupferberg in possession of approx. 15 kg of venison. Enquiries again not yet complete; report to follow.

The escaped Dutch Worker

Pieter Scholtmeijer

who was picked up by the GFP [*Geheime Feld-Polizei*, Secret Field Police] while not in possession of an identify card and was assigned to Wipperfürth Station on 2.11.44, is still in custody pending findings by Wuppertal State Police Station.

The Hereditary Farmer

Karl Wurth

of Neuenherweg was fined 100 M for giving away to 2 Eastern Workers tobacco plants cultivated by him. The sum was paid into the NSV [National Socialist Public Welfare] account of Wipperfürth Savings Bank.

The Freehold Farmer's widow

Ida Köser, née Nasenstein

b. 7.12.1891 in Wüstenmünd, resident in Dievsherweg, who likewise, through her daughter, sold apples to 2 Eastern Workers for payment of 11 M, was also required to pay a 100 M penalty on grounds of unauthorised dealings with foreigners and sale of fruit to the Russians, but refused to do so. She herself perceived, however, that her action was incorrect. File still in preparation.

The State Railways Works Assistant

Fritz Blumberg

b. 14.9.1888 in Erlen, resident in Niederschuweling, no. 7, had handed his radio set for repair to an Italian wireless technician in Kreuzberg camp. The set remained for some days in the camp without German supervision. It was taken into temporary safekeeping, since there is a suspicion that it had been used for listening to foreign news broadcasts. Final report to follow.

In the course of the week various Eastern Workers' camps in Gummersbach and Wipperfürth were inspected. In Gummersbach written materials were found and examined, but no indications of illegal organisations or their propaganda were observed.

In addition, inspections were made of scattered farmhouses in the countryside, although nothing of note was found. It was apparent, however, that the requisite separation between the rural population and the Eastern Workers and foreign employees that has been called for is not always being maintained. For this reason the 100 M fine against the farmer, Wurth (cf.

above), was imposed and action to be taken against Köser is under consideration. Efforts are being made to ensure that the rural population, in particular, come to a greater realisation that itinerant [foreign] workers should be reported without delay to police stations, especially Secr. State Police stations.

On the night of 19.11 in the Bergmausen [*sic*] district, enemy aircraft dropped the customary leaflets 'People of Cologne, Help Yourselves!' and 'Men and Women of the Rhine Industrial Region'. All copies collected were destroyed; a sample, with accompanying report, was submitted to Cologne State Police Station.

In conclusion, it should be mentioned that the firm Schmidt & Clemens in Berghausen arranged for the broadcast of the speech by the President of the Russian Liberation Committee, General Vlasov, to be heard in the form of a communal listening session for the Eastern Workers. As well as the male and female Eastern Workers, Russian prisoners of war were also present in the press shop, which was crowded. The address by General Vlasov was heard with interest, and salient passages were met with nods of the head by some listeners. Individual listeners were so deeply impressed merely by hearing their own mother tongue that tears came to their eyes. The majority of the Russians described the speech as very good.

It has been brought to our attention in confidence that hopes have arisen in individual cases that the formation of an anti-Bolshevik army will make possible an early return home for the Russians living in Germany and will mean liberation from Red terror for Russians with pro-German views.

[Signature]
SS-Obersturmführer [Senior Company Commander]
and Kriminalkommissar [Detective Superintendent]

Translation*
Women citizens of the Soviet Union who are under the yoke of the fascist hangmen and dogs in Germany!

Dearest daughters, sisters, women! I send you warmest greetings, and don't ever forget your beloved Ukraine, where you were born and where you have lived, but these dogs have robbed you of your freedom because they have conquered you and not let you live. You were quickly loaded into goods-wagons and brought here, to work for cabbage for 3 or 2 weeks, which there was hardly any of. You have had to sleep in camps, first thing in the morning you heard the words 'Out of bed!', and the police were already standing by the window where the bread rations were handed out. But now we won't have to wait much longer. If any of us who have been particularly worked up by the fascist dogs goes up to a German, he will say the whole wide world is free, there is no oppression. But they can't see their own

---

*[English version of (an evidently rough) German translation of leaflet appended to the Weekly Report. (Transl.)]

hideous faces. They don't work with their own hands, they rob and steal, they invade weak countries, they plunder them and are satisfied. Well, I don't think [they] are going to [last very long]. They are being driven out like dogs. You already know their soldiers are struggling day and night, they have spilled their hot blood and are stained with it. They took 2 years to conquer our beloved Ukraine, but the Red Army cleared them out in 3 months. They have no right to show their faces in a foreign country they have forced they way into. Our Bolsheviks will show them that spring follows winter as night follows day. I put this appeal to you: 'Never betray your bleeding hearts, even if they maltreat you and drink your heart's blood – be stronger than steel! The enemy will be defeated and victory will be ours!' Their young people live the good life, they are young and happy, but we shall never know what happened to our youth, we shall only remember the life in prisons that we lived in our youth in Germany. Don't believe these enemies and parasites when they say our Bolsheviks will do you harm. Yes, my dear friends, today on 25th April our families at home are celebrating, but we know the food these dogs and parasites are giving us to eat, we are sitting and waiting in misery. Read this sheet and think about your own young life. Have you had freedom under Hitler? That's right, we have had the freedom not to leave the prisons and concentration camps. We know very well what your lives are like in the camps. I am writing you this letter and I ask you to preserve it as you would your own heart, until we arrive.

This letter has been written by Russian people living under the fascist yoke in German hands.

In certain places there were in fact quasi-partisan battles, notably amidst the rubble of bomb-shattered Cologne in the autumn of 1944, when foreign workers, escaped prisoners of war, German anti-fascists and young anti-regime members of the 'Edelweiß Pirates' came together, carried out surprise attacks on military supply sites and high-ranking NSDAP and Gestapo officials, and mounted full-scale assaults on units of the Gestapo, Wehrmacht and police.[29]

Aside from this, foreign workers represented by far the largest category within the monthly statistics of arrests compiled by the central office of the SS Reich Security Service. The following tables, for the months of December 1941 and of June and August 1943, give an overall view of the structure of political persecution in Germany during the war, and hence, indirectly, of the areas and forms of resistance.[30]

1. Numbers of arrests recorded in daily reports by State Police (Gestapo) Stations and Central Stations, December 1941

Altreich and Ostmark*

State Police Stations and Central Stations	Total	Communism/Marxism	Opposition	Church movement Catholic	Church movement Protestant	Jews	Economic	Refusal to work German	Refusal to work Polish	Refusal to work Belgian	Refusal to work Dutch	Refusal to work Other	Prohibited contact with Poles or POWs
Aachen	113	14	9			(8)	13	10	16	9	15	24	3
Allenstein	144	7						6	115		1	21	1
Berlin	605		21	1	1		18	158	81	42	44	220	4
Braunschweig	162		13			1	11	20	70	14	2	26	5
Bremen	131	2	3		1	1	13	31	25	7	14	31	3
Breslau	635	2	25			(3)	1	15	473	1		101	14
Chemnitz	76	9	16		1	4	4	16	17	1		4	4
Darmstadt	88	3	2	3		12		19	26	1	1	10	11
Dortmund	186	1	7	6		1	3	99	6	7	1	50	5
Dresden	330	10	30		4	15	1	31	158	14	1	46	20

*['Old Reich' and 'Eastern March' (Austria). German versions of place-names, e.g. Allenstein (= Olsztyn) have been retained. (Transl.)]

1. Numbers of arrests, December 1941 (cont.)

	Communism/ Marxism	Opposition	Catholic	Protestant	Jews	Economic	German	Refusal to work — Polish	Refusal to work — Belgian	Refusal to work — Dutch	Other	Prohibited contact with Poles or POWs	Total
Düsseldorf	8	37	2	1	2	6	62	22	11	12	33	7	203
Frankfurt/Main	19	29	7		28	6	21	37	5	4	30	6	192
Frankfurt/Oder	1	8	5				12	99			13	2	135
Graz	1	6		1			2	6			14	1	36
Halle	5	11			1	1	37	11		2	15	11	94
Hamburg	9	46			2	11	156	69	25	18	108	4	448
Hannover	1	30			5		46	109	12	9	27	7	246
Innsbruck	8	16	3		3							1	31
Karlsbad		13	6			2	5	9			4	3	42
Karlsruhe	14	55	6	1		4	25	23		2	25	32	187
Kassel	1	2					3	17			9	4	36
Kiel		14				1	28	9			43	1	96
Klagenfurt	4	18					1	10			6	2	41
Koblenz		3	1			4	5	11	1		1		26
Köln	1	6				6	6	5	2	6	7	1	40
Königsberg	5	2			3	7	46	155		1	70	6	295
Köslin		5				1	8	16			2	5	37
Leipzig	3	16			4	14	21	96			61	7	222
Linz	2	18	1		1	2	6	31	2		18	11	92

Region												
Magdeburg	364	4	26		3	1	53	153	26	6	68	24
München	261	5	7	2		18	13	119	10	1	83	3
Münster	171	2	27	2		1	28	46	40		24	2
Nürnberg	110	2	18		1		13	56	6	2	10	1
Oppeln	129	2	8	4	5		12	83	1		12	2
Osnabrück	94		5		1	16	4	25	2	47	1	9
Potsdam	43		3	1		3	7	22	1		9	1
Regensburg	127	3	6		1	3	3	86		3	2	7
Reichenberg	117	20	17		1		9	15			47	5
Saarbrücken	98	6	11			2	33	12	1		26	6
Salzburg	79		3			9	21	20		1	16	16
Schneidemühl	99		3	1		6	1	73			2	5
Schwerin	191	2	13			4	34	105	6		12	19
Stettin	138	1	14	1	1	10	17	66	4		17	12
Stuttgart	207	6	21	8	7	4	55	40		2	50	3
Tilsit	123	1	11		1	2	9	73			24	1
Trier	15		2	2		4	3	1			2	1
Troppau	66		24		10	6	4	19	19		15	2
Weimar	286	14	39		10	3	26	94		8	38	34
Wien	366	64	69				13	94	1		106	14
Wilhelmshaven	102		18		3	1	15	24	10	31	3	4
Commanders of Sipo & SD, Luxemburg	26		11	2				1			1	
Commanders of Sipo & SD, Metz	83	2	30		1	1	7	18	18		10	7
Commanders of Sipo & SD, Strasburg	134	2	30			5	3				40	4

1. Numbers of arrests, December 1941 (cont.)

Protectorate and Eastern Regions

State Police Stations and Central Stations	Total	Communism/ Marxism	Opposition	Church movement Cath.	Church movement Prot.	Jews	Economic	Refusal to work	Prohibited contact with Poles or POWs
Prag	422	93	229			44	6	50	
Brünn	475	36	336		1	31	29	12	
Bromberg	128		47			1	4	68	8
Danzig	68	1	11			1	2	50	3
Graudenz	113		7				1	103	2
Hohensalza	52		7					28	17
Kattowitz	363	5	193		1	14	4	142	4
Litzmannstadt	163		110			14	1	35	3
Posen	180		80		1	4	3	30	12
Zichenau	515	4	66			16		428	1

Total number of arrests, December 1941

	Altreich and Ostmark	Protectorate and Eastern Regions	Total
Communism/Marxism	266	139	405
Opposition	927	1,116	2,043
Catholic ⎫ Church	61	3	64
Protestan ⎭ movement	12	—	12
Jews	129	125	254
Economic	228	50	278
Refusal to work	6,412	996	7,408
Prohibited contact with Poles or POWs	363	50	413
Sum totals	8,398	2,479	10,877

2, Digest of statistics of arrests compiled by the SS Reich Security Service Central Office for the *Regierungsbezirke* of Münster, Arnsberg (Dortmund) and Dusseldorf, June 1943 (August 1943 figures in parentheses)

State Police Station for the *Regierungsbezirk*	Dortmund		Düsseldorf		Münster	
Total taken into custody	1,520	(2,813)	1,341	(1,765)	1,293	(1,974)
Reasons for arrest						
Communists/Marxists[a]	2	(2)	19	(16)	22	(58)
Opposition	15	(35)	7	(25)	41	(49)
Resistance[b]	—	(—)	10	(2)	4	(—)
Church movement	2	(1)	6	(2)	—	(3)
Jews	—	(—)	14	(10)	1	(—)
Economic[c]	3	(11)	—	(4)	4	(?)
Strikes etc. by nationality						
German	32	(28)	40	(83)	58	(69)
Soviet	1,063	(2,373)	520	(690)	836	(906)
Polish	204	(95)	114	(108)	123	(179)
Baltic	—	(—)	—	(—)	—	(—)
French	86	(75)	129	(225)	33	(86)
Dutch	61	(91)	246	(268)	280	(78)
Belgian	28	(55)	51	(110)	36	(69)
CSR [Czech]	—	(—)	2	(6)	10	(4)
Balkan	6	(—)	29	(43)	49	(27)
Italian	—	(—)	12	(10)	—	(2)
Other	11	(21)	54	(46)	2	(4)
Contact with foreigners	28	(26)	35	(1)	36	(36)
Other punishable offences	—	(—)	51	(98)	—	(—)

[a] i.e. Social Democrats.
[b] The term 'resistance' includes all forms of oppositional activity not included under other headings.
[c] E.g. black-market activity.
— = no arrests reported.

As an illustration of the conflicts that could lie concealed behind these bald statistics – whereby, for example, everyday disputes about the speed of work might intersect with conflicts between German and foreign workers, hence taking on a resistance dimension – we may cite the following report emanating from the August Thyssen steel works:[31]

Re: violent behaviour by Russian POW 40481

Yesterday (Wed. 4th Aug.) an incident took place, the nature of which is made clear by the following account given by the bricklayer U[. . .].

'I have been working for 5 weeks in the Thomas slag mill with a gang of 12 female Eastern Workers (excavation work). 4 days ago I repeatedly observed the Russian POW 40481 engaged in urging the women workers to work more slowly. He stated first in Russian, and then actually to me in German, that the work was much too hard for girls and that in Russia girls did not need to work.

'I repeatedly and energetically sent the prisoner of war away.

'On Wed. 4.8.43 at 3.30 p.m. the Russian concerned came back again as a shunter with the grading machine and again went straight up to the female Eastern Workers. The yardmaster Hugo St[. . .] told me that he had requested the Russian not to distract the women workers from their work, whereupon the prisoner had become abusive and threatened him with his fists. During this time the Russian was standing next to the women and leaning against a wooden plank as he was speaking. I went up to him and took the plank away from him and requested him to move away. Without making any rejoinder, he jumped at me and threw me to the ground. I was able to hold the Russian down with a half-nelson, but only with difficulty, as he possessed colossal physical strength. I might observe at this point that my authority with regard to the foreign female workers was also at stake.

'After I had released the Russian, he at once mounted the shunting loco.'

The prisoner of war therefore:

1 Urged female Eastern Workers to adopt a slower pace of work.
2 Threatened yardmaster Hugo St[. . .].
3 Physically assaulted bricklayer Hugo U[. . .].
4 In front of foreigners, undermined the authority of members of the German supervisory staff.

We have made a request by telephone today to Sgt. W[. . .] to arrest the Russian immediately upon his return from work. We ask you, in addition, to remove the prisoner from the camps of the August-Thyssen-AG works and to serve upon him the heaviest punishment customary in such cases. We should be grateful if you could notify us of the measures that are taken.

The relationships between German and foreign workers were not always those of *Herrenmensch* and *Untermensch*. In many ways work colleagues of different nationalities had close mutual ties within the workplace, and viewed supervisors and surveillance personnel as the common enemy. There were repeated examples of aid and support being given in little ways: help with food, or protection for those who were exhausted by work. The use of foreign labour, however, also altered the position of German workers, notably because the latter no longer had to do so many of the dangerous, physically taxing or generally lower-grade jobs. Many German workers settled with depressing speed into their new and more prosperous roles and ignored the misery before their very eyes.

Yet the attitude of the great majority of Germans cannot be characterised either as spitefulness towards the 'aliens' or as solidarity. The most common attitude was indifference tempered by occasional sympathy. During the war people had enough worries of their own; the hardships of the foreign workers were of no especial significance. A case such as the one documented below was exceptional.[32]

Memorandum from Franz Otto Colliery to Duisburg Gestapo, 13th October 1943

We wish to inform you herewith of an incident which occurred underground here on 9.10 in Franz Otto Colliery, Duisburg Neuenkamp.

At the end of a shift the foreman S[. . .], Karl, b. 24.10.03 in Duisburg, who is in charge of coal-extraction from the faces of one district of the pit, ordered one of the Russian prisoners of war employed there to stay on longer and help extract a wedge of coal that had remained in the rock.

Since the Russian refused, despite repeated requests, to comply with this instruction, S[. . .] attempted forcibly to compel him to perform this task.

In the course of the altercation the apprentice face-worker Lapschieß, Max, b. 24.4.03 in Gelsenkirchen, resident here at Essenbergerstr. 127, turned on the foreman and defended the POW in a manner such as to encourage the latter to strike the foreman on the head with his lamp. S[. . .] received a gaping wound on the face which has required stitches, and he has since been on sick leave. He is a diligent man and a member of the colliery Political Action Squad.

We should be grateful if you could make it clear to Lapschieß, who has already been in a concentration camp (1935–39), that his interference with instructions issued to the Russian prisoners of war constitutes a disturbance of the colliery's operation and that he may under no circumstances take the part of a POW.

This morning Lapschieß declared in impudent fashion to my face that he would continue to intervene if Russian prisoners of war were assaulted. No previous instances of ill-treatment or any other kinds of dispute with Russian prisoners of war have occurred here.

Documents such as the following by the German resistance appealing for solidarity with the foreign workers reached only a small circle of readers.[33]

*Article from the illegal Lower Rhine Communist Party newspaper 'Freiheit'
(Freedom), May 1942*
Growing solidarity is fatal for Hitlerian fascism.

Happily the German people's solidarity with the foreign workers and
civilian prisoners is generally continuing to grow and is driving the
Brownshirt criminals into a desperate state of fear and panic.

In several large firms in western Germany solidarity with the Russian
civilian prisoners has reached such a level that the Nazis have been forced to
hold shop-floor meetings to deal with the threat. What are the workers told
at such meetings?

Because German workers are concerned at the lot of the Russian civilian
prisoners; and because they think that the prisoners' daily rations of food are
too small; and because they maintain that the prisoners (who voluntarily
applied for work in Germany on the basis of fine promises by the German
recruiting agents, as they would otherwise have starved in occupied Russia)
ought to get more food than just 250 grams of bread and a plate of turnip
soup, since with that amount of food the Russians cannot work at all –
because of all this, the Nazi heroes are now ranting and raving against the
German workers. And they are screaming in these factory meetings that
German workers need not worry about the lot of the Russians, and that this
is all the food that has been allocated to the Russians; and this is what they
will have to make do with, period. *This* is what the fat Nazi bigwigs are
telling the workers. And, they say, if German workers have got too much to
eat, they should give away the surplus to charity; and if in future German
workers don't listen to reason and don't make sure they keep their distance
from the foreign workers, then the severest penalties will rain down on the
sinners involved and they can pack their bags for the concentration camp.
This is the way the Brownshirt heroes are threatening the workers. And they
are also trying to explain to them that the Germans are a master race and
ought to behave to foreigners accordingly.

The Nazis' greatest worry is that German workers will talk too much to
the Russians about conditions in Russia before the war and discover that
everything said and written about the Soviet Union in Nazi propaganda is a
fraud. The Nazis are so desperately frightened by the truth about the Soviet
Union, which is emerging more and more, that they have now taken to
separating Russian workers from German workers with barbed wire in the
factories where they are working. The tin god of the DAF, Dr Ley, has let fly
with an article attacking the growing solidarity of the German working class,
in which he writes: 'Increasing numbers of foreign workers have been
employed in Germany recently, and the German worker would therefore be
well advised in future to keep a greater distance between himself and the
foreign workers and to abandon the old habit of international Marxist
solidarity.'

If the Brownshirt bigwigs are so desperately afraid of the growing
solidarity with the foreign workers, to which German workers are giving
practical expression by letting them have food and clothing and shoes from

the small amounts they have themselves, then that is the best possible proof that German workers are on the right path. And we can only assure Hitler's minions that an avalanche is on the move, the avalanche of international solidarity, which will set off even sooner the avalanche of the struggle against Hitler and the war. The hour marking the end of Hiterlerian tyranny will soon have struck.

'International solidarity' on this broad scale, however, linking German and foreign workers, was never more than wishful thinking. Despite individual acts of support, the normal attitudes towards 'alien labour' remained ones of mistrust or, at best, detachment. Even Germans who were not of a Nazi cast of mind were fearful of the moment when the liberated foreigners would seek revenge for the injustices that they had suffered.

EIGHT

Young people: mobilisation and refusal

Repression and 'emancipation' in the Hitler Youth

The National Socialists had set particular store by winning over young people, whom they believed they could mould to their purposes and whom they needed, equally, as cannon-fodder for the war that lay ahead. The central features of National Socialist youth policy took shape accordingly. These were the assimilation of young people as fully as possible into the Hitler Youth (*Hitlerjugend*, HJ) and then into the Labour Service and the armed forces; education based on an extreme racialist ideology and on militaristic norms of behaviour involving incorporation and subordination within hierarchical structures of command; and, not least, the bestowal of comparative privileges on active members of the Hitler Youth as future cadres of National Socialism.[1]

In practice, contradictions arose between these objectives of youth policy, and more especially between the different methods of realising them: contradictions which fragmented and obstructed the apparently unitary programme of totalitarian assimilation. For example, military call-up robbed the Hitler Youth of many badly needed older youth leaders. Competition between the rival authorities of school and Hitler Youth[2] – whose mutual relationship was only ever clarified from case to case, never fundamentally resolved – gave rise to zones of conflict in which young people could play the one off against the other: skipping Hitler Youth duties, for example, by citing school obligations, or badgering school teachers with appeals to the 'higher' call of the Hitler Youth and the Party.[3] Not least, the ideological content of National Socialism remained much too vague to function as a self-sufficient educational objective. In practice young people selected from competing information-sources and values that were on offer: fragments of ideas of racial and national arrogance, mingled with traditional pedagogic humanism; the model of the front-line soldier, along with the supposition that there was an especially profound and valuable 'German' culture; backward-looking agrarian Romanticism, along with enthusiasm for modern technology. Which of these sources of identification and orientation really caught on with young people depended on local, temporal and personal factors that are not susceptible of generalisation. At any rate, the only conclusion that can be drawn from the wealth of memoirs of youth and school that have been published, especially in recent years,[4] is that education produced no universal, generation-wide effects. Such memoirs cover a wide span: the member of the Hitler Youth who enjoyed the privilege of having a father in the Party; the sceptic who had picked up enough during the last years of the Weimar Republic to keep his distance from the regime; the outsider who procured a measure of freedom through activities in a specific field which the Nazis fostered, and thereby came to realise that he was suddenly developing 'virtues' which the regime demanded.

> In his attempt to get somewhere, my father had staked everything on the new rulers. [. . .]
>
> Although my father did not greatly concern himself about me – my mother spent frequent spells in the sanatorium in any case and our 'family life' could only be termed intermittent – I availed myself of the earliest opportunity of translating his sententious maxims into action. It was in the third form of the primary school. Some pupils, myself included, were to be punished: beaten with the cane. I no longer recall why. We had to stand in a line and bend over. When it was my turn (the teacher's son was also in the form and was my deadly enemy), I straightened up defiantly and shouted: 'No one's going to beat me!'
>
> I am fairly certain that I did not shout, 'I am a German boy and no one's going to beat me!' – even then, that would have been too grandiose for me. But that, basically, was exactly what I meant. I should add that that was the full extent of my rebellion against the 'reactionary bum-tickler', as my father was fearlessly disposed to call him within the bosom of the family. I ran from the classroom and arrived home out of breath and howling. I no longer remember whether anything much happened as a result of my revolt against the authority of the school – which means that it probably did not.[5]

The former pupil of a reform-orientated 'free school' supported by convinced democrats and socialists had to endure the official *Gleichschaltung*, the introduction of state-backed National Socialist ideology in school subjects, and the activities of a Hitler Youth unit, but he had nevertheless learned enough from the now-discredited 'system' to be able to preserve his distance from National Socialism:

> I spent my secondary-school days in a shell. I had had my vaccination jab; as a latch-key child, I had spent too much time on the streets – I was a politically wide-awake city kid, and my roots went down too deep in the

democratic soil. That kept me going then, and it still keeps me going now. But in those days you withdrew. At sixteen and seventeen you crawled inside yourself. Friendships were based on feelings. You bypassed politics; to adapt a phrase of Friedrich Theodor Vischer's, politics went without saying. In two senses: because you were constantly condemned to listening to Nazi speeches, your disgust, mercifully, kept on being reinforced; at the same time, your scepticism and self-imposed distance made you anxious and alert enough to pick up what was going on. In a certain sense – psychologically at least – you were armed.[6]

The boarding-school pupil Peter Brückner was able to elude the demands of National Socialism until about 1937–38 and, at the cost of becoming a loner, to uphold his own non-conforming identity. But the tightening control over what was taught in schools, as well as the facts of boarding-school life, then brought him up against problems which at his age he could hardly hope to solve:[7]

> So, while I had escaped from National Socialism, and had got well clear of it, it caught up with me again in an unexpected way: in gymnastics and sport – a subject on to which the ideological claims of the Nazi state and the rhetoric of its leaders were grafted particularly easily. Hitler spoke of the 'defiant embodiment of masculine strength' as the new ideal for humanity; the gymnastics teachers reaped the benefit.[. . .]
> Uncomprehending, I watched my fellow pupils wax enthusiastic at this new development. For a while the gymnasium and the cinder track became the preferred arenas for the expression of social needs – even for my friend Werner F. Young people's pleasure in using their bodies, in fending off their sexual instincts, their liking for physical competition, and the ideology of the Nazi state all came naturally together on the playing fields of the 'Third Reich'.

This pressure could not be simply defied, because that would have meant having to leave school:

> What could I do? My position as an 'outsider' was no longer a safe one, still less a happy one. A sixteen-year-old who is aware of his shortcomings in gymnastics and sport, who is getting caught up in many different kinds of argument – often stimulating ones – and who is slowly learning to assert himself is dealt a blow in a weak spot when his future career is put under threat. ('Where am I going?') It is self-evident, in retrospect, that he is going to dramatise his situation; evil premonitions could be perfectly realistic in those days.

In deciding partially to give in to the challenge – by showing willingness at least to compete in some sports – the sixteen-year-old found himself suddenly deriving pleasure from orderliness, from the development of his own strength, from improving his performance: the very virtues which National Socialism and 'its concept of the will as an axis of oppression' proposed to cultivate through sport and gymnastics and to mobilise in order to create the desired type of the ruthless 'warrior':

> I had already begun to 'improve' myself in the winter of 1938–39: I enjoyed the state of physical fatigue after a sports lesson, liked running on the snow, and even found that gymnastics had a certain charm. The masochistic high point, however, was that I began to be enthusiastic about order and discipline in the sphere of 'physical training', of all things. One moment the gym was a swirling confusion of running, shouting schoolchildren; the next – a whistle from the teacher, and we were instantly standing in serried ranks, still gasping for breath.

The life stories of young people under the swastika often reveal the most contradictory juxtapositions of impressions. If there was any common factor, it was an education in the heedless, ruthless pursuit of genuine or inculcated interests: what Ernst Wiechert termed the 'boxer ethos'. The next memoir-extract makes plain how the adoption of specific key concepts and modes of behaviour deemed important by the regime also took place in people who, having recourse to their own experience and their social background, did not get caught up by National Socialism 'body and soul':[8]

> No one in our class ever read *Mein Kampf*. I myself had only used the book for quotations. In general we didn't know much about National Socialist ideology. Even anti-Semitism was taught rather marginally at school, for instance through Richard Wagner's essay *The Jews in Music* – and outside school the display copies of *Der Stürmer* made the idea seem questionable, if anything. [. . .] Nevertheless, we were politically programmed: programmed to obey orders, to cultivate the soldierly 'virtue' of standing to attention and saying 'Yes, Sir', and to switch our minds off when the magic word 'fatherland' was uttered and Germany's honour and greatness were invoked.

The way, especially, in which almost all teachers peppered their lessons with stories from the First World War served to make war seem ever-present and a matter of course: 'It was as though they had never lived in times of peace.' Pupils, however, were not mere passive targets of militarist indoctrination; they themselves sought out the fascinating stories of fighting and adventure to be found in the literature of the war:

> A large part of our compulsory reading in German lessons was world-war literature. But we also devoured it on our own account. As a rule these were books like *Seven at Verdun* or *Bosemüller Group*, in which, amidst all the horrors of modern warfare, the comradeship of the front was still triumphant and if you died you were at least awarded the Iron Cross. Occasionally there were variations: the youth-movement hero, the sensitive

'wanderer between two worlds'; the relentless fighter of the 'bestial Bolshevist hordes'; or the despiser of mankind, the knight in technological armour, the aristocratic, freebooting twentieth-century hero of [Ernst Jünger's] *Storms of Steel*. The UFA films, either seen in the cinema or shown to the school instead of lessons, also served their turn. We did not become National Socialists, but we did become the willing cannon-fodder of the National Socialists, softened up for the Second World War.

War was normal; force was 'legitimate', particularly when it paid off. Hitler's achievements in foreign policy between 1936 and 1939 had already accustomed the Germans to regard the combination of violent conduct, risk-taking and assertion of the 'legal right' to efface the 'shame of Versailles' as a sure-fire recipe for success.

We had all – teachers as well as pupils – been caught up long since in the giddy whirl of the new regime's great successes. The growth of Germany's power impressed us.

The mood in March 1938 was particularly thrilling. I stood in front of the display copy of the local newspaper and read and re-read the news: 'The Greater German Reich has been formed. Austria, the Eastern March, is part of Germany once more!' A gentleman standing by said to me: 'Yes, my boy, you can be proud – we are living in great times!' And I felt this too. We were living in great times, and their creator and guarantor was Hitler. Adolf Hitler, for us, was the impressive Führer figure. We took the picture we were given for the man. This did not prevent us from mimicking the stereotyped openings of his speeches, as a joke. But we awaited each speech with the tingling expectation that he was about to announce a new German success. We were seldom disappointed.

Such enthusiasm was certainly compatible with criticism. But characteristically the two managed to exist side by side, disjoined from one another: there were manifestly no universal standards of evaluation, and no possibility of working the differing impressions and perceptions into one consistent viewpoint:

Criticism was not lacking. Many things happened which were straightforwardly condemned. The pogrom in November 1938 was an example: the 'Crystal Night'. People were ashamed that this could take place in Germany. People said: 'How can something like that happen here? It's a disgrace.' But also: 'What can we do about it?

In this instance even a young person could see that he was in the clutches of a police state, one which otherwise caused him little bother. Memories then came back of the many occasions when you had said too much and had then toned your words down, for fear of possible denunciation. That was humiliating. But since nothing happened, it could quickly be forgotten. Besides, for us young people the risk was not all that great: we gave our consent to the state and could plausibly claim that our criticisms sprang from this affirmative point of view.

For those who took part in the Blitzkrieg campaigns, this lack of compunction, feeding on successes as easy as they were brutal, was reinforced further. And the bitter envy of those young men who had not yet been called up was exacerbated by the thought that others might be coming back from the war laden with decorations before they themselves would have a chance of 'being there':

> After the defeat of France, success seemed to be within easy reach. My Labour Service was behind me, and I was released to take up my university studies. But it seemed intolerable to imagine having to live in a post-war period without having seen front-line service. Since England was all that was left to conquer, I volunteered for the Marines. The dashing blue uniform also had something to do with it. Before I could wear it, the Russian campaign was under way.

Even the recognition of the inevitable approach of defeat did not immediately lead to a change of heart:

> The expectation of victory gradually evaporated; but defeat was unthinkable. It was simply impossible to imagine what could happen after it. There were no other choices: either we hold out, we thought, or we perish. Germany and National Socialism were even more indistinguishable for us than ever.

The central agency of National Socialist youth policy was the Hitler Youth,[9] whose leader Baldur von Schirach had occupied the offices of the Reich Board of German Youth Organisations as early as 5th April 1933 and was appointed by Hitler as 'Youth Leader of the German Reich' on 17th June 1933. By the end of 1933 all youth organisations, apart from the Catholic youth bodies – which for the time being remained protected under the Reich's Concordat with the Vatican – had either been banned (like the labour youth movement) or been more or less voluntarily *gleichgeschaltet* and integrated into the Hitler Youth (as were the non-political *bündisch* youth movement and, during late 1933 and early 1934, the Protestant organisations).

By the end of 1933, therefore, the Hitler Youth already incorporated 47 per cent of boys aged between 10 and 14 (in the so-called *Deutsches Jungvolk*) and 38 per cent of boys between 14 and 18 (in the Hitler Youth proper); on the other hand, only 15 per cent of girls between 10 and 14 were assimilated (in the *Jungmädel-Bund*) and 8 per cent of those between 15 and 21 (in the *Bund Deutscher Mädel*). The Hitler Youth Law of 1st December 1936 called for the assimilation of all German youth, and was given backing by growing pressure on those still outside to enrol 'voluntarily'; later, two executive orders ancillary to the Hitler Youth Law, issued on 25th March 1939, made 'youth service' compulsory and further refusal a punishable offence.

In the first years after 1933, for many young people, membership of the Hitler Youth was far from being felt as mere compulsion. There were many links with the youth activities of the Weimar period; varied leisure pursuits were offered; and at the lower levels – which in an everyday sense were the important ones – the leadership often consisted of former youth leaders or other people with practical youth experience.

In addition, the Hitler Youth uniform provided many opportunities for waging sharper and often highly aggressive conflicts with traditional figures of authority: schoolmasters, fathers, foremen, local clergy. To a certain degree, therefore, the Hitler Youth functioned as a sort of counter-authority. The countless activities of the Hitler Youth, not to mention the many posts within an organisation involving millions, also fed the appetite of many young people for recognition and action, as the memoirs of Melita Maschmann show:[10]

> The insatiable thirst which many young people have for action and movement found ample scope in the high speed action programmes of the Hitler Youth. It was part of the National Socialist youth leaders' method that almost everything took the form of competitions. Not only were there contests for the best performances in sport and at work, but each unit wanted to have the best-kept home, the most interesting travel album, the top collection for the Winter Relief Fund (*Winterhilfswerk*); or at least was supposed to want to. [. . .] Even during peacetime these perpetual contests introduced an element of unrest and artificial excitement into the life of the groups.

For many young people in the provinces, where the youth movement had not succeeded in spreading widely before 1933, the arrival of the Hitler Youth often meant a first chance to pursue leisure activities within any kind of youth organisation: the opportunity to build a youth club or sports field, or to go on weekend or holiday trips away from the familiar narrow home environement.

The emancipatory openings for girls were even greater.[11] In the *Bund Deutscher Mädel* (League of German Girls) girls could escape from the ties of domesticity and from the female role-model of child care and devotion to family (though this model was in fact propagated by the National Socialists themselves). They could pursue activities which, on the conservative model, were reserved for boys, and, if they worked as functionaries for the BDM, they might even approximate to the classic 'masculine' type of the political organiser who was never at home. Such opportunities for emancipation remained limited and were progressively revoked by the National Socialists' blanket discrimination against women. Yet the features of the ideological aim that were undoubtedly reactionary proved, in many practical day-to-day respects, to have a modernising effect.

With the consolidation of the Hitler Youth as a large-scale bureaucratic organisation, and with the gradual ageing of its leadership personnel in the course of the 1930s, its attractive force for the young began to wane. Political campaigns against former youth-movement leaders and supposed youth-movement styles of behaviour within the Hitler Youth led to the disciplining and purging of units. The pursuit of total assimilation brought into the ranks of the Hitler Youth those young people who had previously proclaimed their antipathy merely by their absence. Disciplinary and surveillance measures to enforce 'youth service' criminalised even harmless everyday pleasures such as meetings of friends and gangs.[12] Most of all, the assertion of sovereign power by the Hitler Youth *Streifendienst* patrols, whose members were scarcely older than the young people on whom they were keeping check, provoked general indignation. On top of this, even before the outbreak of war the Hitler Youth had become more heavily taken up with pre-military drill.

Accordingly, the second half of the 1930s reveals a growing crisis in the Hitler Youth, a crisis which during the war years developed into a massive opposition movement on the part of groups and gangs of young people. The SOPADE 'Reports on Germany' for 1938 already recorded this radical shift of attitude among the young, from initial attraction to growing rejection:[13]

> Young people are more easily influenced in terms of mood than are adults. This fact made it easier for the regime to win over young people in the first years after the seizure of power. It appears that the same fact is now making it hard for the regime to keep young people in thrall. Naturally, the mood of youth is influenced by the popular mood generally, and reports on youth reflect the same dissatisfaction and disenchantment as do the general morale reports. But beyond this, young people have reason for special disappointment. They were made particularly large promises which for the most part were incapable of fulfilment. The great mass of young people today can see that the well-paying posts in public administration and the Party apparatus have been filled by comrades who had the good fortune of being a few years older. Set against these reduced prospects are increased demands in all spheres. In the long run young people too are feeling increasingly irritated by the lack of freedom and the mindless drilling that is customary in the National Socialist organisations. It is therefore no wonder that symptoms of fatigue are becoming particularly apparent among their ranks. [. . .]
>
> Young people are causing the relevant Party agencies much anxiety. Both boys and girls are trying by every means possible to dodge the year of Land Service. In Greater Berlin in May 1938 a total of 918 boys and 268 girls were

reported missing, having secretly run away from home because they did not want to go away on Land Service. Police patrols in the Grunewald, the Tegel Forest and the Wannsee district periodically round up whole lorry-loads of young people, some Berliners, some from the provinces. There is a section of youth that wants the romantic life. Whole bundles of trashy literature have been found in small caves. – Apprentices too are disappearing from home much more frequently and are drifting in the hurly-burly of the big cities.

From this period at the latest there were now clearly opposing opinions of the Hitler Youth among young people:

> Our camp community was a small-scale model of what I imagined the 'national community' to be. It was an absolutely worked-out model (Melita Maschmann, BDM leader)[14]

> Everything the HJ preaches is a fraud. I know this for certain, because everything I had to say in the HJ myself was a fraud. (Youth, Karlsruhe, 1942)[15]

The thesis that the Hitler Youth successfully mobilised young people fits only one side of the social reality of the Third Reich. The more the Hitler Youth arrogated state powers to itself, and the more completely young people were assimilated into the organisation,[16] the more clearly visible became an emergent pattern of youth nonconformity. By the end of the 1930s thousands of young people were declining to take part in the leisure activities of the Hitler Youth and were discovering their own unregimented styles in spontaneous groups and gangs. Indeed, they defended their autonomous space all the more insistently as the Hitler Youth *Streifendienst* and the Gestapo applied ever more massive pressure. In 1942 the Reich youth leadership was driven to declare:

> The formation of cliques, i.e. groupings of young people outside the Hitler Youth, was on the increase a few years before the war, and has particularly increased during the war, to such a degree that a serious risk of the political, moral and criminal breakdown of youth must be said to exist.[17]

The leadership could no longer get out of this by saying that the people involved had been conditioned by the Weimar 'system': by Marxism, clericalism or the old youth movement. The 14- to 18-year-olds who made up this opposition in the late 1930s and early 1940s were boys (and to a lesser extent girls) whose socialisation in school had largely taken place under National Socialist rule. It was the very generation, indeed, on whom Adolf Hitler's system had operated unhindered that turned out so many 'black sheep'.

Who, then, were these young people who caused the Hitler Youth, youth workers and, increasingly, the police and the courts so much trouble? Amidst the wealth of evidence of nonconformist behaviour, the activities of three groups stand out particularly clearly: groups which resembled one another in their rejection of the Hitler Youth but which differed in their style, in their social background and in their modes of action – the Edelweiß Pirates, the '*Meuten*' and the swing movement.

Edelweiß Pirates[18]

The first Edelweiss Pirates appeared at the end of the 1930s in the western parts of the Reich. The names of the individual groups, their badges (metal edelweiß flowers worn on the collar, the skull and crossbones, pins with coloured heads), their get-up (usually a checked shirt, dark short trousers, white stockings) and their activities all varied, but pointed towards one single underlying model. '*Fahrtenstenze*' (Travelling Dudes) from Essen, 'Kittelbach Pirates' from Oberhausen or Düsseldorf (named after a stream in north Düsseldorf) and 'Navajos' from Cologne[19] all regarded themselves as 'Edelweiß Pirate' groups. This understanding was not something abstract, but took on concrete reality during weekend trips into the surrounding countryside, when groups from the whole region met up, pitched their tents, sang, talked, and together 'clobbered' Hitler Youth patrols doing their rounds.

The enemy – the Hitler Youth, the Gestapo and the law – also soon categorised the groups under a single heading, having first hesitated lest the 'youth-movement' (*bündisch*) label would save them the bother of needing to analyse new, spontaneous forms of oppositional activity and hence construct corresponding new sets of prohibitions.[20] It quickly became clear, however, that while it was possible to make out precursor groups and so-called 'wild' or unauthorised *bündisch* organisations in the early 1930s, there was no continuity of personnel (the 'delinquents' of 1935–37 had long since been called up for the front line) and there was no continuous intellectual tradition.

The Edelweiß Pirate groups, then, arose spontaneously, as young people aged between 14 and 18 got together in the evenings or at weekends to make the most of their spare time away from the control of the Hitler Youth. The age make-up of the core group, with a surrounding cluster of younger boys and older war-wounded men and men in reserved occupations, was not fortuitous: boys of 17 and 18 were conscripted into the Reich Labour Service and then into the armed forces, while boys of 14 had reached the school-leaving age and could thus escape from the immediate sphere of day-to-day Hitler Youth control. They were taking their first steps into the world of work: as apprentices, or increasingly – thanks to the shortage of manpower caused by the war – as relatively well paid unskilled workers. This personal watershed, always a critical moment in the socialisation of working-class youth in any case, thus became at once doubly more significant: negatively, as marking a liberation from direct Hitler Youth control, positively as involving the premature adoption of an adult role.

To this increased sense of self-esteem, and real increase in autonomy, the continuing obligation of Hitler Youth service up to the age of 18 could contribute very little. The war reduced the Hitler Youth's leisure attractions: playing fields and club buildings had been bombed, official hiking trips were cut down and finally discontinued, many former Hitler Youth leaders were called up. Instead there was repeated paramilitary drilling, with mindless exercises in obedience which were all the more irksome for being supervised by Hitler Youth leaders who were scarcely any older than the rank and file, yet who often stood out by virtue of their grammar- or secondary-school background. 'It's the Hitler Youth's own fault,' one Edelweiß Pirate from Düsseldorf said, explaining his group's slogan, 'Eternal War on the Hitler Youth'. 'Every order I was given contained a threat.'[21]

A leaflet of the Oberhausen Kittelbach Pirates likewise gives precise expression to this contempt for the state youth organisations (junior and senior) and their representatives, bringing out the gulf between the different realms of social experience in parodic terms:

> Why are 15- and 16-year-olds still in the Jungvolk? They should be in the Hitler Youth. But the slackers don't want to spend their summer holidays in the country helping the farmers. That can be left to 14-year-old girls and old boys and old dears of 70 and 75. The young fellows don't know how to fill their time in the holidays. But they don't want to work. Well, send them out into the country, so they learn how to work too.[22]

The self-assurance of the Edelweiß Pirates and their image among their contemporaries were unmistakable, as an Oberhausen mining instructor found in the case of his trainees in 1941:

> Every child knows who the KP [common abbreviation for Kittelbach Pirates] are. They are everywhere; there are more of them than there are Hitler Youth. And they all know each other, they stick close together. [. . .] They beat up the patrols, because there are so many of them. They never take no for an answer. They don't go to work either, they are always down by the canal, at the lock gates.[23]

What did the Edelweiß Pirates do with the free time that they had won through opting out of the officially organised activities? They met in gangs comprising former school friends, work colleagues, neighbours. The overriding factor (as in many youth peer-groupings in the post-war period) was the territorial principle: they belonged together because they lived or worked together. They met in a nearby park, or bar, or at a street corner; in a square, by an air-raid shelter, on a bomb site; by the canal and, not least, at the fairground. The gangs usually consisted of about a dozen boys and a few girls. The fact that girls were involved was enough to distinguish these oppositional groups from the strict sex-segregated state youth groups, the *Bund Deutscher Mädel* and the Hitler Youth. The presence of girls at the evening get-togethers, and more so on the weekend trips into the country, gave the adolescents a relatively unrestricted chance of sexual experience. In this respect they were much less inhibited than their parents' generation, particularly the representatives of National Socialism with their positively obsessive fixation on the repression of sexuality. None the less, sexual life in these spontaneous groups was no doubt much less orgiastic than contemporary unofficial informants believed, or wanted others to believe, when they sought to construct a trinity of delinquency out of (sexual and criminal) depravity, (anti-organisational and anti-authoritarian) rebellion and (political) antagonism.[24]

The high point of leisure was the weekend, when the young people could go off on trips. They hiked, hitchhiked or cycled dozens of kilometres into the Neanderthal, to the Blauer See at Ratingen near Düsseldorf, the Entenfang in Duisburg, the dams in the Bergisches Land, Altenberg cathedral or as far afield as the Rhine valley at Neuwied near Koblenz, over a hundred kilometres away. Armed with their rucksacks, sheath knives and bread-and-butter rations, sleeping in tents or barns, they spent a carefree time with like-minded peers from other cities, away from adult control, though always on the watch for Hitler Youth patrols, whom they either sought to avoid, prudently calculating their own strength, or taunted and fell upon with relish. An important basis of this need repeatedly to create as much space as possible between themselves and their daily working and living conditions was the wish to escape from the 'educative' incursions of adults, and from the denunciations, spying, orders and punishments issued by the National Socialist institutions that were inevitably bound up with these in practice. The old reason for hiking that had inspired the youth movement – to withdraw from the constraints of the world of adults – was intensified and took on a political charge.

It is an astonishing fact that several of these 14- to 18-year-olds undertook long journeys during their holidays, as far as the Black Forest and the Tirol, to Munich, Vienna and Berlin – and this in wartime, despite a ban on travel, the restrictions of freedom of movement caused by the food ration-book system, and police controls. The boys made do with casual work, hitched lifts, joined up with others like themselves, and in the process demonstrated the existence and vitality of informal structures of support and communication even in the bureaucratised war economy of the German Reich.

While the long holiday journeys and shorter weekend trips opened up realms of experience that were normally out of the reach of working-class children in those days (and especially so in wartime), the daily meetings after work determined the groups' cohesiveness and structure, created specific forms of communication and made possible the development of clearly defined and distinctive identities that marked off the Edelweiß Pirate working-class youth sub-cultures from the dominant official style of the Hitler Youth. In these evening gatherings people killed time, gossiped, told stories, played the guitar and sang songs – especially hiking songs or popular hits, with words that spoke of foreign lands, adventure, 'rough fellows', beautiful girls. No cliché of commercial entertainment was left unused; but the Edelweiß Pirates also appropriated these banal stereotypes for their own ends. For one thing, they were not singing the Hitler Youth songs prescribed as 'suitable for young people' or the fighting songs of the chauvinistic German military tradition; they were singing the songs that were permitted to the citizenry as non-political compensation for the burdens imposed by the regime – adult hit songs, which dealt furthermore with adventures not allowed to the young, the pleasures of boozing and love. In addition, the Edelweiß Pirates developed a remarkable knack for rewriting the words of the hit songs, inserting new phrases or lines or whole verses which catapulted their own lives into this dream world. The hits thus became a means of articulating longings and demands for an existence other than the grey reality of war.

The Edelweiß Pirates turned the traditional songs of the hiking and youth movements to similar use. These were adapted or reworded so as to relate to their own realms of experience, and became signals of demarcation and protest, either because the songs themselves were disapproved of or even banned by the Hitler Youth, or through the substitution of the names of the Nazis, Gestapo or Hitler Youth for those of the foes mentioned in the original texts. The classic instance of this, perhaps, was from a popular glorification of the Russian White Guards, where a reference to the Soviet secret police was simply replaced with a National Socialist reference: 'Into hiding we must go/From the henchmen of the Gestapo.' Some further examples of Edelweiß Pirate songs illustrate the tone and outlook:

In Junker's Kneipe bei Wein und Pfeife	We all sat in the tavern
da saßen wir beisammen.	With a pipe and a glass of wine,
Ein guter Tropfen von Malz und Hopfen	A goodly drop of malt and hop,
der Teufel führt uns an.	And the devil calls the tune.

Hei, wo die Burschen singen
und die Klampfen klingen,
und die Mädel fallen ein.
Was kann das Leben Hitlers uns
geben,
wir wollen frei von Hitler sein.

Hark the hearty fellows sing!
Strum that banjo, pluck that string!
And the lasses all join in.
We're going to get rid of Hitler,
And he can't do a thing.

Wenn die Sirenen in Hamburg
ertönen
müssen Navajos an Bord.
In einer Kneipe von einem Mädel
fällt uns der Abschied nicht schwer.
Rio de Janeiro ahoi Caballero,
Edelweiß-Piraten sind treu.

The Hamburg sirens sound,
Time for Navajos to go.
A tavern's just the place
To kiss a girl good-bye.
Rio de Janeiro, *caballero*, ahoy!
An Edelweiß Pirate is faithful and
true.

Des Hitlers Zwang, der macht uns
klein,
noch liegen wir in Ketten.
Doch einmal werden wir wieder frei,
wir werden die Ketten schon brechen.
Denn unsere Fäste, die sind hart,
ja – und die Messer sitzen los,
für die Freiheit der Jugend
kämpfen Navajos.

Hitler's power may lay us low,
And keep us locked in chains,
But we will smash the chains one
day,
We'll be free again.
We've got fists and we can fight,
We've got knives and we'll get them
out.
We want freedom, don't we, boys?
We're the fighting Navajos.[25]

Und im Graben der Chaussee
liegt der Streifendienst, Juchhe,
sieht uns starten, Edelweißpiraten,
nur mit Schmerz und Weh.

Out on the high road, down in the
ditch
There're some Hitler Youth
patrolmen, and they're getting black
as pitch.
Sorry if it hurts, mates, sorry we
can't stay,
We're Edelweiß Pirates, and we're
on our way.

An Rhein und Ruhr marschieren wir,
für unsere Freiheit kämpfen wir,
den Streifendienst, schlag' ihn
entzwei
Edelweiß marschiert, Achtung die
Straße frei.

We march by banks of Ruhr and
Rhine
And smash the Hitler Youth in
twain.
Our song is freedom, love and life,
We're Pirates of the Edelweiß.

Hör Eisbär [also Rübezahl*], was wir
Dir jetzt sagen,
Unsere Heimat ist nicht mehr frei,

Polar Bear, listen, we're talking to
you,
Our land isn't free, we're telling
you true.

---

*A mountain giant from the Riesengebirge.

schwingt die Keulen ja wie in alten Zeiten,	Get out your cudgels and come into town
schlagt HJ, SA den Schädel entzwei.	And smash in the skulls of the bosses in brown.[26]

What stands out in these songs is certainly the thirst for freedom – expressed, as regards positive identification, in the motifs of faraway adventure, and negatively in the calls to fight the Nazis. It is also noteworthy that only the individual, or the gang, serves as a basis of identification; large-scale social entities and abstract values, whether borrowed from the labour movement or from the dominant Nazi ideology, manifestly play little part. The complete absence of echoes of the socialist and communist song tradition also needs explaining: possibly those songs were never so popular among young workers (apart from the activist minorities) as folk songs, hiking songs and hits. At all events, their words did not serve, or no longer served, to express the feelings of the new generation. Certainly, the absence of explicitly socialist songs was not due to the fact that they were politically taboo, since the songs the Edelweiß Pirates did sing were provocative enough. Their words put pleasure, excitement, group solidarity and the direct, tangible joys of life into the foreground; not abstract allegiances. An equally noteworthy new feature was the scorn for work, or more precisely the wage-relationship, a topic which in the traditional proletarian songs was oddly conspicuous by its absence:

Meister gib uns die Papiere,	Master, give us our cards,
Meister gib uns unser Geld,	Master, give us our pay.
denn die Frauen sind uns lieber,	We've had enough of slaving,
als die Schufterei auf dieser Welt.	Women are better any day.[27]

All this must have been provocation enough for the Hitler Youth, and for a good many non-fascist adults too. For the Edelweiß Pirates, however, dissociating themselves and emphasising differences in- volved, in addition, taking positive action of their own in order to provoke their Nazi opponents and the intolerant adult world. Reports of brawls with members of the Hitler Youth (especially the disciplinary patrols), of assaults on uniformed personnel, and of jeers and insults directed at Nazi dignitaries, are legion. Such activities appear to have been one of the gangs' chief preoccupations. They sprang from a complex cluster of motives. There was the wish to generate excitement, to stave off boredom, to 'go to town'. There was also the need to get back at authority, which was an inescapable presence in everyday life and which held the isolated individual at its mercy through its numerous bodies, office-holders and bosses. All the humiliations that the members of the gangs had endured between clocking on and clocking off came back to mind when they gathered at their regular meeting-places to jeer at the 'big shots' behind their backs, or when they knocked a *Jungvolk* Pack Leader off his bicycle and robbed him of his badges and dagger of honour. And, not least important, the only way the groups could maintain their sense of self-esteem, in face of the constant pressure from above, was to undertake some form of action: to 'show them a thing or two'. Certainly, there was no let-up in the complaints made by National Socialist officials about the excesses of the Edelweiß Pirates:[28]

> I therefore request that the police ensure that this riff-raff is dealt with once and for all. The HJ are taking their lives in their hands when they go out on the streets.

a Mühlheim SA unit reported in 1941. The Düsseldorf Hitler Youth reported to the Gestapo in April 1942:

> For the past month none of the Leaders of 25/39 Troop has been able to proceed along the Hellweg or Hoffeldstraße (southern part) without being subjected to abuse from these people. The Leaders are hence unable to visit the parents of the Youth members who live in these streets. The Youth themselves, however, are being incited by the so-called *bündisch* youth. They are either failing to turn up for duty or are seeking to disrupt it.

And the Düsseldorf-Grafenberg branch of the National Socialist Party reported to the Gestapo on 17th July 1943:

> *Re: Edelweiß Pirates question* The said youths are throwing their weight around again. I have been informed that assemblages of young people have become more conspicuous than ever, expecially since the last terror [bombing] raid on Düsseldorf. These youngsters, aged between 12 and 17, hang around into the late evening, with musical instruments and young females. Since this riff-raff is to a large extent outside the Hitler Youth and adopts a hostile attitude towards the organisation, they represent a danger to other young people. It has recently been established that members of the armed forces are also to be found among them, and they exploit their membership of the Wehrmacht to display a particularly arrogant demeanour. There is a suspicion that it is these youths who have been inscribing the walls of the pedestrian subway on the Altenbergstraße with the slogans 'Down with Hitler', 'The OKW [*Oberkommando der Wehrmacht*, Military High Command] is lying', 'Medals for Murder', 'Down with Nazi Brutality' etc. However often these inscriptions are removed, within a few days new ones appear on the walls again.

Be this as it may, the conflicts between the Edelweiß Pirates and the authorities continued to escalate, and each party did its share to give the other a hard time. The prospects of success, of course, were far from equal. On the one side was a power apparatus whose drive for perfection led to ever more irrational measures of compulsion and surveillance; on the other were gangs of young people who had nothing going for them other than their great numbers and their ability to retreat into the foxholes of everyday normality.

The Gestapo and Hitler Youth brought to bear an armoury of repressive measures that ranged from individual warnings, round-ups and temporary detention (often followed by release with the public branding of a shaven head) to weekend imprisonment, reform school, labour camp, youth concentration camp or criminal trial. Thousands were caught in the net; for many the hunt ended in death, and not only for the Cologne Edelweiß Pirates whose so-called ringleaders (among them the 16-year-old Barthel Schink) were publicly hanged in the Hüttenstraße in Cologne-Ehrenfeld as late as November 1944.[29] On 25th October 1944, as the curtain was coming down on the Third Reich, the national leader of the SS and head of the German police, Himmler, issued an ordinance for the 'combating of youth cliques', therewith capping a long series of bans and prosecutions that had been used in the attempt to defeat the protest movement.[30] In a single day of raids, on 7th December 1942, the Düsseldorf Gestapo broke up the following groups 'at a stroke': 10 groups comprising 283 young people in Düsseldorf, 10 groups with 260 people in Duisburg, 4 groups with 124 people in Essen, and 4 groups with 72 people in Wuppertal. The Chief Public Prosecutor for Cologne referred on 16th January 1944 to the fact that 'the Secret State Police, since the beginning of the growth of the cliques, [has] dealt with between 1,000 and 1,200 cases on its own authority, using Special Procedures (cautions etc.)'.[31]

As long as the National Socialists needed workers in armaments factories and future soldiers for the front, they could not exterminate German youth in the way they exterminated the Poles and the Jews. They were forced to use more sophisticated methods – they owed as much, indeed, to their ideological concept of the 'healthy stock of German youth'. But a sub-culture without organised structures only rarely throws up 'ringleaders' who can be easily singled out. An alternative leisure style, to which many adhere and with which very many more sympathise, cannot be penalised in blanket fashion. A changed, more sceptical attitude towards the dominant norms of work, authority, social order and morality can be dealt with and punished in individual cases, but not when a considerable portion of the younger generation begins to subscribe to it.

The institutions of the National Socialist state, accordingly, reacted to the Edelweiß Pirate movement with manifest uncertainty. Some state functionaries regarded the misdemeanours as silly childish pranks, the result of wartime youth deprivation and of the waning appeal of the Hitler Youth, robbed of its leaders by military conscription. Others scented large-scale conspiracy and looked for secret structures, plotters behind the scenes – in other words, projected their own familiar schemata on to a movement they did not understand. These widely differing assessments of the Edelweiß Pirates have not been resolved to this day. But the Edelweiß Pirates were neither merely 'deprived children' (or delinquents) nor unimpeachable political resistance fighters. Indeed, their significance is precisely that they combined behaviour that deviated from the dominant social norms with a semi-political rejection of National Socialism, since National Socialism and the whole weight of its institutions and machinery of repression had come to stand for an authoritarian, hierarchical and militaristic norm.

The social make-up of the Edelweiß Pirates movement can be well illustrated by an analysis of the 80 or so volumes of files which the Düsseldorf Gestapo Central Station compiled on 19 Edelweiß Pirate groups in Duisburg between 1938 and 1944. These groups comprised about 240 named members.[32] The numbers of those undetected cannot be determined, seeing that the phenomenon was one in which spontaneous everyday association shaded into more unequivocal gang-style features. The total number of adherents of the Edelweiß Pirate groups, however, must have been many times greater than the 240 whose names were known to the Gestapo.

As far as age was concerned, the dominant group consisted of 16- to 19-year-olds, who had passed beyond the authority of school and often also of their apprenticeship instructors but had not yet been called up for military service. Almost all had gone to elementary school (hardly any to schools for the retarded); very few had attended or were attending schools that would take them beyond the minimum leaving age. The central factor in the emergence and underlying outlook of the Edelweiß Pirate groups, then, is that almost all of their members had already entered the world of work. The number who had completed an apprenticeship was also relatively small. Most members of the gangs were simple unskilled or semi-skilled workers. It is a striking fact that they show a relatively frequent change of job, which was the only way, under the laws of the Third Reich, for a worker to obtain higher wages or better working conditions. About one in four had changed jobs at least once. Many had got involved in clashes with superiors, recurrently took absence without leave, reported sick or worked only as much as they wanted and at the speed they wanted. Such behaviour did not always imply a conscious aim of sabotage, of the sort ascribed to 15 young workers by the management of the Oberhausen zinc concern Altenberg AG; these workers had been absent for a total of 1,400 hours between January and July 1941, which represented a loss of production of at least 400,000 kg of galvanised zinc. A memorandum of 10th July 1941 declares:[33]

> It is our presumption that St. is deliberately out to commit deliberate [*sic*] sabotage against the productive capacity of the German Reich by tempting the youths concerned into idling at work. In our view St. must be got rid of without more ado, since we regard this individual as the chief ringleader of the Kittelbach Pirates who are under suspicion of subversive activity. [. . .] The youths mentioned display an extraordinary degree of cynicism and impertinence in their behaviour towards their older work colleagues and superiors, and in our judgement it would be appropriate if these youths were enlisted for compulsory HJ service in order to be taught some discipline.
>
> We have already made great efforts, in harness with our staff council head Pg. Sch., to exercise an educative influence on these youths, but this has so far been without result. We would therefore respectfully request that you back us up in our attempts to educate these youths by providing stronger punitive measures.

If we look at the jobs done by the fathers of the Edelweiß Pirates, it is evident that what we have here is the 'born' proletariat, without exception. It is striking in this connection that in a comparatively high number of instances the fathers are recorded as being dead; there are no systematic records of the numbers of fathers working on the home front as against those in the armed services. This seems to indicate that it was easier for those young people who were not subject to paternal authority to undertake extended weekend excursions, pick quarrels with the boss, or spend their evenings outdoors with friends in contravention of the Decree for the Protection of Young People.

These young people belonged together not only by virtue of their shared social situation and the working-class environment of their parents: they also lived in the same districts of the cities. The gangs had, first and foremost, a territorial identity.

These data do not imply that the Edelweiß Pirates were in any sense a deprived, sub-proletarian, 'delinquent' younger generation. Certainly, relatively few of them could reckon on much likelihood of upward mobility through school or work, and the bulk of them were on the look-out for adventure. But they were in no way pauperised. Data on their earnings indicate an average unskilled monthly wage of just over 100RM, a considerable portion of which was their own to dispose of, as their presence in pubs and their extensive travels show. The social profile of the Edelweiß Pirates is thus one of self-assured working-class young people who were not exactly willing to conform to the norms of working life and who were not loth to get into conflict with those who saw themselves as being in authority. And the Hitler Youth came to realise this too.

All Edelweiß Pirates rejected the Nazis; indeed, this self-segregation, and the development of an alternative style, constituted their own definition of themselves. Few of them, however, had a political point of view, as is only to be expected in the case of 14- to 18-year-olds. They seem, rather, to have set the experience-based content of their own group existence against the demands of systems and abstract norms which they encountered in National Socialism. The Edelweiß Pirates were not content with mere 'inner emigration', with keeping their political opinions to themselves; they wanted to do something against the Hitler Youth. But only a few went beyond small, humdrum acts of provocation. Those few, however, stuck Allied leaflets into people's letter boxes if they found them in the woods, or joined organised resistance groups. In Düsseldorf in 1942 Communists, including the then national Communist Party leader Wilhelm Knöchel, made contact with Edelweiß Pirates such as Werner Heydn, received reports on opinion and morale from him, and gave him stickers and leaflets to distribute. In Cologne-Ehrenfeld in 1944 Edelweiß Pirates joined an underground group which, in the confusion of ruined streets and houses, had offered shelter to German army deserters, prisoners of war, forced labourers and prisoners from concentration camps. They got supplies by making armed raids on military depots, made direct assaults on Nazis, and took part in the quasi-partisan fighting. Indeed, the chief of the Cologne Gestapo fell victim to one of these attacks in the autumn of 1944.

Many members of the Edelweiß Pirate movement thus passed through the whole gamut of nonconformist behaviour, conscious refusal, open protest and political resistance. The common factor in all these acts was the formation of dissident sub-cultural norms among sections of working-class youth. This culture of protest derived its political force from two sources. On the one hand, the rigid power demands of National Socialism could tolerate no nonconformist behaviour; on the other, the conflict over leisure time occurred precisely along the social dividing line between the realm of experience of the working class and that of the middle-class-imbued National Socialist organisations. The awareness of social dichotomy which workers acquired in their daily collisions with bosses, landlords and representatives of authority, in advance of developing any political awareness, took on a sharper form as the Edelweiß Pirates rebelled against National Socialist authority and regimented leisure. Their songs, their style of protest and their demeanour indicated that they had seen through the talk of *Volksgemeinschaft*. Without subscribing to an explicit political doctrine, they set their social experience, in the form of a specifically youth-based sub-culture, against the National Socialist call for integration.

'Meuten'

The relationships between youth sub-cultures and their wider social cultures of origin are by no means unproblematical. The former are not only expressions of shared class experience, which each new generation undergoes; they also enshrine the specific experiences which distinguish the members of the younger generation from their fathers and older brothers and which cause them to find their own styles. An example of a variant of the generation-specific sub-cultures within the working class in this period is the Leipzig *'Meuten'* (gangs).* This movement, which according to Gestapo figures involved about 1,500 young people, reached its high point in the years 1937–39.[34]

In many respects the activities of these groups on weekday evenings and at weekends resembled those of the Edelweiß Pirates and may therefore be taken as typical of this whole generation of working-class youth. Under this heading come their gathering in parks and regular pubs, their territorial structure (based on friends, neighbours and a common place of work), their journeys to the surrounding Baggersee lakes, their *bündisch*-inspired outfits, their songs of wandering and adventure, their unabashed sexuality, their acts of provocation against the Hitler Youth. But there was also a significant difference. The Leipzig *Meuten* style was assembled not only from *bündisch* elements but from items borrowed from the Communist and Socialist tradition.[35] In the working-class districts of Leipzig – the former Red strongholds where the *Meuten* originated – the Communist tradition seems to have put down deeper roots into everyday life than in the Rhineland and Ruhr.[36] Memories of the times when 'our side' was strong; hopes for a society in which 'everyone would be equal', as in the Russia of Communist Party propaganda (and, more important, as in the dreams of many Germans); speculations about the day when the violent overthrow of the regime would come; lively interest in every news broadcast about the civil war between the Spanish workers and the fascists – these features all demonstrate a certain 'Communist' day-to-day consciousness which, while certainly having little to do with strategy and shifts of party ideology, nevertheless betoken a more politicised class identity than that of the Edelweiß Pirates. This identity was also reflected in the language of the *Meuten*, it was evident in some of their 'ringleaders' (as the Nazi judicial system termed them), and it

---

*[Literally, 'packs'. (Transl.)]

influenced the sub-culture's style. Initiates greeted one another with a garbled version of the Russian Pioneer salutation, 'Be prepared.'

So far as one can tell from the source material, the fact that the Gestapo in Leipzig had a more clearly-defined picture of their quarry appears to have given them the opportunity to impose a more massive and ruthless crackdown. In the main, however, to a disinterested observer the elements of Communist style in the *Meuten* were local variants of a broader basic pattern of working-class youth protest, not a real continuation of Communist resistance activity.

Similar working-class youth groups, either approximating to the more politicised Leipzig type, or even more clearly non-political than the Edelweiß Pirates, existed in Dresden ('*Mobs*'), Halle ('*Proletengefolgschaften*', Proletarian Troops), Erfurt ('*Meuten*'), Hamburg ('Death's Head Gang', 'Bismarck Gang') and Munich ('*Blasen*', Crews or Crowds).[37]

The swing movement

A quite different form of popular culture developed among young people from the (upper) middle class: the swing movement.[38] Its adherents made it their vocation to shun music of the *völkisch* sort, and banal moon-June German hits, in order to listen to jazz and swing numbers, either on records or in live performances. At first some of these events were allowed to take place in public; then, when Hitler Youth officials took umbrage at them, they were banned. In one internal Hitler Youth report on a swing festival in Hamburg in February 1940, which was attended by 500–600 young people, we can hear all the leitmotifs that recur in the lamentations of the authorities when faced by the jazz and rock cultures of the twentieth century:[39]

> The dance music was all English and American. Only swing dancing and jitterbugging took place. At the entrance to the hall stood a notice on which the words 'Swing prohibited' had been altered to 'Swing requested'. The participants accompanied the dances and songs, without exception, by singing the English words. Indeed, throughout the evening they attempted only to speak English; at some tables even French.
>
> The dancers were an appalling sight. None of the couples danced normally; there was only swing of the worst sort. Sometimes two boys danced with one girl; sometimes several couples formed a circle, linking arms and jumping, slapping hands, even rubbing the backs of their heads together; and then, bent double, with the top half of the body hanging loosely down, long hair flopping into the face, they dragged themselves round practically on their knees. When the band played a rumba, the dancers went into wild ecstasy. They all leaped around and joined in the chorus in broken English. The band played wilder and wilder items; none of

the players was sitting down any longer, they all 'jitterbugged' on the stage like wild creatures. Several boys could be observed dancing together, always with two cigarettes in the mouth, one in each corner . . .

With the ban on public functions, the swing movement transposed itself into informal groupings where, naturally, its character became more sharply defined. Swing clubs sprang up, particularly, in big cities like Hamburg, Kiel, Berlin, Stuttgart, Frankfurt, Dresden, Halle and Karlsruhe. They consisted predominantly of middle-class young people with enough education to be able to cope with the English words of the songs and to try out their own foreign colloquial fragments and catch-phrases. Like the Edelweiß Pirates, who in using German-language hits had seized on an element of 'non-political' leisure activity which they had then directed against the claims of National Socialist youth policy, so the 'swing boys' and 'swing girls' took up the watered-down jazz that was perfectly permissible in variety shows and dances and radicalised it for their own purposes – stylising it into an emblem of a culture that rejected the Hitler Youth norms, stripping it of its domesticated dance-floor character in favour of hotter varieties of what in National Socialist parlance was called 'negro music'.

Thus dance music gave way to hot jazz; the dance steps taught in dancing classes gave way to free, spontaneous rhythmic movement and extreme bodily exertion; instead of a rigid demeanour and tidy dress, there was 'jiving' and 'jitterbugging', hair 'grown down to the collar' (to quote the same Hitler Youth report) and a cult of 'casualness' (*Lässigkeit*) and 'sleaziness' (*Lottern*). These catchwords were very much part of the standard repertoire of the 'swing boys'. 'Their ideal is the "sleazy life"', the above-cited Hitler Youth report noted; or as the member of a Kiel swing club, the 'Plutocrats', put it in a letter to a friend who had gone away on a journey:

Be a proper spokesman for Kiel, won't you? i.e., make sure you're really casual, singing or whistling English hits all the time, absolutely smashed and always surrounded by really amazing women.

The characteristic features of the swing scene reflected the difference in social background between these scions of the middle class and the working-class young people in the Edelweiß Pirates and *Meuten*. The latter met on street corners and in parks: that is, outside the confines of the parental home yet in public neighbourhood territory that could still in various respects be called their own. The swing boys and girls had the money, clothes and status to enable them to show their faces at bourgeois inner-city night clubs, besides coming from homes that were spacious enough to let them indulge in their 'jitterbugging' and 'sleaziness' when their elders and betters were out. They had gramophone records, they could get hold of chic English-looking clothes:

> The predominant form of dress consisted of long, often checked English sports jackets, shoes with thick light crepe soles, showy scarves, Anthony Eden hats, an umbrella on the arm whatever the weather, and, as an insignia, a dress-shirt button worn in the buttonhole, with a jewelled stone.
>
> The girls too favoured a long overflowing hair style. Their eyebrows were pencilled, they wore lipstick and their nails were lacquered.
>
> The bearing and behaviour of the members of the clique resembled their dress.

A free-and-easy regime in their parents' houses, or lack of nocturnal supervision, offered ample opportunities for gaining sexual experience. The semi-official National Socialist reports on the swing cliques stress the incidence of promiscuity, group sex, 'sexual intercourse involving minors' and, generally, unabashed pleasure in sexuality (which the reports denounce as moral depravity). The wording and tone of these internal reports as a rule said more about their authors and readers than about the objective behaviour of the young people. Much of what they described is likely to have been a projection of the writers' own anxieties and repressed wishes. At any rate, the writers' own modes of perception added colouring to the facts. Too much was taken literally that was perhaps only bragging; isolated 'incidents' were generalised. Even this caveat, however, does not alter the fact that the young people's sexual behaviour clearly deviated from the National Socialist norm.

The very revulsion shown in the National Socialist reports, and their dramatisation of the phenomenon, indicate that National Socialist officialdom felt itself attacked at the very marrow of its conception of itself and of the state. This is the only way, too, to explain the reaction of Heinrich Himmler, who wanted to put the 'ringleaders' of the swing movement into concentration camps for at least two or three years of beatings, punitive drill and forced labour.[40]

The young people in the swing movement were not anti-fascist in a political sense – their behaviour was if anything emphatically anti-political – but both National Socialist rhetoric and traditional bourgeois nationalism were matters of equally profound indifference to them. They sought their counter-identity in what they saw as the modern and thus 'casual' culture of the national enemies, England and America. They admitted Jews and 'half-Jews' among their numbers – another thing to horrify the Nazis – and gave ovations to visiting bands from Belgium and Holland. All this naturally called forth 'educative' and 'policy' measures on the part of the Nazi state, but it does not explain the vehemence of the state's reaction and the profound consternation that is apparent from Himmler's intervention and from the words of disgust used by the compilers of the Hitler Youth reports.

The image that dominated the thinking of the Nazis who came from the generation of front-line soldiers of the First World War, the Freikorps fighters of the post-war period, and the paladins and vassals of Adolf Hitler was that of the stalwart and soldierly man (and of the housewife by his side – his subordinate, warm-hearted but above all chaste).[41] The renunciatory struggle against inner softness and the suppression of forbidden wishes, especially of sexuality, forced the self, as it were, into a body armour which could function only within a structure of military rigidity, unquestioning acceptance of orders issued by the Führer for the greater good, and dutiful effort that took the body to the brink of exhaustion. The inevitable effect of this internal pressure was that the rigidity and hostility to all that was soft, feminine, sexual or simply different were projected outwards in the form of an aggressive, terrorist search for order. Those whose prescription for all of Germany's youth was their own personal agony of armour-plated self-discipline – Hitler's motto was 'hard as Krupp steel, tough as leather, swift as greyhounds' – could not help seeing the very purpose of their lives being called into question by 'casual' behaviour, sexual freedom, individualism and all-embracing scepticism, especially scepticism about the rallying-cries of the nation. The only fitting response to the 'sleazy life' was hence the rod of discipline and the 'hardness of steel'.

Everyday culture and *Volksgemeinschaft*

The aggressive militancy of the young working-class members of the Edelweiß Pirates and *Meuten*, and the sceptical coolness of the middle-class swing cliques, served as irritants not only in instances where individuals resorted to explicitly political forms of protest but also, far more pervasively, within the culture of everyday life in the Third Reich.

Everyday cultures are the result of the re-processing by human beings of the basic living conditions prevailing in the social and economic systems and authority relations within which they find themselves. Human beings are placed in social classes and groups by virtue of similarities of objective conditions; but they also exert control over these collective forms of existence symbolically. They develop value systems and connexions of meanings which yield possible bases of identity for individuals and groups and which make action possible: in other words, they appropriate their reality by means of culture (using the term 'culture' to connote far more than aesthetic production).[42] A stratified society produces different cultures, interwoven yet contrasting with one another. Although the dominant, hegemonic culture of the

169

ruling classes penetrated the cultures of the social sub-systems to varying degrees, assigning them their status and their spheres of application, it cannot extinguish them entirely.

The social culture of the German working class was rooted in its own everyday relationships, experience and behaviour in this sense. National Socialism certainly deprived it of its political means of expression and shattered its formal organisational relations, but, even within the Third Reich, working-class culture continued to reproduce itself by means of distinctive elements of language and outlook, distinctive forms of social association and ways of marking itself off from those 'on top'. It could not fail to reproduce itself, since capitalism, and hence waged labour and the forms of life consequent upon it, were continuing to reproduce themselves. This everyday working-class culture 'translated' workers' experience of objective class structures into connexions of meaning and patterns of action. It thus actively appropriated reality, albeit while being subject to oppressive restrictions imposed by the institutions of a middle-class culture coloured in turn by National Socialism.

It is fascinating, accordingly, to see how working-class young people, who were not old enough to have many personal memories of the pre-fascist period, nevertheless refused to submit to the Hitler Youth's massive pressures and inducements towards conformity and integration, and instead created cultural forms, in the Edelweiß Pirates and *Meuten*, through which they separated themselves off from fascism and gave expression to their own connexions of experience in their own distinctive way. They created a texture of relations, modes of action and styles of expression which made it possible to adopt a meaningful attitude to everyday life and to repudiate the claims and enticements of National Socialist authority. They created an alternative system of leisure, separated themselves off through dress, songs and demeanour, and emphasised this separation by protesting against, and provoking, the Hitler Youth. They developed values of group behaviour and rules for confronting their much more powerful opponents which enabled them to assert themselves, indeed to feel superior because they were having more fun, and to prove themselves through resistance.

In this sense the Edelweiß Pirates followed the traditional group behaviour of the workers and their commitment of loyalty and neighbourliness, while adapting it in their own fashion in their gangs' modes of communication. Not least, they constructed their own cultural subjectivity. The songs and language of the Edelweiß Pirates and *Meuten* formed a texture of significant references blithely borrowed from different cultural sources. The only factor common to these heterogeneous materials was that they were all taboo within the terms of the dominant *völkisch* ideology: old youth-movement elements, features of the non-political culture of adult leisure, occasional fragments of the traditions of the labour movement, and ingredients of the kind of informal gang behaviour which had existed alongside the political and ideological organisations of Weimar. This assemblage of heterogeneous forms produced a distinctive and unmistakable style: a cultural achievement that should not be underestimated.

The bulk of the older working-class generation, moulded by the experience of defeat in 1933 and the subsequent persecutions, did not accommodate itself to National Socialism but avoided head-on confrontation by withdrawing passively into its own everyday culture. The Edelweiß Pirates and *Meuten*, on the other hand, demonstrated in twofold fashion that the articulation of class culture unavoidably entailed conflict: through the distinctive stylistic features of their movements, and through their militancy and willingness to separate themselves off from National Socialism and enter into confrontation with it.

The younger generation, then, did not represent a seamless continuation of working-class everyday culture; it extended this culture by means of new styles and an astonishing spontaneity. The phenomenon cannot be adequately explained in terms of stale psycho-sociological notions of wartime youth deprivation or pubertal excesses of high spirits – notions which the National Socialist youth welfare authorities, courts and police themselves tried to invoke. Though these factors were no doubt present, and helped to accelerate the spread of the protest cultures, what was also involved was, precisely, the fact that the young people's life-experience had little in common with the world of the Nazi slogans. It is no accident that the nucleus of the Edelweiß Pirates was recruited from among 14- to 18-year-olds who, having left school, were entering the world of work and thus undergoing the critical class experience that would determine their future lives.

The experience of work, and the identity conferred by work, were reflected in the attitudes and behaviour of the Edelweiß Pirates in two ways. As against the schoolboys who were dominant within the Hitler Youth, the Edelweiß Pirates gained the self-confidence that they were doing something 'real', that they were 'grown men' (this male-chauvinist touch takes us right to the heart of the traditional working-class culture) and that they were earning 'real money'. In line with the dual character of capitalist waged labour, however, a second range of values was also evident: as against foremen and employers, the Edelweiß Pirates regarded work as compulsion, something to be evaded as much as possible by 'skiving off', idling and causing trouble. The work-discipline and pride in craftsmanship shown by the traditional skilled workers was little in evidence. In this respect the new generation seems to mark a break in tradition, in the same way that many aspects of the Edelweiß Pirates' leisure behaviour met with incomprehension on the part of the older workers. The Edelweiß Pirates' youth sub-culture, then, was not a straightforward reproduction of its proletarian culture of origin, but added new and often frictional elements which reflected the experiences specific to the younger generation.

The relationship between the middle-class youth culture and the values of the parental generation was even more dissonant. It was, after all, the middle- and lower-middle-class strata that formed the basis of the National Socialist movement, and, if these groups were not entirely fascist, they were almost without exception characterised by authoritarian norms of behaviour and German-nationalist views. And these values seemed to have lost their meaning for the younger generation. Though the political explosive potential of the 'swing boys' was less than that of the Edelweiß Pirates, their 'sleaziness' and 'jitterbugging' carried a much more powerful social and cultural charge.

None the less, the 'swing movement's opposition was likewise rooted in class-specific patterns of experience. The National Socialist reports repeatedly stress the link between swing and a certain level of education. These secondary-school pupils, interested in the rational problem-solving methods of science and technology, familiar with foreign languages and open to the international cultural influences transmitted by the frontierless medium of radio, plainly no longer felt that Nazi phraseology spoke for them or to them. The military drilling to which they were subjected in the Hitler Youth was also repellent. It is nevertheless an interesting point why they were so disgusted by values which had so long held the fascist upholders of the dominant bourgeois culture in thrall – an older generation for whom, to use the Nazi jargon, discipline had become the 'centre of their being' (*Wesensmitte*).

The factors underlying the considerable shifts in middle-class norms and attitudes that have occurred in succeeding generations, starting from the youth movement and later the jazz culture of the 'golden twenties', and extending beyond the wartime swing cliques to the beatnik and rock cultures of the post-war period, have not yet been properly studied. One element in any explanation is likely to be that the process of childhood socialisation of the swing generation took place during a period of very great disorientation within the family, as Germany was hit first by inflation and soon afterwards by the world depression.[43] White-collar unemployment, bankruptcies among smaller firms, salary cuts and falls in income meant that paternal authority was demystified: the father could no longer live up to his role as provider for, and hence master of, the household. It is possible that the first premonitory tremors that were felt in this period were themselves sufficient to deprive the ideal of soldierliness of all appeal as a source of identification, in the eyes of the young people who were to join the swing movement in the late 1930s and early 1940s. At any rate, scepticism, individualism and casualness were elements of a style through which the members of the swing generation registered, above all, their rejection of the middle-class socio-cultural self-image they ascribed to their fathers' generation.

What was the significance of these alternative forms of leisure behaviour for the social policies of the Third Reich?

In the first place, they show that considerable sections of the younger generation held themselves aloof from what National Socialism had to offer by way of education and leisure. At the very moment when the Hitler Youth seemed finally to have established itself officially, with service becoming compulsory, it came up against apathy and rejection on the part of many young people who, when they were able to express themselves by means of clearly demarcated groups and gangs, operated persistently along a border line between passive and active insubordination. Despite manifold forms of repression, these oppositional groupings seem also to have been attractive to many young people who did not join them in a stricter sense.

Secondly, the everyday experience of National Socialism, for both the working-class and the middle-class younger generation, and their need to give meaningful practical expression to their identity, ran so contrary to what National Socialism and its encrusted organisational structures had to offer that young people's creation of their own cultural identity and alternative styles naturally made itself most particularly apparent in the realm that was important for them as an age group: namely, leisure. These sub-cultures demonstrated that National Socialism, even after years in power, still did not have a complete grip on German society: indeed, that parts of society increasingly slipped from its grasp, the more it perfected its formal armoury of methods of organisation and repression.

Thirdly, therefore, the two central projects of National Socialist social policy – the nullification of class reality through the sentiment of *Volksgemeinschaft*; and the mobilisation of the people, militarised and schooled in chauvinism, to smash the perceived threat to traditional values posed by modernity and internationalism – seem to have miscarried even before the end of the Third Reich loomed into sight in the shape of military defeat. The realities of everyday life in class society continued to reproduce cultures of everyday life in the next generation. Crucial generation-specific dislocations within class cultures took place in the bourgeois camp, where the basis of National Socialist doctrines and of the authoritarian ideal of soldierliness was concentrated.

Fourthly, however, National Socialism unwittingly paved the way for these manifestations of modern youth leisure. Its power was sufficient to do extensive damage to the traditional forms within which sections of the working-class and middle-class cultures had communicated and been organised. In their place, however, National Socialism could offer only military discipline, an anachronistic ideology and stifling bureaucracy. It could not provide ways in which meanings in the cultures of everyday life could be mediated. The National Socialists' blueprint of order was not a durable social design. While society was already producing highly civilian forms of sub-cultural survival, the ideals of National Socialism could make themselves manifest, in their ultimate perfection, only in the graveyards that lay scattered across the whole of Europe.

NINE

'Brown revolution'?

The twelve years of the Third Reich form part of the longer material
and human continuity of industrial class society in Germany. Many
long-term trends within Germany – demographic, social-structural,
economic – continued through the epoch from 1933 to 1945, with short-
term interruptions but generally undisturbed. Furthermore, National
Socialism unquestionably absorbed elements of the authoritarian,
militaristic and intellectually reactionay tradition in German history,
while repudiating other traditions and other elements.[1] On the other
hand, these continuities were often not the mere perpetuation by
National Socialism of features that had already been present; they were
one-sided exaggerations, deformations or deflections of traditional
features, even though it took these distortions to make apparent just
what had been latent in the traditions all along.

This may be illustrated by reference to the school system.[2] The
impact of the National Socialists on textbooks in German, history and
biology is evident at a glance; Nazi norms of racial education, and the
destruction of procedures involving staff and pupils in school
administration, tell their own story. But there was continuity here too.
Most German and history textbooks of the Imperial period, and indeed
of the Weimar Republic, were replete with anti-democratic sentiments,
nationalistic emphases, Teutonic archaisms and glorifications of war.
All this could be maintained under National Socialism, or needed only
to be stepped up a degree or two. The dismissal of the few teachers who
had left-wing views[3] and the regimentation of those who supported a
humanistic, child-centred approach to teaching went hand in hand with
the perpetuation of a widely prevalent and long-standing tradition of
corporal punishment, authoritarian teaching styles and, above all,
authoritarian teachers. The Nazi regime was rich in paradoxes,
however, and it is therefore no surprise that while, on the one hand,
there was a broad tendency for modes of behaviour presented and
inculcated in everyday school life to foster the type of personality

favoured by the National Socialists, it was this very continuity and bureaucratic authoritarianism in traditional schools, on the other hand, that offered tough and dogged resistance to the Nazis' jolting experiments in radical change. Leaving aside the eradication of the marginal democratising changes in education that had occurred during the Weimar Republic, the structural transformation of traditional schools into National Socialist ones was thus the result of the implementation of a dual hierarchy: the leadership principle (*Führerprinzip*) within the school, embodied in the head teacher and the 'co-ordinated' (*gleichgestaltet*) teaching staff; and the leadership principle outside the school, embodied in the Hitler Youth. Ironically, it was the existence of, and conflicts between, these two systems, each bent on total assimilation, that gave rise to boltholes to which the individual could retreat, away from the procedural wrangles of the two colossi.

Ideologically speaking, the transformation of the educational system was the result, first, of the reinforcement of the schools' traditional anti-democratic nationalistic and militaristic features; also of the extension of these ideologies through racialism, with its notions of internal and external extermination; and of a shift of emphasis in teaching towards preparation for war, both by means of *Weltanschauung* and through paramilitary training and sport. On the other hand, even in the National Socialist elite schools the problem of reconciling advanced and thorough scientific and technical study with the inculcation of the soldierly, virile virtues was, to the extent that it was acknowledged, not fully resolved.[4] Here, as with the National Socialist transformation of the school system generally, what seems to have been important is not so much the often abstruse elements of instruction in *Weltanschauung* in the narrower sense as the forms of behaviour which the school system instilled and which served to generate the soldierly, masculine fascist ideal.

A problem that throws up similar paradoxes and also seems intractable at first sight is one that had been building up for many years and was causing anxiety, not only to politicians dealing with employment, but also to the members of the population concerned: namely, the role of women wage-earners within the economy.[5]

The employment of women during the First World War in jobs that had previously been 'typically male', the use of women to carry out monotonous assembly-line industrial tasks that came with the modernisation of the 1920s, and, significantly, the growth of white-collar jobs in the commercial, administrative and services sector, of which women were increasingly availing themselves, had disrupted the previous gender-based division of labour. Many men perceived this change as a multiple threat. The self-sufficient, non-dependent type of woman upset traditional role images; the growth of the new female jobs was seen as a symptom of more general disturbing changes in the labour market and in labour relations, as the transition to rationalised mass production took place; and in times of high unemployment, women were regarded as unwelcome competition.

The National Socialists' image of women, apparently so anachronistic, was thus a very welcome one to many men. The notion that women were 'intrinsically' (*wesensgemäß*) different from men, and should therefore be assigned their own appropriate tasks of looking after children and the home, was certainly combined, in the Nazi leaders' speeches and policies, with the idea that women could also do paid work outside the home; but the condition was that this should be 'intrinsically' female work and should not encroach on the activities reserved for men. Ideological and economic considerations were thus in a state of coexistence coloured by limited conflict.

Until about 1935–36, while the issue was still the conquest of unemployment, the Nazis' banal model of 'blood and soil' prevailed, the corollary of which was that women did not belong in factories but should be doing housework or working on the land. When labour shortages built up with rearmament, however, a more pragmatic approach developed. But no small part was also played here by women's own resistance to being ousted from their jobs in favour of men. An Employment Exchange expert complained in 1934, for example:[6]

> The reorganisation and re-establishment of the pattern of female employment, however, on the basis of those occupational categories which are appropriate to the female nature and disposition – the basic aim of the change in the female labour market that is being sought by the state – is meeting obstacles which are rooted in the personal attitudes of the present-day generation of women rather than in objective economic causes.

The granting of marriage loans, made conditional on the woman's giving up work, the 'weeding out' of civil-service posts, and the introduction of laws, decrees and plans directed towards 'a lasting shift in employment and population policy for German women'[7] had only a short-lived impact. By 1939 the number of women in paid employment had risen from 11.5 million (in 1925 and 1933) to 12.7 million, a proportion of 37 per cent; in 1928 the proportion of women in employment had likewise stood at 37 per cent. The figure fell to 35 per cent in 1935 and 31 per cent in 1936, owing to the fact that as the labour market slowly recovered, men received preferential treatment in obtaining jobs. During the first half of the war the proportion rose again, to 38 per cent, as large numbers of men were called up, though the

177

proportion of women in armament production remained below the First World War level; instead, 'alien labour' was increasingly taken on (though of course a large proportion of foreign workers were again women).

Did the ideological rigidities of the National Socialist policy for women, then, simply founder on the realities of an industrialised economy? Did the long-term trend towards modernisation covertly, but irresistibly, prevail? This would be to put matters too crudely and to underrate the Nazis' policies on women, the subtler versions of which were by no means hostile to female industrial employment in all its forms and called, rather, for it to be restricted to certain areas. In fact, the scheme of 'intrinsically female' types of work played a considerable part in the long-term gender-based re-structuring of the labour market. Women were designated to perform repetitive assembly-line tasks because, according to ergonomic theorists, such work was particularly appropriate for them: having a dual role as workers and mothers, women could find in child care, housework and family duties an emotional compensation for the stresses of industrial monotony. In addition, women were to gravitate, as expansions and contractions in the labour market dictated, between waged employment outside the home (especially before marriage) and domestic work within the family – or rather, to do two jobs during booms and one during downturns. This was also the solution to the pressing problem of retaining a fluctuating supply of labour without overloading the social-security system with payments for unemployment and premature disability. The woman, if she was currently not employable, or was no longer employable, was to be supported under the aegis of the family. The special emphasis placed on women's familial role by Nazi propaganda, combined with women's own adaptation to fluctuating and subordinate forms of employment, thus gave rise during the Third Reich to a new, gender-based division of labour that was in conformity with modern needs. Hofstätter had already stated the 'meaning' of this division in 1929:[8]

> Women have a high tolerance for paid employment that leaves them psychologically unaffected, provided they have other sufficiently strong emotional ties outside their employment. The natural tie is the family: love and care for their husband, children and parents. For the true woman, everything in this realm is her 'job'; the highest kind of job.

Dicta such as this, coming from prominent experts, were translated into action by Nazi policies for women that were at first blush utterly anti-modern and irrational.

In many other areas, Nazi social policy, the proselytisers for which had promised to bring back the 'good old days' and banish the vexations of modernity, in fact gave further impetus to secular modernising trends.[9] The National Socialists set out to abolish resistant forms of social and cultural organisation, such as the clubs and associations of the Catholic congregations, small-town systems of local dignitaries, working-class political, trade-union and cultural institutions, and (during the war) the traditional leadership position held by the aristocracy in the armed forces. In direct contradiction of the propaganda slogans of blood and soil, the restoration of *Handwerk* and the destruction of the 'sinful' asphalt jungle of the cities, the urban landscape in fact spread[10] (thanks in part to the build-up of new industrial centres like Wolfsburg and Salzgitter), migration from the countryside into the more lucrative industries of the cities continued, and 'old' middle-class (*mittelständisch*) craft businesses were neglected in favour of industrial concerns concentrating on rearmament.

The four years of rearmament-led boom before the outbreak of war are too short a period to yield a distinction between the intended results of Nazi policies and those developments that the Nazis merely put up with *faute de mieux*. David Schoenbaum's formulation, that National Socialism was reactionary in its goals but revolutionary in its methods, and that the longer-term effects of the regime were modernising by virtue of these revolutionary methods, sheds light on a partial aspect of the reality of the Third Reich. If, for example, we survey those business enterprises that were singled out for honour as 'model' National Socialist firms, we are struck, on the one hand, by attempts to perpetuate a certain paternalistic social tradition of entrepreneurship[11] but, on the other, by social and political measures which are part of a general tendency within the development of industrial societies: attempts to improve the working environment, holidays, and modern schemes of piece-work and incentive payments.[12] Ergonomic theories and policies in the Third Reich were a plain continuation of tendencies towards the rationalisation of production and the parallel 'modernisation' of industrial relations. They took their inspiration equally from 'Americanising' approaches centred around Henry Ford's social model of rationalised high productivity linked to high wages, and from the psycho-technological approaches of the German Institute for Technical Work Training designed to foster social partnership and the 'works community'.

On the other hand, the use of forced labour – foreigners, prisoners of war and inmates of concentration camps – and the establishment during the war of large numbers of forced-labour camps for German 'idlers' indicate that 'modern' achievement-orientated methods were only one facet of the National Socialist ethos of work: the other facet was the use of force against those who, for whatever reasons, were not to be motivated and integrated. Whereas modern liberal industrialised societies believe they can afford to tolerate the existence of marginal groups deviating from the prevailing social and employment norms, National Socialism set up a dual model of the way people were to be mobilised for work. It offered incentives for the achievement-minded, the 'talented' and those who through education or for other reasons were higher up the social scale; for the non-achievement-orientated at the bottom of the scale, it prescribed forced labour, segregation and eventual annihilation.[13]

The social reality of the Third Reich, then, involved these two aspects simultaneously: the dawning of the new achievement-orientated consumer society based on the nuclear family, upward mobility, mass media, leisure and an interventionist welfare state (though much of this still lay in the realms of propaganda and had not yet come into being); and the encroaching shadows cast by a project of social order based on racialist doctrines and terror.

The internal contradictions therefore make it difficult to assent entirely to the thesis that National Socialism administered a particularly powerful thrust towards modernisation, let alone that it carried out a 'Brown revolution', although these hypotheses certainly contain important elements of the truth.[14]

In any case, the explanatory power of concepts and definitional formulae in history is limited. (Not that this seems to mitigate the stubbornness of conceptual disputes; to the contrary. It is obviously easier to achieve agreement on matters of fact than on the ways in which facts should be conceptually combined and organised within an historical and political interpretation.) Historical concepts are always more metaphorical than definitional, because they bring together, in interpretative cast, specific bodies of fact from a complex, contradictory past reality which is irrecoverable in tangible form and which can be reconstructed only on the basis of fragmentary surviving sources, for the purpose of building bridges of understanding between the present and the past. Ambiguity and vagueness are therefore inescapable ingredients of historical conceptualisation, since it is these very features (as in all literary metaphor) that allow the partners in historical dialogue to make their own intellectual connexions with ideas that are under discussion, in the interest of creating a more richly nuanced 'picture' of the past and a wider range of possible contemporary interpretations. Conceptual precision, however, which is equally essential for making agreement possible, also comes into play, in two ways. First, and most important, theory construction must not fly in the face of the empirical historical facts adduced; and secondly, conceptual precision has a vital bearing on both the specialised and the wider public debate and on the incorporation of theories into the existing state of knowledge.

We must bear these problems of historical concept formation in mind if we are not to be defeated by the bewildering complexities and incompatible claims to be found in the debates on fascism, Hitlerism, totalitarianism and modernism. In this instance we are dealing with two highly indeterminate concepts – 'revolution' and 'modernisation' – whose meanings we nevertheless think we know because we repeatedly use the terms in imprecise everyday speech. 'Modernity' in this context is the form of society, extending to the present day, of states which are technologically and economically developed and socially and culturally 'civilised'. Modernity connotes the social and economic structure of an industrial class society, in either a planned or market version; a secularised culture committed to rational procedures of argument; the inclusion of the masses in the political system; a wide-ranging and intricately interlocking communications network; and, of course, a bureaucratic, institutionalised state, in which more and more areas of society come under regulation. Examples of 'pre-modern' societies or institutions, by contrast, are tribal societies or agrarian cultures, involving craft methods of production, personalised (e.g. feudal) relations of dependency, immobile social hierarchies based on 'eternal' principles or forms of life dominated by religion. Different sociological and historical theories of modernisation have given conceptual precision to these vague pre-theoretical notions and have proposed models of the structure of modernity and its development.

Using, then, both our everyday notion of modernity and the models put forward within modernisation theory, we can ask whether and to what extent National Socialism triggered off a 'thrust towards modernisation'. Despite the fact that research into the social history of the period from the 1930s to the 1950s has been very far from exhaustive, four broad categories of answer can be suggested.

First, National Socialism can in no sense be described as out-and-out 'anti-modern'. It was often, indeed, precisely the profuse trappings of antiquated traditionalism or reactionary utopianism in Nazi ideology that served to make more acceptable in practical, social terms the modern technologies and structures they disguised. In addition, the opportunism of those in power and the internal logic of the drive for technological and economic war-readiness quickly swept aside the corporatist and other anti-modern experiments of the early period. As for the relationship between modern means and reactionary utopian ends that was contemplated for the time when the dream of world-wide victory would be fulfilled and the 'ultimate aims' of National Socialism would be implemented, here only speculation is possible. In any case, these vague projects for the future had little practical influence on the solution of immediate problems of social policy.

Secondly, National Socialism adapted readily to long-term trends towards modernisation. In terms of long-range socio-economic statistical data, the years of the Third Reich (or at least the years of peace up to 1939) show no divergence, either positive or negative, from the earlier course of development of industrial class society in Germany. As far as points of detail are concerned, the time-span involved is too short to validate any general claim that National Socialism was responsible for such comparatively small and inconsistent deviations from the longer-term trend as can be found. No particularly powerful new *thrust* towards modernisation can be inferred from the objective data available, although a continuation of the previously existing trend certainly can be. A different conclusion, on the other hand, seems indicated if we move from the hard data to the perceptible, if not statistically provable, shifts in values and changes in social behaviour. There are many indicators that National Socialism greatly loosened the previously firm hold of traditional social environments and systems of values and that, over and beyond its destructiveness, it contributed to the modernisation of everyday cultures. This applies, for instance, to the drive against traditional family-based education and in favour of egalitarianising peer-group work in youth organisations, exemplified in the Hitler Youth's slogan, 'Youth leads youth' and in the BDM's provision of non-domestic leisure activities for girls. At the same time, however, this selfsame example of the role of youth in the Third Reich shows how poor National Socialism was at detaching itself from long-outworn patterns and principles of socialisation and education, as a more modern trend towards the growth of youth sub-cultures spontaneously gave rise to gangs beyond the reach of state policies and, indeed, to forms of behaviour that ran contrary to the desired educational goal of the technically skilled yet soldierly 'warrior'. In this instance the shift in values, which was to be a decisive factor in the formation of the so-called 'sceptical' younger generation of the post-war period, was not a deliberate result or fortuitous by-product of Nazi policies, but was a bitterly combated counter-current. In short, the Nazis' positive drive towards modernisation was in many ways more short-winded than is commonly assumed.

Thirdly, in view of these facts, the concept of the 'Brown revolution' does seem to be somewhat wide of the mark, even if, as many historians urge, we separate the concept of revolution from its customary association with progress and social innovation. Whatever concept of society historians may seek to distil from Hitler's inconsistent jumble of ideas, they must acknowledge that the competition between sources of authority that occurred once National Socialism was in power meant that all attempts at large-scale social reform broke down well short of their goal, ran aground in the shoals of polycracy, or were postponed until such time as 'final victory' had been won. The undoubtedly far-reaching, though not total, destruction of institutions, social environments and traditions that the National Socialists carried out is not of itself sufficient to warrant the term 'revolutionary' as long as it is unclear what functional equivalents might have arisen in their place. Many of the changes in outlook which led to the modern society of the 1950s thus took place through inadvertence, 'on the side', or even as a result of the population's refusal to fall in with what the Nazis had to offer and its retreat into 'normal' private life. Not least, it was in many instances only the war and its consequences that swept away for good those traditions and institutions which National Socialism had merely weakened (the large Junker estates east of the Elbe, for instance). It is only if the character of National Socialism is defined primarily in terms of its chaotic destructive and then self-destructive dynamism – i.e., if it is seen as the progressively more radicalised prolongation of the crisis of the 1920s into the war of the 1940s – that the great cataclysms of 1914–18, 1929–33 and 1939–45 can be construed as one single accelerating destructive process, and hence, in this sense, as a 'negative revolution'. But to do this would, in turn, be to erase from the analysis once again all the aspects of continuity in everyday life from the 1930s to the 1950s, all that was so fatally 'normal'; it would be to revert to the fiction of *Stunde Null* – 'zero hour' – in 1945. The semantic games that have so often been played with the concept of revolution since the 1920s, then, are not of much help in providing a balanced historical assessment of the continuities and discontinuities within industrial class society in Germany.

Fourthly, however, the destructive dynamism of National Socialism and, in particular, its tendency to cloak the social and political inadequacies of its notions of *Volksgemeinschaft* by seeking out ever larger numbers of external enemies, reveals a long-term pathological dimension within modern industrial society itself: a dimension which was transfigured into the utopian vision of a racialist reconstitution of society and which found its apocalyptic fulfilment in the extermination camps. We shall trace this process in the final section of this book.

'National comrades' and 'community aliens'

TEN

Public show and private perceptions

In earlier chapters our primary concern has been to examine the extent
to which the major social groups in Germany were affected by National
Socialist policies, the ways in which they complied with them or resisted
them, and the degree to which the Third Reich either perpetuated or
obstructed longer-term social and economic developments. We shall
now, by contrast, examine the key concept of National Socialist social
policy, the *Volksgemeinschaft* or 'national community', both as project
and as achieved fact, with reference to the relationship between the
stage-managed 'national community' of public propaganda and the
everyday perceptions, needs and behaviour of those at whom the
propaganda was directed. We shall thus be concerned, on the one hand,
with the participation and aversion of individuals vis-à-vis the appeals
and claims of *Volksgemeinschaft*; and, on the other, with the model of
'normality' according to which some people were defined as 'national
comrades' (*Volksgenossen*) and others excluded as 'community aliens'
(*Gemeinschaftsfremde*). What was the relation between the inner and
outer sides of the façade of *Volksgemeinschaft*? – Because one thing is
certain: the *Volksgemeinschaft* of Nazi propaganda was indeed primarily
a façade. Like any façade, it could be impressive and, in particular, it
imposed a divide. But it was scarcely an expression of social reality as a
whole.

The National Socialist movement before 1933 had directed all of its
hectic, dynamic energy towards the vague utopian goal of building a
'national community' within which the individual would assume his
'rightful' place and from which all alien irritants would be expunged.
After the *Machtergreifung* (the Nazis' seizure of power) the vacuity of
this wishful thinking inevitably became apparent to all who were not
prepared to take fragmentary and provisional measures for the real
thing. There was no advance beyond the old mechanisms that had kept
the 'movement' going; the props and publicity of a 'community' ethos
had to serve as promises of a *Volksgemeinschaft* utopia whose ultimate

arrival remained remote. Mass rituals, mass organisations and a string of new drives and campaigns were needed to keep up the movement's dynamic thrust that was now directed on to the nation as a whole. These methods, however, were capable only of generating manic and intoxicated moods for shorter and shorter periods before the trials and tribulations of drab everyday life reasserted themselves. So many ingredients were needed to create the right atmosphere for a mass celebration: a starlit summer sky, say, the backdrop of one of the newly-built 'thingsteads',[*1] a receptive audience, a well-rehearsed mass choir or a choreographed march past – and then a shower of rain could ruin everything. Furthermore, the original expectations that had been attached to such mass rituals – with their climax, perhaps, the entrance of the charismatic Führer – could not be recreated indefinitely; the expectations within ordinary life that remained unfulfilled inevitably soured the mood. In fact, the National Socialists' attempts to create a sort of new 'popular national culture' out of ceremonies and festivals, mass rallies and displays mainly date from the early years after 1933. This 'aestheticisation of politics' (to quote Walter Benjamin), in which specious form did duty for lack of content, merged all existing styles and techniques – other than those that had been explicitly denounced on political grounds – into an unoriginal amalgam that in practice aroused enthusiasm only under exceptional circumstances.

After about 1935 these directly political ceremonies became less frequent, though they never disappeared completely and were regularly resurrected for public holidays and big political functions. Instead the sobering realisation dawned within Goebbels's Reich Ministry of Public Information and Propaganda that durable loyalty, capable of surviving the facts of everyday life, could not be generated by solstice ceremonies alone. The only way to make up for the lack of substance in the *Volksgemeinschaft* idea was to produce passive loyalty, and this was more reliably secured by mass media that offered entertainment and distraction.[2] The growing prosperity of the pre-war years provided a useful further underpinning.

Stylistically speaking, the new consensus-directed musical offerings in the mass media embraced rural folk idyllicism, brash marching music, sentimentalised 'great' works from the concert hall and opera house, and smart modern light music such as 'palm court' tangos and the waltz-dreams of the UFA films. It was even possible, as was shown by one of the most famous 'non-political' UFA films, *La Habanera*, for one and the same song to unite cloying Latin American rhythms, 'deep'

[**Thingplätze*: meeting-place of a Nordic or Germanic 'thing' or assembly. (Transl.)]

Nordic sentiment and a *soupçon* of racialism: '*Der Wind hat mir ein Lied erzählt/von einem Glück: unsagbar schön!*' (The wind has sung a song of happiness/to me: too wonderful for words). Here is a dream, in the heat of the tropics, of the coolness of the north and, underlying all, the rhythm of the Caribbean.

Since National Socialism had no cultural vision of its own, its cultural policies, like its policies in other fields, were either destructive or parasitical. They destroyed those aspects of culture which were dismissed, on political or racialist grounds or out of resentful anti-modernism, as hostile and 'degenerate'. On the other hand, they absorbed wholesale all other forms of cultural endeavour, tricking them out at most with some sort of ideological wrapping. This parasitical, instrumental exploitation of culture ranged from Gustaf Gründgens's Prussian State Theatre and Furtwängler's Berlin Philharmonic (and the exertions of the NSDAP member, Herbert von Karajan) to Hans Baumann's non-Christian yet edifying Christmas carol, '*Hohe Nacht der klaren Sterne*' (Lofty Night of Bright Stars). Christmas, indeed, proved to be an especially useful proving-ground for 'the Nazis' eclectic ceremonialism'.[3]

Even in a field such as architecture,[4] which was seen after 1945 as having been typified by the ostentatious style of domination embodied in the 'New Reich Chancellery' in Berlin or the Reich Party Congress Site in Nuremberg, there was, on closer inspection, no break in tradition whatever in 1933. There were only certain shifts of emphasis (and of course individuals who fell from favour on political or 'racial' grounds were persecuted). Even before 1933 the 'new architecture' of the Bauhaus school had played only a marginal, avant-garde role in Germany. It had been rejected, and not only by a few fanatical Nazis, on the grounds that its technologically-based sobriety erased the differences between architectural functions, that its constructivist glass frontages were alien and cheerless, and that it gave no scope for the symbolic qualities of architecture traditionally expressed in ornamentation and the like. In the Third Reich the stylistic features of the 'new architecture' were by no means entirely suppressed, but they were confined to functional buildings such as factories or transport facilities. Other building projects were assigned different styles according to their social and symbolic roles. This led to the design of public state and Party buildings whose purpose was to serve as overpowering and 'eternal symbols of authority' and which continued the prevailing neo-classicism, but also to an elaboration of the modern monumentalism that had earlier been exemplified in Peter Behrens's AEG buildings.

On the other hand, domestic architecture and the buildings of everyday social life remained the preserve of the regionalist style that had also already developed under Weimar: the style epitomised by the detached one-family owner-occupied house with garden and pointed gable that was typical of so many model housing estates of the Third Reich and proliferated on the outskirts of towns in the post-war era. But again, during the drive for rearmament and the Four-Year Plan, when there was a demand for rapid housing construction in new industrial complexes such as the Hermann-Göring-Werke in Salzgitter and the Volkswagen works in Wolfsburg, there was a purely pragmatic switch to high-rise rented flats in fairly densely populated urban areas, along the lines of the welfare-state housing of Weimar and the Federal Republic. The breach with the *Blut und Boden* doctrine that the 'corrupting' cities should be depopulated was not allowed to be a cause for concern.

The distinctively Nazi dimension in architectural policy was the contrast between public and private that found expression in the tension between the monumentalist and regionalist styles. The monumental public spaces, resembling stage sets, reduced people into mere ornament; the individual was lost within huge perspectives which could be filled only if he was merged into a marching column. The desire to retreat into the private sphere, into comfortable and familiar small spaces, was therefore all the more pressing. Thus the practical effect of Nazi architectural policy – discounting the grotesque bombast of the unfulfilled projects for the post-victory epoch – was a functional split characteristic of modern industrial society in general: a split between barren central urban areas made over to public representation, administration and consumption; technologically-based functional buildings for industrial use; and small-format private residential areas. This split underwent modifications of style after 1945, but not of substance.

The pattern of continuity and discontinuity in other cultural spheres is a similar one.[5] The National Socialist leadership admittedly had, as has already been said, no coherent theory of culture at its disposal, nor even a specific body of cultural output that might have served its own propagandist needs if nothing else. But it would be a mistake to pay too much attention to the banal and grotesque views of the gaggle of aesthetic dogmatists who followed in the Nazis' wake, and not to note the practical effectiveness of Nazi cultural policy, which was not without its pragmatic features. After the war the behaviour of writers and artists under National Socialism was often described as 'internal emigration' (*innere Emigration*);[6] it was said to have been a withdrawal from the official cultural barbarism into the sanctuaries of 'true' art, or a cunning blend of yielding when necessary and standing firm when possible. This certainly accords with the way many artists saw their own actions, although their retrospective accounts all too often exaggerate their differences with the regime and understate the harmony of interests and outlook. The reality was more subtle.

There was, perhaps, a two-pronged strategy of de-politicisation: the National Socialists' destruction of proscribed political content led, in actuality, to the same end-result of non-political cultural production as was created by those artists whose response to the superficial calls for loyalty (or to the Nazi leadership's occasional grotesque incursions in cultural affairs) was to retreat and distance themselves. Cultural producers strove to uphold the high standards of the years before 1933; and they were wholly supported in this by politicians concerned for their own prestige. The artists, however – reluctantly, with relief, or with a nod and a wink, according to temperament – renounced all political references in cultural production beyond the minimal lip-service that was required. Instead they established forms of artistic production and popular entertainment that were technically polished and devoid of all contemporary messages or references (and that could, furthermore, be salvaged without too much difficulty for use in the post-war world). The tendency, however, for cultural production to become non-political, harmless and lacking in contemporary relevance, which artists who kept their distance from National Socialism held up as an achievement of their 'internal emigration', fell in almost entirely with Goebbels's Ministry's policy of giving 'national comrades' light, relaxing entertainment in the second half of the 1930s and later, particularly, on providing distractions from the hardships of war.[7] Just as the artists set their sights on what was timeless and universally human, so the German population wanted, and received, cultural fare that was uncontroversial and that promised them an eventual return to normality. Indeed, the quest for introspection, private harmony and harmless normality that supposedly arose from the shock of the collapse of 1945, and which turned the cultural life of the 1950s into such a desert of provincialism, in fact owed its origin to these earlier causes: the population's need for rest and calm in the thirties, the retreat by artists in the face of dogmatic Nazi claims and demands, and the formidable expansion of a pragmatic light-entertainment culture on the Goebbels model in broadcasting (including experimental television), films, variety, theatre, music and literature.

The indistinguishable blurring of 'political' and 'non-political' perceptions can be illustrated by a popular magazine such as the *Berliner Illustrirte*, whose number for 13th April 1939 announced the macabre news: 'Gas Masks for German Children Now Ready'.[8] The cover picture echoes classical western Madonna-and-Child portraiture, while at the same time unabashedly lauding technological achievement, offering 'human interest' kitsch and playing on latent fears of gas warfare. Indeed, the whole of this issue, both pictures and text, alternates between non-political idyll and prettified barbarism. Fashion, technology and 'all-too-human interest' set the tone for a picture report on the Führer's visit to a *Kraft durch Freude* ship; Hitler's manner, incidentally, is winning and jovial rather than martial and imperious. Next to this is a reminder of atrocities which the British are alleged to have committed against Boer women and children interned in concentration camps in 1902. After 'Fashion Ideas for Spring', sensationalist photographs from the USA and advertisements for cars ('Opel – the Reliable One') comes a political story on the Austrian *Anschluß* packaged for popular consumption: 'It Won't Do, Chancellor!' – a story which recurs in different form a few pages later, in a travel advertisement:

> Your travel agents will tell you everything you need to know, especially about the attractive new trips to the Ostmark [Austria] and the Sudetengau [the German-speaking region of Czechoslovakia annexed in 1938].

and in an advertisement for:

> Spa Casino, Baden bei Wien. [Baden, near Vienna]
> Roulette, Baccarat – Chemin de Fer. [. . .]
> *Cercle privé.*
> Restaurant & Bar, Dancing, Music.
> Luxury Coach from Vienna Opera.

Aggressive foreign policy and the threat of war thus assume a reassuring, entirely normal aspect; tourism, following in the train of the advancing Wehrmacht, helps itself to the new acquisitions. Private and public commingle: the *Herrenmensch*, filled with self-assurance, means no harm; the world is his for the enjoyment, or becomes his by force, in accordance with the law of the stronger. A few pages before the travel advertisements is a brief photo report giving the latest news from Prague: 'The Reich Protector of Bohemia and Moravia Takes Up His Official Duties'.

Colonialist propaganda typically blending motifs of cultural mission and sentiments of superiority imbues the two photo-reportage stories from outside Europe, which again contain technically superb photographs and sport a slick, witty style calculated to play up the spiciness of faraway places. An Italian fort in the Libyan desert now serves as a centre for disseminating the higher culture; while Gotthard Schuh's report from Dutch Sumatra spells out the cultural achievements of the Nordic colonists:

> Instead of human flesh, it's leg of pug and fillet of fox terrier. Heathen cannibals have been turned into consumers of canines.

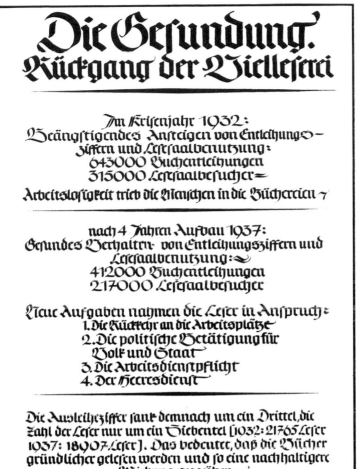

1937, four years after the burning of the books: Essen City Library hails the decline in reading

'Healthy Recovery
Decline in Indiscriminate Reading

1932, year of crisis:
Disturbing increase in numbers of books borrowed and in use of the reading room:
643,000 titles borrowed
315,000 reading-room users
Unemployment sends people into the libraries

1937, after 4 years of reconstruction:
Healthy response in numbers of books borrowed and in use of the reading room:
412,000 titles borrowed
217,000 reading-room users
Readers are engaged in new tasks:
1. The return to employment
2. Political activity for the people and the state
3. Labour Service duty
4. Military service

Thus, numbers of loans have fallen by one-third, but the number of readers has fallen only by one-seventh (1932: 21,765 readers; 1937: 18,907 readers). This shows that books are being read more thoroughly and will therefore have a more lasting effect'

The Nazi 'movement': a self-portrait. The dynamism of the marching troops sweeps all before it, wounded and bystanders included

'Ensure Victory over Hunger and Cold. We are Making the Sacrifice (sc. giving money)'

'The Fuhrer and the People Care. Protect Mothers and Children'

'Your Sacrifice Helps To Build the Future.'

The amorphous ideals of *Volksgemeinschaft*. (Top) Conquering the distress caused by the old 'system'; (bottom left) petty-bourgeois idyll;

(bottom right) 'self-sacrifice' as a down-payment on a better future. (Winter Relief Fund designs)

National Socialist May Day celebration in Penzberg, Upper Bavaria. Miners in the front, Nazi ranks at the back: note the contrasting loyalties indicated by the different styles of salutation

The hidden meaning of a reconstruction slogan. '*All pulling together*': anyone getting in the way will be crushed. Carnival in Essen, 1935

The Führer myth was not all martial poses at mass rallies: Hitler also played the jovial statesman concerned with everyday life. A Strength through Joy (KdF) cruise, 1939

High spirits and horror: a Krupp gun in the Shrove Monday procession, Essen, 1937

'*Mother, we're back home again*': successes in foreign policy improved the Führer's credit rating. The reincorporation of the Saar into the Reich, 1935 (the slogan is in local dialect)

4

Racing-car aces of the 1930s: Rosemeyer and Caracciola in conversation with the Leader of the National Socialist Drivers' Corps, Hühnlein

Ceremony to install a new police chief in Essen, 1937. The slogan exhorts the audience to support the police

'*The national community in action*' – or at any rate on parade

Clichés of *Volksgemeinschaft* propaganda: the middle-class family as portrayed by the Winter Relief Fund designers. Note the combination of archaic stove and modern dress

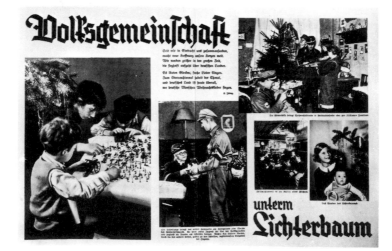

'*The national community under the Christmas tree*'

1933: raids in working-class districts are the order of the day

'*1000 SA and Police Comb Breilsort in Frohnhausen District*'

Der Friedenskämpfer (The Peace Fighter), illegally produced in 1942 by German resistance fighters in Düsseldorf and Berlin, reported on Nazi crimes in the occupied countries and reproduced drawn versions of photographs secretly taken by soldiers (see also next page)

Der Friedenskämpfer (cont.)

'Innocent Russian women, men and children are dragged by the SS bandits to the place of execution'

'An entire Russian fa[...] a few metres from th[...] mass grave of murder[...] innocent people. The [...] stricken with terror, desperately protests h[...] innocence'

'In the name of the German people! In the name of every individual German!'

'How much longer wi[...] tolerate this shameful outrage? Bring down Hitler! Fight the SS [...] Gestapo! Call a halt [...] tyranny!'

'The family . . . at the edge of the mass grave (see title picture) seconds before the husband, wife and children are murdered by shots in the neck. The wife desperately flings herself behind her husband and child to ward off the bullets'

The 'Beauty of Work' campaign meant discipline as well as the 'improvement' of working conditions. A Nazi magazine juxtaposes working breaks 'before' and 'after' 1933: time for a rest (left) and for callisthenics (below)

'The way things used to be. Young workers taking a break. Not any more!'

The reality of work: miners in a Krupp pit

Russian prisoners of war clearing bombs (Kalkum Bomb Disposal Squad)

'*We Want to Win*'

'*Toughening the Body is the Best Remedy against Cold*'

(Top and left) The League of German Girls and the Hitler Youth: sport encouraged toughness and competition but also offered adventure

(Below) Behind the glittering façade of the rallies and marches: frustration and wasted energy. 'Youth Day' in Essen

(Top) 'Wild' (unauthorised) 'cliques',
Cologne, 1940
(Left and below) 'Swing Youth',
Hamburg, 1940

'*Full sails;*' and '*That's some motorbike: a poem of a machine.*' Archaic symbolism and the new technology

The wife of the racing driver Bernd Rosemeyer subtitled this picture *The new Manuela – Bernd's great love*

Women at work: '*Sporting Girls – Working Girls! these young workers know that sport keeps them young and attractive and also sustains and increases their joy in their work . . .*' (from *Krupp: Magazine of the Krupp Works Community*)

A conservative schoolmaster caricatures the sports ballyhoo: Olympic year, 1936

A change of camera angle betrays the reality behind the propaganda façade. Opening ceremony at Waldthausen Park, Essen, 9th July 1935

A few days later: the front view of everyday life in the Third Reich. Fashion show in Gruga Park, Essen, 25th July 1935

Staatsschauspieler

geht in die Luft

Heinz Rühmann, dem am 20. April vom Führer der
Titel „Staatsschauspieler" verliehen wurde, ist
wie allgemein bekannt nicht nur ein Freund des Film-
himmels, er ist ein ebenso begeisterter Freund des
Flugplatzes. Alle voraussichtlich ist er auf dem Flugplatz
Rangsdorf bei Berlin anzutreffen, wo sein eigenes Flugzeug, „Motte" genannt, seinen Standplatz hat. Als
unsere Bildberichterstatter ihn kürzlich daselbst in
Rangsdorf knautschte, war in gerade im Begriff, mit
dem Flugzeug seines Sportkameraden General Udet
einen „Erkundungsflug" zu veranstalten.

Hinter'm Steuerknüppel
Heinz Rühmann, der wir demnächst auch als Sportflieger
in einem großen Terra-Spielfilm erleben werden

'State Actor Reaches for the Sky'

Im Scheinwerfer

Frau am Steuer
Links: Grethe Weiser, Ursula Deinert, Lilian Harvey
Rechts: Lilian Harvey als Marie Kelemen und Willy Fritsch
als Paul Banky
Unten: Lilian Harvey, Rudolf Platte, Willy Fritsch, Grethe Weiser

Lilian Harvey
in 2 neuen Filmen
„Frau am Steuer", „Ins blaue Leben"

'Lilian Harvey in 2 new films
Frau am Steuer (Lady in Charge)
Ins blaue Leben (Into the Wide Blue Yonder)'

Light entertainment: Heinz Rühmann and Lilian Harvey, film stars of the 1930s (and of the 1950s)

(Left) *'German workers – you must know the world, to love your native land.'* Foreign travel is more a matter of propaganda than a reality (from *Krupp: Magazine of the Krupp Works Community*)

(Below) Farmhouses make way for blocks of flats; identical family homes bestride the countryside. Even in the Third Reich, despite 'blood and soil' propaganda, the 'modernisation' of peasant life continues.

Old Makes Way for New'

'Saving Makes Your Wishes Come True'

*'The German Homesteader (*resident of new owner-occupied housing estates*) Homestead estate in Manzell am Bodensee'*

'*The history of the German people is the history of its infantry*': the model of soldierliness in a school-book timetable, 1939

The counter-model: '*The orgiastic effects of this Jewish music are clear from the drawing.*' 'Casual' 'swing boys' and 'swing girls', from an article on Benny Goodman, 1944

Nur noch Verbrecher vermehren sich heute im deutschen Volke wirklich.

Es treffen auf:

Männliche Verbrecher — 4,9 Kinder

Eine kriminelle Ehe — 4,4 Kinder

Eltern von Hilfsschulkindern — 3,5 Kinder

Die deutsche Familie — 2,2 Kinder

Ehe aus der gebildeten Schicht — 1,9 Kinder

'The only people really contin multiply in Germany are criminals. Relative figures: Male criminals 4.9 children; Marriages involving criminals 4.4 children; Parents of children in Special Schools 3.5 children; The German family 2.2 children; Marriages in the educated classes 1.9 children.'
From a Nazi schoolbook: racia social policy. Deviant behavio ascribed to 'biology'.

The 'battle for the birth-rate'. Not every child is welcome; not every marriage is allowed. A doctor conducts a 'genetic health' examination to determine whether a marriage loan can be granted

'Healthy and unhealthy genetic stock:' 'national comrades' and 'community aliens' ('feeble-minded'), from a secondary-school biology textbook

'How to knock out your opponent:' within the 'national community', too, the weak must give way to the strong. From a schoolchildren's magazine

So schlägt man den Gegner t. o.

'He's known to everyone in Koblenz: the Winter Relief Collector in the pubs and taverns, Georg Schütz. He's an indefatigable collector. Every day he does his rounds through the city's places of refreshment, and his collecting box is his constant companion. He's collected a lot of contributions for the Winter Relief in this way: his self-sacrifice is an example to everyone who hasn't yet done his bit for the community.'

Donations are the touchstone of loyalty. This 'indefatigable' collector for the Winter Relief Fund is 'known to everyone' in the *Gaststätten* in Koblenz.

'And now: Everything in one Pot for the Winter Relief Fund.' Essen carnival, 1935

Without in any way making an obtrusive ideological fuss about it, the report suggests that these *Untermenschen* are unlikely to be stirred to any further cultural advance for the time being.

Not so the modern German, turning to Nature as a restorative after the daily stresses of civilisation. Camping and canoeing provide relaxation and privacy, and recharge the batteries of social virtue:

Relax, take a break:
For once, stop being the working man
And live for yourself.
All you need
Is a folding boat and a tent;
Wherever there's water, sun and blue sky
There's a path for you to wander.
If you want to paddle,
You can paddle;
If you want to dream,
You can let yourself just drift along.
With a folding boat and a tent
You're independent and free.

The consumer-goods market promotes the individualism and freedom of movement that the political system is attempting to obliterate. The ambivalence of this publicity for normality is barely disguised.

The relative harmony of the image of cultural consensus based on normality – from which only the 'adversaries' and the 'degenerate' were eliminated, and on which the Nazis' dogmatists intruded only occasionally – was little ruffled by the defamatory campaigns against 'degenerate' modernism.[9] Here the National Socialists were at one with the bulk of the population, which swung between incomprehension and destructive vandalism, and they also had on their side the spokesmen of more traditional academicism in the arts, which remained far more prevalent in the 1920s than the modernism that now dominates textbooks about the period. Indeed, the present-day rehabilitation of the visual art of the nineteenth century has rendered more questionable the stock view that was so common after 1945, that only abstraction is 'modern' and that realism is 'kitsch'. It is thus possible today to assess in a more impartial spirit the positive qualities, as well as the clichés, of realist art in the Third Reich.

The Nazis' political intervention into an aesthetic debate, and the use of state power to repress certain new areas of modern art, is of course one of the particularly infamous aspects of their cultural policy. If we are looking at cultural activity from the viewpoint of social history, however, we must also acknowledge that the cultural offerings that remained available met with a comparatively broad and affirmative

193

reception among the population. Few tears were shed for abstractionism, and there was considerable approval of the symbolic language of power and brutality displayed in works of art that expressed a more specifically Nazi point of view.[10] Pictorial imagery based on an aesthetic of force had by no means been absent from earlier and recent art, and it had given rise to striking and technically accomplished works. In any case, culture in the Third Reich in no sense involved a blanket rejection of modernist styles. Elements of the Bauhaus style recurred in industrial architecture, in functional furniture and consumer goods, in design generally, and in advertising – including advertising for political purposes, such as the campaigns for the Winter Relief Fund. National Socialist cultural policy drew a dividing line only between the exalted sphere of 'true' art, which had to be non-tendentious and inspiring – or ideologically significant in the eyes of the dogmatists – and the functional styles of everyday popular culture, where modern forms suited to practical needs and purposes (and, above all, to industrial mass production) not only continued to play a role but increased in importance and in so doing paved the way for the chrome and plastic culture of the 1950s.

This overlapping and cross-fertilisation of forms of cultural reception, styles, functions and meanings made itself felt in the minutest details of de-politicised everyday culture. It can be seen in the small aesthetic forms typical of everyday life under National Socialism: stickers for the Winter Relief Fund, toy figures which could be acquired for a 'donation', or the cigarette cards put out by tobacco firms.[11] Martial images, promising adventure and demanding sacrifice, existed cheek by jowl with 'harmonious' forms appealing for community spirit and co-operative effort and occupying a stylistic terrain somewhere between conventional academic graphics and aggressive modern publicity design. The toys, particularly, which ranged from plastic versions of old-fashioned metal soldiers and mini-Panzers and -Stukas to figures from the tales of the Brothers Grimm, were masterpieces of small-scale design, and undoubtedly meant more to young children growing up under National Socialism than a handful of school lessons in 'racial biology' devoted to the measuring of skulls. This juxtaposition of the warlike and the idyllic in the public-relations tactics of the Winter Relief designers symbolises the ambivalent relationship that existed between the militant *Volksgemeinschaft* of Nazi propaganda and the retreat into privacy and 'self-interested' consumption that occurred in practice.

The tension between public show and the retreat into non-political privacy is also evident in the everyday activities of the National Socialist mass organisations – those bodies, at any rate, that involved more than the mere empty discharge of duties (as in the Reich Air Raid Protection Association). The most important organisations here were the NSV (National Socialist Public Welfare)[12] and the *Kraft durch Freude* (KdF) division of the German Labour Front.[13] The former ensured participation and a degree of meaningful activity by taking over the running of public welfare services. In this it was not so much recording (much-trumpeted) new achievements as continuing to carry out tasks which the previous welfare associations had been performing before they were banned, *gleichgeschaltet* or cut back. *Kraft durch Freude* (Strength through Joy) acted as a cheap travel agency and instigator of leisure activities, selling itself – by dint of ample propaganda, much of it inflated – as a thoroughly modern leisure service. The combination of de-individualised, prefabricated leisure provision with an atmosphere which the participants found agreeably non-political was criticised in a SOPADE report, as early as 1935, on the grounds that it was a move to 'create activity and excitement with the avowed aim of preventing any real communal activities or any voluntary sociality from taking place'.[14] Yet even staunch Social Democrats could be impressed, as a report from the following year shows:[15]

> KdF events have become very popular. Even ordinary workers can afford these walking trips, since they are generally cheaper than private hikes.
>
> Almost all national comrades rate KdF as one of National Socialism's really creditable achievements. KdF sports courses are enjoying greater and greater popularity, even among older people. Everyone can take part. [. . .]
>
> KdF is now running weekly theatre trips into Munich from the countryside. Special theatre trains are coming to Munich on weekdays from as far away as 120 km. It has therefore been made easy for people from the countryside to go to the theatre in the city. The trips are very popular. [. . .]
>
> I attended a KdF swimming course in which over 50 took part, and I have to admit there was very little Party atmosphere. The participants were all ordinary people. There were scarcely any 'Heil Hitlers'. Coming from the old workers' sports clubs as we did, we felt at home, so to speak. I was doubtful about taking part in a KdF function at first, but there is really no alternative. I was all the more pleasantly surprised to find that there was absolutely nothing National Socialist about the way the course was organised and run.
>
> It is pretty generally the case now that you can't avoid *Kraft durch Freude* if you want to travel or take part in sport. So a lot of our comrades who used to be in the Outdoor Club, for example, are availing themselves of the opportunity of going on trips with KdF. There is simply no other choice.

Although the National Socialists went all out in the direction of the 'aestheticisation of politics', in order to indoctrinate their *Volksge-*

meinschaft ideal into existence, the result of the stage-management of public life was only to render it empty and to provoke the retreat into non-political privacy though this was indeed enough to secure passive consent and approval for the 'normality' that was achieved. Even the regime's own symbols of the new 'normal' leisure life-style, the 'People's Wireless Set' and the Volkswagen car,* served in practice to promote individualism in leisure and transport, albeit in the standardised form determined by the needs of mass consumption in a modern industrial society.

---

*The KdF car did not in fact go into series production before the outbreak of war.

ELEVEN

Order and terror

The consent which the people accorded the regime, however, and which found expression in the Führer myth and in numerous transactions of everyday life, had a further, highly sombre dimension. The population was more than merely implicated reluctantly in the use of terror: terror – or more precisely, specific manifestations of terror – met with popular approval.[1] This phenomenon has already been touched on in connection with the approval and lack of all moral scruple shown by the population at the time of the murders of 30th June 1934. But it went further than this. It is true, admittedly, that National Socialism stemmed and eventually halted specific spontaneous forms of Brownshirt terrorism, such as those which the SA had begun to commit in March and April 1933, but even the bureaucratically regulated species of terrorism that followed was a blend of order and terror: a pattern of norms and sanctions, outsiders and victims.

The terror, directed against political or social 'trouble-makers', was not only not concealed from the population – as many who pleaded for excuses were to suggest after 1945 – but was highly visible, was documented in the press during the Third Reich, was given legitimacy in the speeches of the Reich's leaders and was approved and welcomed by many Germans, at any rate while its targets were 'enemies' on the left and, later, the 'asocial'. Indeed, it was the sheer ruthless severity of the measures taken against the left in the first months of 1933 that was taken as a promise that 'order' would be restored and the threats to it repulsed with maximum force.[2] A typical expression of this expectation, which was shared even by those middle-class conservatives who kept their distance from the NSDAP, is the sermon preached by Friedrich Dibelius, the General Superintendent of the Protestant church in Brandenburg, on the 'Day of Potsdam', the occasion of the solemn opening of the Reichstag on 21st March 1933. The sermon was delivered in the presence of Hitler and Hindenburg in the Potsdam Garrison Church (the burial place, symbolically enough, of Frederick the Great):[3]

A new beginning in the history of the state is always marked, in one or another way, by the use of force. For the state *is* power. New decisions, new attitudes, transformations and upheavals always signify victory on one side and defeat on another. And if the life and death of the nation are at stake, then the power of the state must be employed effectively and with vigour, whether internally or externally. [. . .]

If the state carries out its duties against those who undermine the foundations of state order – against those, in particular, whose coarse and corrosive words destroy marriage, expose faith to contempt, and slander all who lay down their lives for their fatherland – then let the state carry out its duties, in God's name! But we should not deserve the title of a Protestant church if we did not add, with the candour of Luther himself, that the duties of the state must not be tainted by acts of personal arbitrariness. Let order be established; but then let justice and love hold sway once more, so that all men of honour may rejoice in their nation.

Consent to the use of terror as an emergency measure in order to restore 'order', and approval of its use as a means of excluding those who were alien to the 'national community', or who were defined as alien to it, were attitudes which many Germans shared with Dibelius in 1933. (This did not, however, prevent members of the later 'Confessional Church' from opposing Hitler on matters of religious policy.)

It is a disturbing fact, none the less, that even in subsequent years, as emergency institutions such as the Gestapo were consolidated rather than dissolved and extended their hold on society by means of totalitarian controls and sanctions, many Germans continued to see the political police as a means whereby their notions of order could be imposed on all who seemed guilty of deviations from the norm. This is shown by the denunciations and depositions made by members of the public who reported breaches of the 'Malicious Offences Law', under which people telling political jokes, for example, or 'grumblers, carpers and fault-finders' (to use the terminology of a propaganda campaign of 1934) were brought before Special Courts.[4]

Many older people today, looking back on the Third Reich, still see it as having had two strong points in its favour that made up for a lot: people could leave their bicycles unlocked outside their front doors; and long-haired layabouts were hauled off into Labour Camps. Even if such attitudes fell short of a demand for the death penalty or the gas chamber (though these demands were common enough), they testify to the existence of popular consent to a specific form of terror, namely dealing with non-standard behaviour, or non-standard categories of person, by bundling the individuals concerned into camps and subjecting them to drill even if not to annihilation. It should not be forgotten that a complementary part of the stock folk memory about unlocked bicycles that were safe against theft was the knowledge that gypsies were being arrested as 'theft suspects' and imprisoned in concentration camps.

The second mythicised memory of order and terror – the use of drill in labour camps – ties in rather closely with an everyday notion with a long pedigree. It was being claimed back in 1866 that the victory of Königgrätz had been due, not to the needle gun, but to the thrashings administered by Prussian schoolmasters. Sanctions against acts of nonconformism, such as idling at work or behaving unconventionally in public places, are a commonplace in the history of education in industrial class societies.[5] Pedagogic theory and practice not only called for docile compliance but sought to instil it, if necessary, by force, through the imposition of prison-like conditions and humiliating and physically gruelling drill. The fact that the Weimar Republic brought in some constitutional and humanitarian reforms of the Wilhelminian system was one of the very things that was held against the Republic by a not inconsiderable portion of the population. In establishing 'strict discipline', therefore, National Socialism could rely implicitly on disapproval of these mollycoddling aberrations of the 'interregnum' and could revert to the doctrine of order of the Imperial era with little fear of opposition. The old system was not simply restored, however: the liberal and constitutional features which it had acquired despite all the militaristic and authoritarian deformations of the nineteenth century were now stripped away. It is quite clear that the long prison terms in concentration camps given to alleged professional criminals, so-called 'asocial' gypsies or 'recidivist' homosexuals were approved of by wide sections of the population, including many who criticised the detention and torture of political opponents of the regime.[6]

To understand how the National Socialist version of the enforcement of norms of social discipline differed from earlier methods customary in bourgeois society, it is necessary to examine the ruling ideas and cast of mind of members of the Nazi movement itself. Heinrich Himmler gave voice to his notions of 'norms' and 'order' with positively obsessive frequency, and scarcely less often to his view that order had to be achieved by the ruthless use of force. Even at the moment when the victorious Wehrmacht was coming up against the first major block to its progress, Himmler found time to worry about the minutiae of 'order'. Midway through the winter battle outside Moscow, the 'Reich Leader of the SS and Chief of the German Police' went to the trouble of instructing his deputy Heydrich on the subject of swing. He wrote from the Führer's headquarters on 26th January 1942:[7]

Dear Heydrich,
   I enclose a report which Reich Youth Leader Axmann has sent me about the 'swing youth' in Hamburg.

I know that the Secret State Police have already intervened once. In my view, however, this mischief must be destroyed rot [*sic*; analogous misspelling in original] and branch. I am against mere half-measures here.

All the ringleaders, and I mean ringleaders both male and female, and all teachers with enemy views who are encouraging the swing youth, are to be assigned to a concentration camp. There the youth should first be given thrashings and then put through the severest drill and set to work. I think that any sort of labour camp or youth camp would be inappropriate for these youths and worthless girls. The girls should be put to work weaving and do land work in the summer. The spell these people should spend in concentration camp must be a fairly long one, 2–3 years. It must be made clear that they will never be allowed to go back to their studies. We must investigate how much encouragement they have had from their parents. If they have encouraged them, then they should also be put in a KL [*Konzentrationslager*] and their property confiscated.

It is only by intervening brutally that we shall be able to prevent the dangerous spread of this anglophyle [misspelling in original] tendency at a time when Germany is fighting for her existence.

Please send me further reports. I should be grateful if this action can be conducted in co-operation with the Gauleiter and the senior leader of the SS and police.

Heil Hitler!

Yours, H.H.

The 'swing youth' phenomenon, as will be remembered from Chapter 8, sprang up in large cities among young members of the (upper-) middle class whose tastes in music, life-style and opinions inevitably seemed utterly 'un-German' in the eyes of National Socialist observers. The observers' disgust was matched by 'vigorous measures' on the part of the police authorities. Swing festivals were banned, and transgressions of this ruling fell within the extensive catalogue of offences that were 'handled' by the Gestapo.

Swing, though, would not go away. Recurrently, young people at dance-band concerts would burst out into storms of enthusiasm as soon as the music livened up, and they would besiege the band leaders with requests for swing numbers. On 27th August 1942 the Security Service of the SS reported on a concert in Hamburg by the Willi Artelt band:[8]

The band leader was performing in an apparent state of ecstasy. He was conducting with his back hunched and with rolling eyes; the audience was roaring in accompaniment. The discords provoked thunderous storms of applause.

Another report comments on a guest appearance by the Wolff band at the Caricata Bar in Hamburg:

The band played primarily German hits, but in a heavily 'jitterbugged' style. [. . .] The applause after these English hits was extraordinarily loud and was in sharp contrast to the applause bestowed on the German numbers. Among other items, the English hit 'Sweet Sue' was performed, using the words '*Lest das Mittagsblatt, lest das Tageblatt*' [Read the midday paper, read the daily paper]. Since the 'swing youth' have always sung the words in the amended form, '*Lest das Mittagsblatt, lest das Tageblatt, alles Lüge, alles Dreck*' [. . . all lies, all rubbish], and that is how they are always known, this piece reaped particularly loud applause.

Similar reports came in from Hanover, Dresden and Berlin. According to a National Socialist report of 10th August 1942, the youthful 'regulars' in the 'concert cafés' of many big German cities were

so plainly opposed to respectable light music conforming to German taste, and are demanding jazz music, sometimes in no uncertain terms, that the bands are gradually giving in, and the wilder, 'hotter' and more jazzified the music they play, the more unrestrained the applause they obtain from young people of this type.

In 1944 the editors of the *Völkischer Beobachter* deemed it necessary to devote a whole page of the 29th June issue of their supplement, the *Illustrierter Beobachter*, to a denunciation of swing. Pictures and extracts from American articles on Benny Goodman, the 'King of Swing', were assembled, with forged quotations and malicious comments added. Three photographs, showing Goodman, Goodman's hands holding his clarinet, and a couple dancing at a concert, carried the following captions:

The Jew Benny Goodman (Gutmann). With his swing band he not only receives the top radio fees, but exerts a positively sinister influence on American youth. 'My music is more immoral than all the courtesans in history put together,' he himself boasts.

Hands of a criminal. The hands of the swing Jew Benny Goodman, described as 'definitely a criminal's hands' by a Milwaukee music magazine held in high regard by experts.

No dance floor here. But the boys and girls who have been seduced by the 'immoral' music of the 'Pied Piper of New York' jerk their way between the aisles in a cinema.

If the public behaviour of swing fans, harmless enough in all conscience, was enough to arouse the indignation of the National Socialist guardians of order, then the 'goings-on' inside the private swing cliques could only make them lose control entirely. These young people, with the run of their parents' homes, played records of hot jazz, danced and affected a 'casual', 'English' style; worse still, they availed themselves of the unregimented sexual opportunities open to them.

The reports on the 'swing youth' by the National Socialist authorities are replete with sexual detail: 'sexual intercourse among minors', group sex, 'perversions', homosexuality, 'racial violations'. Sexual behaviour in the young swing cliques was undoubtedly more casual than the National Socialist norm countenanced; equally clearly, however, the monitoring reports, with their uptight fixation on sexual noncon- formity, were exaggerated. The episodes they describe do not necessarily all have a factual basis, although the accounts are certainly accurate enough as documents of their authors' own sexual preoccupations. The result of the official ban on swing was that most young people, while retaining their preference for this kind of jazz, gave expression to it only in private; for a minority, however, the restriction of the music to the private sphere led to the formation of cliques that were more entrenched and more clearly set on opposition to the Nazis' cultural ideals.

The 'swing boys and girls', however, also continued to take advantage of the music played in city dance halls that was intended, in line with Goebbels's prescriptions, to keep the home front in good heart during the war. The Third Reich's cultural policies were caught in a quandary of their own making, split between attempting to provide a *völkisch* culture patched together from the aesthetic principles of the pre-war middle class and making concessions to public taste with apolitical, international dance music (stripped of all avant-garde, modernist features) and the escapist glamour of the UFA films. The 'swing youth' exploited this ambivalence. Not content with the fare provided by the Reich Ministry of Public Information and Propaganda, they appropriated it in ways that were utterly unwelcome to the authorities.

In the first place, they defied the constraints that had been imposed: if certain kinds of music were suitable for cheering up adults, particularly soldiers on leave, then they were all right for the young too, and so much the worse for the tightened regulations for the 'protection of young people' and the *völkisch* pressures of education in schools and the Hitler Youth. And where a UFA hit number took up some rhythmic ideas from international jazz, toned down and blended into a well-mannered palm-court style, then the swing fans wanted hot jazz and applauded every dissonant departure from harmonic blandness. Where the use of German words and the kitschy re-shaping of melodies was meant to efface the music's international jazz roots, then the 'swing boys' insisted on the original. For them, the fact that what the Nazis called 'negro music' was American in origin was not an inherent defect: it was a seal of quality. The second way in which the members of the swing movement appropriated popular music was connected with this: they carried over the features of the music, and their response to it, into their everyday behaviour. Relaxed surrender to the rhythms; spontaneous bodily movements instead of coached dance-steps; unexpected discords instead of conventional harmonies – all these were expressive of a loose, easy-going attitude to life in general and a desire to escape from the rigid demands of social order, school discipline, the paramilitary drill of the Hitler Youth, the 'keenness' of Nazi officials and the ever-present call of duty. Their musical taste was paralleled by a cool style of behaviour modelled on English and American film stars and by chic casualness in dress. A diary entry of the period records:

> And so we casually sleazed our way into the small hours with night-club swing.

To which a Hitler Youth commentator adds, not inaccurately: 'Their ideal is the "sleazy life".' This catch-phrase sums up the style of the 'swing youth' succinctly. Their aim was to spurn the duties laid down by those in authority, to throw off inhibitions of behaviour, and to defy sexual taboos.

This, though, explains Heinrich Himmler's reaction to swing, at first sight so inexplicably violent. His sense of outrage and his call for severe punishments is not without traces of panic. Even as a young man, Himmler went into a flap when faced with 'unbridled' sexuality or with actions 'neglectful of duty'. His diaries, for all their stiff impersonality, are full of such touches.[9] After reading an erotic book, *Das Lustwäldchen* (The Pleasure Grove), he brands it 'the poetry of demolition'. What sort of defensive walls must he have built within himself, that they could be 'demolished' by pornography? When by chance he came across 'The Priest and the Acolyte' (a piece attributed to Oscar Wilde), his whole evening was ruined. As he confided to his diary:

> An idealisation of a homosexual person. Pictures atrocious. Evening: 10.30, dreadful mood.

Just as literature about sex drew him on, only to throw him into confusion and strengthen his resolve to remain 'chaste' until marriage, so he also learned to dance, but only in order to be able to conform, with stiff formality, to the safe conventions of social obligation and intercourse. His real longing was for the military life – but again, more for the idea and principle of the thing than for the arduous reality of basic training, which had actually caused him great suffering:

> At last I have been in uniform for the day again. It is still my first love, when all is said and done.

This note is from December 1919, a year after his premature departure from officers' school.

Himmler's strange traits of character were not untypical of his generation. He was born in 1900 and grew up in a middle-class household. His father, a *Gymnasium* master (and later headmaster), had made the upward social move for which his own father had paved the way. The young Heinrich Himmler was prepared for 'life' in accordance with the same formula for success: if you wanted to get on in the world, you had to steer your ambitions up the conventional pathways of the social hierarchy. With tyrannical solicitude his parents drummed home the message that power was to be acquiesced in unquestioningly, that the favour of the powerful was to be sought through the zealous – indeed, ultra-zealous – discharge of duty, and that the absorption of a rigid code of behaviour would ensure automatic correctness of behaviour when the individual entered the higher social spheres in which his destiny would be decided. The busy schoolmaster read and corrected Heinrich's diary; Heinrich's mother converted her under-used reserves of love and energy into steadfast care and attention, permitting her son no independent life outside the narrow framework of a pedantically regimented daily round. This tension, between a father who was seldom at home but whose norms and authority were all the more threatening an internal presence, and a mother who continued to stuff her twenty-year-old son with 'goodies' but had also crammed him full of rules of cleanliness and good manners, produced a personality which needed an external armouring of authority and obedience to serve as protection for the softness concealed within. A few early bohemian outbursts were soon broken off; Himmler had no gift for enjoying himself, he suffered from a bad conscience and he concealed the episodes from his family.

This concentration on socially acceptable duties – the insertion of stabilising tension bolts into a personality which, though slowly becoming firmer, still remained fragile – came under critical threat when, with the collapse of the Empire and his premature departure from officers' school, he was deprived of the gratifications of drill and the opportunity to ascend the social ladder. Just as prestressed concrete, however, needs to be solidly anchored in order to create a complex equilibrium of tension and pressure and avoid collapse, so there were many in Himmler's generation who turned to terrorism when the structure of duty and social mobility within traditional society crumbled. A new order was called for, they believed: a fascist upheaval backed by terror would blast society apart, and their damaged personalities would find new points of anchorage in its exposed foundations.

This psychological ambivalence, in Himmler's case, is shown by his attempts during adolescence to extract affection and attention from the parental 'authorities' (as a military recruit, he bombarded his mother with almost daily petitions for letters, 'goodies', money and, above all, notice), while on the other hand, the fiancée of his elder brother Gebhard, after committing an alleged faux pas, received a letter from Heinrich in which, rather than leave the job to his brother, he took it upon himself to give her a dressing down:

> If your union is to become a happier one for you both, and is to be of benefit to the nation, the foundation of which must be healthy and happy families, then you must be taken in hand with barbaric severity.

The early hints apparent in the young Himmler's letters and diaries, and the tyrannical principles which were later enjoined on the nation as a whole in the speeches and directives of the 'Reich Leader of the SS and Chief of the German Police', are of a piece with a host of other autobiographical documents and memoirs from the middle-class pre-war generation, Freikorps men and the SA 'old guard'. The ideal is that of the 'soldierly' man, with an inner hardness which enables him to kill off his own desires and weaknesses, is transmuted externally into murderous fantasies and, once he has the actual power to commit them, finds its fulfilment in acts of terror and mass slaughter.[10]

In metaphorical terms, the stereotyped fantasies of violence of these fascists can be seen as corresponding to the 'national war colours', the black, white and red of the Nazi flag. (See pp. 34–5 above). White represents the dream of the taming of sexuality, the neutralising of women into the images of the exalted lady, the sister of mercy or the bloodless corpse; white also denotes the empty city square after machine-gun fire has 'cleansed' it of menacing, demonstrating masses; it stands for 'purity' and 'cleanliness' in general; and, not least, it also stands for the controlled marching columns or the rigid architectural blocks which do not actually fill the empty square but extend its soullessness into the environment beyond. Red is the 'bleeding pulp' to which all those guilty of insubordination will be reduced; the 'flood' of enemy workers; the 'Reds'; and, especially, the threatening Amazonian figures of the female revolutionary soldier. Black represents the spells of pleasurable exhaustion into which a man can sink when he has gone to the limits of his strength and beyond, in ecstatic submission to duty and the Führer's calls for action. This condensed account of Klaus Theweleit's interpretation of a large corpus of autobiographical documents of Freikorps fighters can only hint at the central core of the National Socialist doctrine of order: its inner 'meaning'. But it explains why the 'casual' life-style of the 'swing boys and girls' struck at the *Wesensmitte* of the National Socialist philosophy and why it provoked a response in the form of terror.

What the young people who had been committed to a concentration camp on Himmler's orders could expect may be illustrated by an account of conditions in the Moringen youth concentration camp near Göttingen.[11] There, as subjects for research in 'racial biology', they were assigned to 'blocks' from which only a few were released (i.e. 'set free' to become cannon-fodder for the Wehrmacht). The rest waited until they reached the age of majority, whereupon they were transferred either to a mental asylum (with the prospect of becoming victims of euthanasia) or to an adult concentration camp. But there were very few so-called 'feeble-minded' people in the Moringen camp: of the 1,231 'pupils' (*Zöglinge*) committed up to the middle of 1944, 1,018 had completed elementary schooling and 36 secondary schooling. Rather, it was their social behaviour, put down to 'racial biology', that was made the basis of their allocation into 'blocks':

> Pupils who are difficult, deviant in character, suffering from emotional inadequacies, hyperactive, excitable, discontented in disposition, bad-tempered, incorrigible mischief-makers or determined petty criminals – i.e. pupils who are continually at odds with the community – are clear custody cases. In line with the practice of the Institute of Criminal Biology and of this camp, these pupils are termed 'trouble-makers' [*Störer*] and, as soon as they are identified as such, assigned to S Block (*Block der Störer*) [Trouble-Makers' Block]. Between 5 and 10 per cent of pupils are assigned to this block. Upon attainment of the appropriate age they are either transferred to a concentration camp or, as soon as the Community Aliens Law has been enacted, will be transferred to an appropriate institution of the *Land* Welfare Association.
>
> Pupils with personality weaknesses, who are unsettled and lacking in drive, who cannot pass any of the proficiency tests and have an unfailing tendency to aberrancy, are also custody cases without exception. They are allotted to D Block (*Block der Dauerversager*) [Persistent Failures Block] and later transferred to concentration camps or to half-open or closed institutions. D Block accounts for between 10 and 15 per cent of pupils.
>
> Those who are primarily unstable, irresponsible or lacking in independence, who are severely at risk and liable to recidivism, go into G Block (*Block der Gelegenheitsversager*) [Occasional Failures Block].

The author of this report (dated July 31st 1944) – a senior regional court judge, no less – concluded with the following assessment:[12]

> The negative human material detained in Moringen Youth Protection Camp provides valuable data for educational purposes, in the sense that it displays in coarse and in some instances unadulterated form the defects which can be found, in initial outline, in young people who although not yet depraved are at risk, in so far as risk is biologically determined. Work on the negative cases, therefore, is also of considerable significance for positive work.

Just as the young Himmler justified the repression of sexuality as 'racially superior chastity' and decked out his anti-Semitism and hatred of negroes with spectres of 'oriental' sexual debauchery, so the system in Moringen youth concentration camp used 'racial biology' to lay down a standard of social behaviour based on unquestioning performance of duty and unconditional conformity, and set out to 'eradicate' the 'community aliens' who did not meet the standard. National Socialist racialism, in other words, entailed a rigorous principle of social order: it was a Procrustean attempt, based on terror, to reduce the bewildering diversity of an industrial society, linked with the international world outside, to a racially pure 'national community' whose social structure and norms of achievement had been given the legitimacy of 'science'.

TWELVE

Racialism as social policy

The violence and brutality of the National Socialists were not directed only against political dissidents or foreign countries: 'traitors' or the 'racially inferior'. Nor were the racial doctrines of National Socialism merely an unreal utopia fleshed out with biological absurdities – though they were not without their bizzare features. What should not be forgotten is that fascist racialism provided a model for a new order in society, a new internal alignment. Its basis was the racialist elimination of all elements that deviated from the norm: refractory youth, 'idlers', the 'asocial', prostitutes, homosexuals, the disabled, people who were incompetents or failures in their work. Nazi eugenics – that, is, the classification and selection of people on the basis of supposed genetic 'value' – was not confined only to serilisation and euthanasia for the 'valueless' and the encouragement of fertility for the 'valuable'; it laid down criteria of assessment, categories of classification and norms of efficiency that were applicable to the population as a whole. The goals were 'people of German blood and Nordic race: four-square in body and soul';[1] social conformity; and 'German hard work':

> Satisfactory performance or failure in work effort, or as regards incorporation into the national community, are often better measures of the total hereditary value of a kinship group [*Sippe*] than the results of brief medical investigation. They are therefore of particular value for investigating and assessing applicants for marriage loans, as indeed for all cases of eugenic assessment.

Such 'assessments' found their way not only into Nazi social policy but into day-to-day Gestapo procedures.

Whereas the persecutions of Jews and of those ideologically opposed to the NSDAP have long been on the record, post-war German society found it hard to bring itself to enquire into the wider aspects of Nazi social-Darwinist practice. Comparatively little is known about the use of euthanasia or about standard psychiatric procedures during the

Third Reich. Victims of compulsory sterilisation and homosexuals who were held in concentration camps generally received no reparations after the war. Refractory teenagers, the 'work-shy' and the 'asocial' continued to be socially ostracised, although people who regretted that there were no more concentration camps to put them in generally kept their mutterings private.

The National Socialist utopia of the *Volksgemeinschaft* had a double thrust: its 'internal' aim was to engineer the conversion of a society of fractured traditions, social classes and environments into an achievement-orientated community primed for self-sacrifice; its 'external' aim was to segregate and eventually 'eradicate' (*ausmerzen*) all those who, on real or imaginary grounds, could not be allowed entry into the *Volksgemeinschaft* – 'aliens', 'incurable' political opponents, the 'asocial' and the Jews.

What, then, was the relationship between National Socialism's generalised racialism and its anti-Semitism? The image of 'the Jew' as the root of all evil, 'pulling strings' behind the scenes, was an ideological synthesis of diffused anxieties about civilisation and separate, self-contradictory racialist notions, all focused on to a political target. The very diversity of actual modern Jewish experience was taken to point to the existence of the mythical hate-figure of the essential 'Jew' lurking behind the most disparate surface appearances. The intellectual, culturally assimilated Jew stood for detestable modernity; the religious Orthodox Jew matched the traditional hate-image of Christian anti-Semitism; the economically successful Jew stood for 'money-grubbing capital' and liberalism; the Jewish socialist represented abhorrent 'Bolshevism' and 'Marxism'; the 'Eastern Jew' from the alien culture of the ghettos was a suitable target for the aggression and arrogance of the civilising and colonialist missions of the imperialist era. Unlike traditional anti-Semitism of a religious or nationalistic cast, the anti-Semitism of the NSDAP was thus directed not against selected characteristics of the Jews but against an abstract object, 'the Jew' as such: an artificial racialist construct. This all-encompassing image entailed an all-encompassing 'final solution', for the very reason that the mythical target of 'the Jew' served to conceal the otherwise obvious fact that a racialist interpretation of world problems bore little relation to reality. The ostracism and, later, annihilation of Jewry therefore stood at the head of the long list of measures for racial purification. The sheer rigidity of the machinery of destruction also helped the Nazis to deceive themselves that their pursuit of the fantasy of a 'new racial order' for Europe was proceeding in a systematic and efficient fashion. The more the Nazis' unmasking of racial enemies failed to deliver the promised concord of *Volksgemeinschaft* and the solution of society's real problems and contradictions, the more radical and ruthless had to be the destructive pressure exerted against the 'community aliens'. The fact that the mass murders were kept secret does not gainsay this. They were the defining core of the Nazis' programme.

Since the fate of the Jews, who constituted the largest group among the victims of National Socialist racialist policies,[2] has been documented in extensive detail, we shall not provide a further account here. It is only recently, on the other hand, that historians and the public have turned their attention to the second major population group which the National Socialists proposed to exterminate in its entirety: the gypsies.[3] The hate-image of the gypsies which the Nazis propagated fused two figures of Nazi demonology: the 'alien', whose culture is a source of mistrust and distaste; and the 'asocial', who refuses to submit to the values of work discipline and stable social relations. This labelling of deviant behaviour was made additionally ominous by the Nazis' racialism, according to which the causes of 'incurable' nonconformity were hereditary.

It is true that the gypsies were subjected to police surveillance and discriminated against in many ways before 1933, because of their different culture, their unwillingness to accept the work discipline of industrial society and their unsettled mode of life. The National Socialists at first merely continued this tradition, though with extra severity. A further level of proposed discrimination, however, began to become apparent in research publications in racial biology, a field given new respectability by National Socialism. An important role was played here by the former Tübingen neurologist Dr Robert Ritter. From 1936 onwards Ritter headed a so-called 'Establishment for Research in Hereditary Science' in Berlin, which, after various changes of name, became the 'Institute of Criminal Biology' and was merged during the war into Himmler's Head Office for Reich Security. Ritter's *idée fixe* was that a hereditary disposition towards criminality was produced by inter-breeding with 'blood' of 'criminal stock'. From the point of view of 'criminal biology', accordingly, there were basically three human groups: those of straightforwardly 'good type' (*gut Geartete*), those totally deficient as to 'type' (*Ungeartete*), and a large intermediate group whose degree of educability and adaptability could be determined by 'expert' genetic opinion and 'pedagogic' practice.[4] 'Gypsy half-castes', however, were clearly of 'inferior value' and a focus of criminality. (Ritter and Himmler had a higher opinion of the small number of gypsies of supposedly 'pure race'.) Being 'ineducable', 'gypsy half-castes' were not to be dealt with by the legal system, where the purpose of punitive measures was at least potentially remedial; they were 'biologically depraved' and as such were to be singled out for biological 'eradication' by Himmler's police (which in the first instance meant sterilisation).

Ritter expounded these basic ideas in two studies of 1940 and 1941. He wrote:[5]

> Primitive man does not change and cannot be changed. [. . .] Instead of punitive measures, suitable provision [should be] made [for] preventing the further emergence of primitive asocials and the offspring of criminal stock by way of segregation of the sexes or sterilisation. [. . .]

> [. . .] As a rule [gypsy half-castes are] highly unstable, lacking in character, unpredictable, unreliable, as well as slothful or unsettled and hot-tempered: in short, work-shy and asocial.

The 'gypsy question', in Ritter's view,

> can be considered solved only when the majority of the asocial and unproductive gypsies are placed in large work camps and the further reproduction of this half-caste population is terminated. Only then will future generations of the German people be freed of this burden.

The gypsy policy of the National Socialist state followed these general lines, albeit with some tactical time-lags. The semi-official commentary on the Nuremberg race laws by Globke and Stuckart in 1935 declared the gypsies, like the Jews, to be of 'alien type' (*Artfremde*); and coercive measures rapidly increased. In the crucial decree announcing 'Preventive Police Measures to Combat Crime' issued by the Prussian Minister of the Interior on 14th December 1937, gypsies were already listed among the escalating category of the 'asocial':[6]

> Such persons shall be deemed asocial who, through behaviour which is inimical to the community (but which need not be criminal), show that they are not prepared to be members of the community. The following are instances of asocial persons:
> (a) Persons who, by virtue of petty but repeated infringements of the law, are not prepared to comply with the order that is a fundamental condition of a National Socialist state (e.g. beggars, vagrants [sc. gypsies], prostitutes, drunkards, persons with contagious diseases, especially persons with sexually transmitted diseases who fail to adhere to the regulations of the health authorities).
> (b) Persons, regardless of any previous convictions, who evade the obligation to work and who are dependent on the public for their maintenance (e.g. the work-shy, work evaders, drunkards).

> The use by the police of the powers of preventive arrest shall apply in the first instance to asocials with no fixed abode. Under no account shall political considerations play a part in determining whether a person is to be designated as asocial.

In the wave of mass arrests of the 'asocial' and 'work-shy' that ensued, gypsies were among those assigned to the concentration camps. A decree to 'Combat the Gypsy Nuisance' of 8th December 1938 provided for a further stepping up of established police powers of arrest, and this was followed after the outbreak of war by the 'Custody Decree' of 17th October 1939, which stipulated the committal of all gypsies and gypsy half-castes to assembly camps. The first deportations of 2,500 gypsies into occupied Poland took place in the spring of 1940, but were continued on a systematic basis only from the autumn of 1941 onwards (when 5,000 Austrian gypsies were deported to a special section of the Lodz Jewish ghetto). Himmler's 'Auschwitz Decree' of 16th December 1942 ordered the 'assignment of gypsy half-castes, Roma gypsies and Balkan gypsies' into the so-called 'gypsy camp' within Auschwitz-Birkenau concentration camp. A total of about 20,000 gypsies from 11 countries were subsequently deported to Auschwitz. Although no gassings of gypsies took place there at first, the gypsy camp was broken up in August 1944, in view of severe epidemics and the advance of Soviet troops, and its inmates were murdered. Altogether, according to research estimates, about 219,000 gypsies were murdered in the territories controlled by the Nazis, including about 15,000 of the 20,000 gypsies who had been living in Germany in 1939.

The same principles of conformity with social and cultural standards, especially work-discipline, as were invoked in the elimination of the gypsies from the 'national community' were also applied 'internally' in disciplining and regimenting the 'national comrades' themselves. Closely linked to the 'gypsy question' was the more general problem of 'vagrancy' or the 'travelling population',[7] which had earlier been a source of disquiet for welfare associations in the Wilhelmine and Weimar periods. The highways had then been populated by a shifting, complex and highly variegated army of journeymen, men seeking work, young people seeking adventure, beggars and tramps, and the welfare bodies and public authorities had sought in vain to impose order on this confusion. The principal criterion proposed was a division of the 'travellers' into those willing and those not willing to work. In this respect the National Socialist public welfare authorities' call for a fundamental distinction between 'respectable and non-respectable travellers'[8] chimed entirely with long-standing reformist efforts on the part of non-fascist welfare workers. In 1934, for example, the strict Catholic *Land* Administrator for Kassel, Wuermling, wrote:[9]

> The goal of legislative and administrative measures should not be merely to follow the line of least resistance and channel the travelling population along highly orderly lines; the aim must be to remove entirely the destitute

vagrant's right to exist. It cannot be denied that this aim will be achieved only with great difficulty, but if ever there was a fitting time for achieving it, it is now, when the state is in fact in a position to act if there is resolute co-operation between the judiciary and the police.

This sweeping proposal, made when millions were still unemployed, makes plain the essence of the thinking behind the plans for a new order in social policy. Welfare workers, demoralised by shortages of funds, by the pluralistic decision-making processes of democracy and by a greater self-assertiveness on the part of their clientele, were looking for a fundamental restructuring of the welfare system by a state which had apparently become much stronger after 1933. Above all, in the new society those who worked hard and efficiently would be assigned their rightful place; deviant and disturbing behaviour would be eliminated as socially unbeneficial.

As labour shortages set in during the rearmament boom of 1936–37, the economic argument was added to the argument from social order. The long-serving administrative head of the German Association for Public and Private Welfare, Hilde Eisenhardt, said in 1938:[10]

> We need their hands to help us in the great economic programme that lies ahead, and we therefore cannot continue to allow people who are capable of work to spend months and years on the open roads.

The implications were spelled out in plain language by Oberführer Greifelt, a member of Himmler's personal staff, in a report on the results of the national 'Work-Shy' campaign conducted in 1937–38:[11]

> The tight situation in the labour market necessitated the work-discipline principle that all persons who were unwilling to participate in the working life of the nation, and were merely scraping by as work-shy or asocials and making the cities and main roads unsafe, should be dealt with by coercive means and set to work. Following the lead of the 'Four Year Plan' department, the Secret State Police took energetic and vigorous steps in this matter. At the same time, vagrants, beggars, gypsies and procurers were picked up by the criminal police and, finally, those wilfully refusing to earn a living were apprehended. Considerably in excess of 10,000 asocials are currently undergoing a diet of work training in concentration camps, which are eminently suited to this purpose.

National Socialist policy towards social outsiders rested on approaches to the question similar to those that had earlier been advocated by non-fascist policy-makers, academics and welfare workers. At first it pursued the same solutions, albeit more harshly and by discarding constitutional restraints. The new elements which the Nazi state introduced – not infrequently to the applause of professional social and welfare workers – were the legitimation, based on racial biology, of the distinction between those eligible for training and the 'biologically degenerate' (who were to be separated out) and the use of the concentration and extermination camps. Even though many welfare workers may not have approved of the murder of the socially 'unfit' and the nonconformist, their calls for 'incurable' cases to be segregated, taken into compulsory 'protective custody' and maintained at minimal expense helped pave the way for the concentration camps and the gas chambers.

The committal of 'asocials' to concentration camps in accordance with the crucial 1937 decree instituting 'Preventive Police Measures to Combat Crime' was followed in 1940 by the establishment of work education camps. According to a decree of Himmler's of 28th May 1941,[12] these were

> intended exclusively to receive those refusing to work or reluctant to work whose activities are tantamount to work sabotage. The purpose of committal is education and training; the aim is not punishment, nor is it to be officially recorded as such. [. . .] Detainees are to be made to do arduous work, so that they can be forcibly brought to realise that they behaviour is detrimental to the nation, so that they can be trained to work in orderly and regulated fashion and so that they may serve as a warning and deterrent to others.

If, however, several weeks of forced labour in a work education camp failed to achieve their 'educational' purpose, and it was noted that the person concerned was once again refusing to work, then the concentration camp loomed.

It is true that only a small number of German workers were detained for 'idling' at work, but such cases formed only one item in a long catalogue of warnings and punishments involving the workplace and beyond. Their chief significance was not the 'education' or 'training' the inmates received but the deterrent effect they had on the great mass of workers, who were faced with a constant reminder of the consequences that could flow from insubordination, slow working and absenteeism. Indeed, as far as can be ascertained from the scattered information available, punitive detention in specific camps far more commonly involved foreign workers than Germans. In the course of the war, on the other hand, complaints by industrial firms about 'idling' by young German workers increased to a quite extraordinary degree, with the steps taken to combat it again ranging from special 'educational' and 'training' terror measures to detention in youth concentration camps.

The extent to which the state-police punitive system had bitten into everyday working life is demonstrated by statistics from Krupp's steel casting works in Essen, which reported 5,426 cases of 'idling' to the

Gestapo between the end of September 1939 and the end of 1944.[13] (The numbers of warnings issued which never went beyond the factory, and of threats to inform the Gestapo, will have been considerably greater.) Of these 5,426 members of the workforce who were reported, 224 were dismissed from their jobs, 105 were drafted into the Wehrmacht, 584 received a warning, 553 received a 'disciplinary penalty' (usually a fine), 204 were taken into juvenile detention or reform schools, 23 received an 'official warning', 224 received court sentences, 132 were taken into 'protective custody', 313 were sent to work education camps and 6 to concentration camps.

Even the brutal conditions in the work education camps, with their procedures for 'educating' 'national comrades' adjudged guilty of nonconformist behaviour, were intended solely to break the will of the inmates and, through the harshness of their methods, to serve as a deterrent to others. In the process the factitious distinction between 'educable' national comrades and the 'biologically depraved' – who, being 'asocial' and 'ineducable', were subjected to sterilisation, concentration-camp detention and 'annihilation through labour' – tended to dissolve. Instead of the dualism, tricked out in racial biology, of 'national comrades' and 'community aliens', there was a continuum of police-enforced pressures to conform, stretching from initial sanctions against nonconformist behaviour, via 'education' and 'training' by means of terror, to systematic extermination.

National Socialist racialism, then, was by no means merely a murderous ideological farrago, involving the spurious 'scientific' designation of races of 'lesser value'; it was also the instrument and ideological expression of the enforcement, through terror, of conformist social behaviour within the so-called 'national community' itself. In this repect one of the purposes of Nazi racialism, in both a theoretical and a practical sense, was to provide norms for, and to regulate, social behaviour. There were two reasons, inherent in the structure of its concept of race, why this was so.

First and foremost, the vagueness of its biogenetic concepts meant in practice that people's social behaviour served as a central criterion of their supposed 'racial character'. This is made plain by the following extract from an 'expert opinion' submitted by the Racial Hygiene Research Centre within the Reich Public Health Office, dated 10th July 1944:[14]

[. . .] Although membership of the Gypsies in terms of blood is denied by family X, the racial diagnosis as regards the members of family X is undoubtedly 'Gypsy' and/or 'Gypsy-Negro-Hybrid'.
This verdict is based on
1. racial and psychological features

2. anthropological features
3. genealogical data
4. the fact that the family is regarded as Magyar by Hungarians. [. . .]

These few data are sufficient on their own for family X to be regarded as presumptively Gypsy. Itinerancy and unsettled journeying as a family unit are characteristic of Gypsies as far as Central European conditions are concerned. Whereas the external appearance of the members of family X is not entirely typical Gypsy, and in fact – with the exception of the mother – suggests Negro-Hybrid, the gestures, affectivity and overall behaviour are not only alien-type [*artfremd*] but in fact positively indicate Gypsy descent. The false show of civility of manner, the moulding of emotional impulses (in any case superficial in themselves) to prevailing external circumstances, the lack of discernment and poor judgement on matters of factual evaluation and inference, and the deficiency as regards opinions and instability of personal attitudes indicate, for all the artfulness and cunning, what is essentially a high degree of naivety and primitivity. This type of slackness is not encountered among settled Europeans with a developed work sense. With family X, in addition, certain peculiarities by way of histrionic expressions, the manner of engaging in bargaining and the attempt to curry favour and create a good impression by using varying emotional moods, testify to the specifically Gypsy character of the alien-type primitivity involved. [. . .]

In addition, the theory of the cross-breeding of different hereditary characteristics implied a graduated categorisation of people ranging from the 'educable', via those 'educable with difficulty', to the 'ineducable'. Again, in practice, this scheme could be operated only on the basis of the observation of everyday behaviour. Thus Ritter's 'Institute of Criminal Biology' (Ritter, incidentally, also pronounced on the gypsy question) had devised a 'scientific' procedure for screening the 'pupils' of the concentration camp for young people set up at Moringen in 1940, using criteria that were unambiguously concerned with conformity of behaviour.[15]

These two basic features of National Socialist racialism – eking out biological grounds for 'suspicion' by using indicators of deviant social behaviour; and systematically extending the classification of types of behaviour from descriptions of small, excluded groups to include norms which could cover practically everyone – can be found not only in the treatment of the gypsies but also, for instance, in a sphere which, according to Nazi propaganda, represented the 'positive' and 'constructive' side of their racial scheme. This was their designation of 'woman' – '*die Frau*' – as the 'German mother'.[16] The campaign to steer women into housework and the bearing and rearing of plentiful offspring – a campaign backed up by awards of the quasi-decoration, the Cross of Motherhood – was only one facet of the Nazis' policies on women and population control. Marriage loans, for example, which could be 'paid off' by arrivals of children ('*abgekindert*'), were granted only to women who were 'genetically healthy'. Those who did not meet this condition not only were turned away empty-handed but, if they had (or were thought to have) hereditary diseases, could be compulsorily sterilised, in accordance with a law of 14th July 1933. In addition, the executive orders ancillary to the Nuremberg Laws, which prohibited marriages between Jews and 'Aryans', extended the categories of those covered to include gypsies and negroes. Children who had been born to liaisons between German women and non-white occupation troops in the Rhineland – 'Rhineland bastards' – were compulsorily sterilised. This '*Berufsverbot* for mothers' (Gisela Bock's phrase) was the complement to the Third Reich's policy of encouraging fertility. (See also Plate 18.)

When the 'Law for the Prevention of Progeny of the Genetically Unhealthy' was announced in 1933, the Reich Minister of the Interior, Frick, issued a rallying cry in support of the 'differentiation' of birth-rates: 'We must once more have the courage to classify our people according to their hereditary value.' Not the least important criterion bearing on sterilisation was general 'social usefulness', which proved to consist of obedience to the paramount norms of hard work, conformist behaviour, orderliness and efficiency. A questionnaire issued to doctors called for possible sterilisation cases to be assessed, in part, in the light of their responses to questions about 'general moral notions':[17]

Why do we learn? Why do we save, and for whom? Why is it wrong to set fire to a house – even your own house? If you find 5RM, what should you do with it? 20RM? 200RM? How do you see your future? What would you do if you won first prize in the lottery? What are loyalty; piety; deference; modesty? What is the opposite of courage?

The formulators of National Socialist racial policy quite explicitly wanted to prevent the reproduction of families which they labelled 'alien' or 'asocial'. In this they were continuing a tradition of eugenic and demographic thought going back to the Imperial period, when there was concern that academic and middle-class families which were 'German through and through' were reproducing at a lesser rate than families from lower social groups – more specifically, the non-'respectable' orders. Even utterly non-fascist medical writers had argued in favour of a differentiated population policy, in order to encourage 'better' genetic stock (defined as 'better' in terms of sociological 'success'). On the other hand, there was little public support before 1933 for views such as those of Karl Binding and Adolf Hoche, who had called in 1920 for 'the authorisation of the destruction of lives not worthy of life', on the grounds that people suffering from certain incurable mental illnesses were mere 'ballast existences', 'empty human shells' and 'mentally dead'.[18]

At first, in 1933, the National Socialists opted for the more 'restrained' policy of social isolation and sterilisation for the 'genetically unhealthy'. This could include compulsory sterilisation of people, such as schizophrenics and severe alcoholics, whose illnesses could at best only be postulated as hereditary but not scientifically proved to be. In addition, the Genetic Health Courts, which subjected the people concerned to a degrading examination procedure, commonly operated with non-medical criteria of 'correct' behaviour which could be totally arbitrary. One verdict of such a court noted:[19]

> In addition, there is the appellant's behaviour, both in life in general and towards the legal system. He has twice been sentenced for larceny and once for aggravated larceny, and is at present in detention on strong suspicion of grand larceny. That his feeble-mindedness is inborn is proved by its having appeared in early youth (failure at school) and in virtue of the fact that there are no external circumstances that might have induced it.

The court passed a similar judgement in another case:

> Failure in the intellectual sphere is matched by complete failure in life, as well as by H.'s attitude towards the legal system.

In many cases there was an elision of criteria: conjectural mental illness, an unconventional and suspect life-style, and dissident, prohibited political opinions. Bruno T. from Wermelskirchen, who had been 'constantly attacking senior officials of the NSDAP in long written documents sent to the *Land* Administrator and other offices', was taken into 'protective custody' in 1936. The public health officer for the Rhine-Wupper *Kreis* cited 'psychiatric' reasons for the decision:[20]

> I examined T. in Wermelskirchen on 25.4.1936 and became convinced that he was mentally ill. Some years ago T. published a very muddled pamphlet discussing political and reformist ideas. During my examination his behaviour was quiet and orderly, but it revealed unmistakably pathological ideas of a megalomaniac nature. A characteristic example is what he said, quite seriously, at the close of the examination: 'It's strange: they all believe Hitler, but they don't believe me.' I inferred schizophrenia or progressive paralysis and advised the local police authorities to take T. in for observation in a closed institution as a mentally ill person who posed a danger to the community.

By 1945 a total of between 200,000 and 350,000 people had been sterilised.

With the outbreak of war, the National Socialists' ruthless pursuit of their programme of 'eradication' reached a new level, when Hitler issued a secret order, backdated to 1st September 1939, in accordance with which the allegedly incurable mentally ill were to be singled out and murdered. In an operation which was conducted by a group of initiates numbering only a few dozen – doctors and administrators of the so-called 'Public Ambulance Service Ltd.' (*Gemeinnützige Krankentransport GmbH*) – about 70,000 people were murdered up to August 1941. The operation was then shelved, after numerous protests, particularly from the churches. This episode, like many other cases in which institutional doctors or relatives took up the cause of mentally ill people in their care, shows not only that there was resistance to the Nazis' policy of 'eradication' but that such resistance could be successful. It contrasts all the more starkly with the silence in the countless cases when the measures for eliminating 'community-alien' groups within the population were accepted and even approved, provided that they were applied within a framework that was outwardly legal.

Majority public approval was certainly accorded to the terror which the National Socialists directed at another minority: homosexuals.[21] The Nazis' fundamental hostility to homosexuality should not be underrated on the grounds that some leading individual National Socialists were homosexuals. The infamous denunciation of the head of the SA, Ernst Röhm, in 1930 by, of all bodies, the Social Democratic press, which had banked on winning votes by its appeal to 'healthy popular feeling' – and, in so doing, besmirched its own liberal tradition – was taken up once again after the so-called 'Röhm putsch' of 1934 and used by the National Socialists in legitimation of their recourse to murder. The fascists' deadly hostility to homosexual 'deviations' from the norm had two sources. One was their dominant image of the 'strict' soldierly man, obliged to repel with brute force all temptations to 'soften' the identity and sexual role indoctrinated into him and seeing homosexuality as a target for his projected aggression. The other was their racialist programme, which had as its goal the strengthening of the 'healthy body of the nation' and which sought to 'eradicate' homosexuality because it deflected sexual energies that were needed in the 'battle for the birth-rate'. Accordingly, the liberalisation of homosexuals' lives and legal status which had begun under the Weimar Republic (the repeal of Paragraph 175 had been planned in the draft penal code of 1929, but was never implemented) was abruptly terminated in 1933. The homosexual sub-culture, its bars and clubs, were smashed, and in 1935 Paragraph 175, which made homosexual acts a prison offence, was considerably tightened up. Merely the indication of sexual interest, not even the consummated act, was made a punishable offence, and the way was thus made clear for denunciations and arbitrary police action.

In 1936–38 homosexuality was frequently the publicly cited ground for proceedings taken against former youth-movement leaders and against priests and clergy who were out of political favour. Concurrently, the increase in the numbers of 'asocials' being sent to concentration camps after 1937 included many homosexuals. In the camps they were left to stagnate at the bottom of the hierarchy, terrorised by the guards, victimised by the criminal prisoners and often enough despised by the political prisoners too. In 1943 a secret order by Himmler laid down the death penalty for all cases of homosexuality falling within the purview of the SS and the police.

No homosexuals obtained reparations after 1945, because Paragraph 175 was in formal terms 'lawful'; only a few even dared to make application, since the paragraph in its harsher form survived until 1969. Even those who had survived the Third Reich without being held in camps had undergone twelve years of profound damage to their lives and their identities.

This example shows that it is not enough to cite the numbers of ascertainable victims of National Socialist racialism. Besides the different groups that have been mentioned already, there were also the millions who only just escaped the net, who were 'merely' threatened with detention in a labour camp, who were 'merely' interrogated and cautioned by the Gestapo, or who were 'merely' oppressed, burdened and robbed of the freedom to articulate their needs by the sheer existence of an ever more elaborate and sophisticated system of discrimination.

Although the National Socialists' use of terror against 'community aliens' tended in practice to be somewhat unsystematic, so that huge, ambitious schemes might at first not be implemented, while far-reaching actual expansions of the concentration-camp state, causing thousands of deaths, could result from the decisions of a moment, the regime can nevertheless be seen overall to have possessed an inner dynamism making for ever greater radicalisation. The goal was a utopian *Volksgemeinschaft*, totally under police surveillance, in which any attempt at nonconformist behaviour, or even any hint or intention of such behaviour, would be visited with terror. This fundamental goal is also evident in a law projected by Himmler[22] which ultimately fell foul of internecine squabbles between the judiciary and the police but which nevertheless represented, at each of its many draft stages, a strategic summation of all the separate measures which the Nazis had hitherto implemented or planned. The two crucial paragraphs from the last draft of this 'Law for the Treatment of Community Aliens' of 1944 deserve quotation. (Later paragraphs of the draft dealt with co-operation between the judiciary and the welfare authorities, arrangements concerning sterilisation, the imposition of the death penalty etc.)

[. . .] Article I
Community Aliens (*Gemeinschaftsfremde*)
§1
'Community aliens' are such persons who:
1 show themselves, in their personality or in the conduct of their life, and especially in the light of any unusual deficiency of mind or character, unable to comply by their own efforts with the minimum requirements of the national community;
2(a) owing to work-shyness or slovenliness, lead a worthless, unthrifty or disorderly life and are thereby a burden or danger to the community;
or
display a habit of, or inclination towards, beggary or vagrancy, idling at work, larceny, swindling or other less serious offences, or engage in excessive drunkenness, or for any such reasons are in breach of the obligation to support themselves;
or
(b) through persistent ill-temper or quarrelsomeness disturb the peace of the community;
3 show themselves, in their personality or in the conduct of their life, mentally disposed towards the commission of serious offences (community-hostile criminals [*gemeinschaftsfeindliche Verbrecher*] and criminals by inclination [*Neigungsverbrecher*]).

Article II
Police Measures against Community Aliens
§2
1 Community aliens shall be subject to police supervision.
2 If supervisory measures are insufficient, the police shall transfer community aliens to the *Gau* (or *Land*) welfare authorities.
3 If, in the case of any community-alien persons, a stricter degree of custody is required than is possible within the institutions of the *Gau* (or *Land*) welfare authorities, the police shall place them in a police camp.

This projected law crystallised once again the National Socialists' design of abolishing the most basic principles of constitutionality: the principles that definitions of offences should be unambiguous; that conviction should be based on crimes committed, not on imputed 'inclinations'; that legal proceedings should be clear and subject to scrutiny. Instead, elastic terminology gave the police unlimited powers of discretion and degraded the judicial and welfare authorities into mere police tools. A penal code based on acts was transformed into one based on mentality; constitutionality had given way to a police state.

Superficially, the elastic terminology used to define 'community aliens' was directed against a limited group of drinkers, vagrants or work-shy people on whom a series of different projected laws and drafts for 'looking after' the incorrigibly delinquent had set their sights since 1920.[23] In practice, the criteria defining 'community aliens' could take in anyone who offended against the norms of everyday social behaviour. Himmler's proposed law would thus have been a perpetual latent threat to practically everyone. Draconian penalties against those whom the police singled out and termed outsiders served to reinforce all other 'national comrades' in their readiness to discipline themselves and fall into line.

Discriminatory, and ultimately racialist, approaches to noncon-formist social behaviour did not begin in 1933. From the turn of the century there had been a marked increase in theoretical schemes designed to bring about a sweeping 'scientific' improvement and reconstitution of the 'social body'.[24] Endemic infectious diseases like tuberculosis and cholera had been successfully dealt with by a combination of medical intervention, hygienic discipline, technological innovation and social isolation; in the same way, it was asserted, eugenic measures could be used to eradicate hereditary diseases. Furthermore, crime and anti-social behaviour could be curbed by a combination of environmental improvement, social reform, aid to individuals via welfare relief and education, while the biologically inferior 'residue' could be separated out and eliminated.

The belief that social problems could be finally and scientifically solved by a joint application of educational and social reforms and measures of racial hygiene and improvement of the hereditary stock was especially widely canvassed in the popular-scientific literature and was by no means restricted to extreme right-wing circles. The prominent biologist Ernst Haeckel, for example, whose popular-science bestseller *The Riddle of the Universe* was widely read in the labour movement (where it helped to shape the scientific *Weltanschauung* of a whole generation of Social Democrats), wrote in 1915, in *Eternity: Wartime Thoughts on Life and Death, Religion and Evolution*:[25]

> One single cultivated German warrior – and they are now falling in their masses – has a higher intellectual and moral life-value than hundreds of the raw primitives whom England and France, Russia and Italy are pitting against them.

The social Darwinism of the National Socialists, then, not only had roots in relatively offbeat nineteenth-century racial theories (Gobineau, Houston Stewart Chamberlain etc.), but could claim support from well-established academic schools of thought in psychology, medicine, criminology and social welfare. These scholarly disciplines were by no means 'fascist' in character, but they were receptive to arguments, modes of perception and schemes for action which entailed the separation of people into groups according to their social usefulness, defined in terms not only of environmental but of notionally hereditary factors. Wherever health, welfare or educational practitioners came up against limits to their work's effectiveness, academic theorists and practitioners alike were inclined to hold immutable hereditary factors responsible. The implication lay ready to hand: for the sake of future generations, these limits to social and medical intervention should be clearly drawn, and such intervention should be complemented by eugenic measures and selection from the genetic stock on the basis of social usefulness. This optimistic view, that scientific and industrial progress in principle removed the restrictions on the possible application of planning, education and social reform in everyday life, lost its last shreds of innocence when the National Socialists set about engineering their 'brave new world' with compulsory sterilisation, concentration camps and gas chambers.

We understate the racialism of the Third Reich if we limit our attention to the pornographic smears of *Der Stürmer*, the grotesque cranium measurements performed by the anthropologists, and the sadism of the myrmidons of the concentration camps. These phenomena are blatant enough. Surely more dangerous, because subtler and more intimately connected with everyday behaviour and discourse, was the ostensibly mild racialism which purported to be helpful and constructive yet which moved, almost apologetically and in passing, to advocating the eradication of those of 'inferior value'. The document which follows exemplifies the kind of almost unsensational racialism that was typical of academic publications of the period. It is reprinted here unabridged, so that the reader can see how a scientific discussion which is filled with sympathy and concern for people (or at least certain categories of people), which appeals to research findings and rational methods of formal argument, and which repeatedly invokes common sense and its audience's practical experience can nevertheless be imbued with the insanity of racialist thinking and the terrorism of the 'final solution'. The document is an address by the Stuttgart *Land* Youth Medical Officer Dr Eyrich, delivered to the Württemberg Conference of Welfare Institutions on 8th November 1938 (as chance had it, the eve of the *Reichskristallnacht*); it was originally published in the well-established *Zeitschrift für Kinderforschung*.[26] It is only one instance of a host of comparable scientific and popular publications.

Children and the Welfare Institutions: a Genetic Approach

It is appropriate that a medical speaker, addressing a conference on welfare institutions, should place at the centre of his discussion the people who are brought up in these institutions. Young people in institutions have proved to be the most stable element within the shifting patterns of institutional life in recent years. Regulations and procedures within institutions can be changed; the people who inhabit them are the work of nature.

The reputation of these inmates is not a good one. People are thankful if they need have nothing to do with them. The old notion of a corrective education is still a widespread one. The common conception is of those cases where the only remedy is strict severity appearing in the guise of welfare education [*Fürsorgeerziehung*]. Even today such instances are far from extinct: after painting a youngster's misdeeds in the blackest colours, a court will decide that education in a welfare institution is the only answer. – Such confidence in the limitless capabilities of welfare education does us honour. But we should prefer to dispense with the honour and point out that such cases are being referred to us too late in the day. We very much hope that they will not come to us in this way in the future.

When people speak of institutional education, they are thinking of children who have been trouble-makers at school. But in addition to them we find quite different kinds of young people within institutions: the deaf and hard of hearing, the blind and weak-sighted, crippled children, the feeble-minded, children with retarded and inhibited physical and mental development. They cannot be educated in normal schools, and because of their infirmity they need special schooling and training in order to be able to lead at least partially useful and productive lives.

Such cases shall not be the primary topic of this discussion, nor shall the particular medical tasks which arise from the special nature of institutional upbringing or which affect delinquent children in institutional care. These tasks are difficult to solve, while also being of considerable significance for public health. (It can, incidentally, be mentioned in this context that the introduction in Württemberg three years ago of thorough clinical examinations of all delinquent girls who have left school has immediately raised the number of young girls known to be infected with venereal diseases to three times the previous figure. This indicates the enormous scale of the infectious contacts involved.)

The underlying concept common to all welfare education is that of neglect [*Verwahrlosung*]*. Those subject to the risk of, or to actual, neglect are taken into educational care. The law assumes that neglect is an occurrence which affects the young person from outside, through the negligence of those responsible for his upbringing or through some other inadequacy in his education. The upbringing required by the courts in such cases is a substitute

---

*[The word *Verwahrlosung* also refers by extension to the effects of neglect, thereby taking on rather different connotations. In these cases it has been translated as 'delinquency'. (Transl.)]

upbringing. It is based, correctly, on the assumption that the deficiencies of upbringing that have been established must first be rectified and eliminated. And in every case which is brought promptly enough to our attention, we are able to eliminate that element in the young person's faulty social development which is due to neglect. But it is well known that the elimination of neglect and the transfer of a young person into properly regulated education is in many cases not enough. Not even the best educator is spared the frequent experience of seeing that his goal of returning a fully useful national comrade to the national community simply cannot be attained, and that he has come up against limits to his efforts which plainly have been set by nature: limits of disposition and heredity. He is also forced to recognise that these boundaries are much more tightly drawn with these young people than they are with others, whose physical and mental adaptiveness and hereditary scope offer him far wider opportunities. Lofty plans are therefore out of place as far as the upbringing of young delinquents is concerned. It is often only after the effects of neglect have been dealt with that the young person's true nature emerges, about which education can do nothing.

It is well known that our ideas concerning the significance of heredity in human mental and social development have been enormously extended and deepened during the past ten to fifteen years. It is now known for certain that forces rooted in the genetic make-up give outward shape to the essential internal features of the life of each individual, be it the life of a genius or a criminal. Nearly ten years ago the psychiatrist Johannes Lange, who has recently died so young, published a book whose title expresses this new understanding. It is called *Crime as Destiny* [*Verbrechen als Schicksal*] (Leipzig, 1928). We can say now that it is a classic; it is a milestone in the development of the human sciences. The book is not a weighty scientific tome. It describes in masterly fashion the life-histories of pairs of criminal identical twins. The impression left by this work is utterly compelling. Presented here before our eyes are the careers of genetically identical people. Their lives differ in many respects, but in essentials they are staggeringly uniform. The separate pairs of twins show many differences as regards externals, but in each case they are a pair of violent criminals, or of confidence tricksters, or of prostitutes, or of homosexuals, or whatever. The effect of a book of this sort is stimulating and exciting. Since it was written, the number of pairs of criminal identical twins known to us has increased considerably. Lange's findings have not been challenged in any essentials.

What sorts of cases do we find in educational institutions? The external manifestations of delinquency are uniform. It starts with truancy, loitering and dissolute behaviour, and generally the police are soon involved. With girls, three-quarters of delinquency cases involve sexual depravity. But anyone looking deeper will see that this uniformity is superficial and that there can be very different underlying roots. The task, therefore, is to separate these apparently similar phenomena into groups that are intrinsically different. It is a difficult and awkward task in many respects, but today it is, in fundamentals and in practical terms, soluble. This

225

assertion is not refuted by the fact that we still encounter individual cases which at the outset cannot be assessed for certain. Medical diagnosis faces similar difficulties in other spheres.

Viewing large numbers of institutionalised pupils, one cannot but be struck by the fact that in many instances a disturbance within the family unit is the original factor in delinquency. That is to say, we find illegitimate children, semi-orphans, full orphans, an astonishing number of step-children, and a host of children of divorced parents or of marriages that have broken down in other ways. These are external circumstances which have led to a form of defective development which takes the form of delinquency. It is not necessary in the first instance to attribute the delinquency to faults on the children's part or to genealogical inferiority.

In addition to these groups, we find those young people who have committed minor criminal offences, among which a large proportion of the sexual offences must also be reckoned. From the perspective of a lifetime such episodes are insignificant, provided that inappropriate treatment does not endow them with a significance that will dog the youngsters for ever. These, then, are typical offences of puberty, sometimes more a sign of youthful thoughtlessness or of overbrimming and above-average vitality than of criminal mentality.

From time to time – on the whole, infrequently – we also encounter young people in welfare educational institutions whose difficulties are the first warning signs, or indeed the first clear symptoms, of approaching mental illness. Under this heading fall cases of incipient dementia praecox and manic-depressive dementia, diseases of the central nervous system caused by syphilis acquired while in the womb, the onset of epilepsy, brain diseases caused by encephalitis, and so forth.

According to a survey by the Reich Ministry of Justice, in the year 1937 in Germany a total of 3,258 men and women were being held in preventive detention as dangerous habitual offenders. Of these, the following had committed punishable offences:

before completing their 18th year	1,356 =	41.6 per cent
between 18 and 21	1,020 =	31 per cent

i.e. 72.6 per cent had committed offences before the age of 21. There can be no doubt that a considerable proportion of this 72.6 per cent will have undergone education by the welfare authorities and, having left school, will have come back before the courts unreformed. It is to these elements, above all, that welfare education owes its public reputation – and unjustly so. For those former pupils who win through in later life have no reason – thanks to this very reputation – for drawing special attention to the fact that they too are 'former pupils of welfare institutions'. If we were to examine other groups of asocials in a comparable way, e.g. vagabonds or prostitutes, we should undoubtedly find similar patterns. Yet we must recognise, at all events, that as far as a certain proportion of our children and young people in welfare education are concerned, the phenomenon of delinquency needs to be interpreted in a quite different way from that appropriate to cases of damage done by conditions in the social environment and from cases of youth crime. The former phenomenon indicates the start of a purposive and unalterable tendency towards criminality or pernicious anti-social behaviour. We also know that the vast majority of cases here are born criminals or asocials by hereditary disposition. We cannot say at present how large a share this group represents within the total number of pupils in welfare education, but what is certain is that this share is a very small one within the overall total and that it would be quite unjustified, on the basis of what we know of this group, to lump all institutional pupils together with born criminals. The latter are the group with lowest genetic value among our institutional population. Their mental make-up has been studied in detail quite recently (Stumpfl, *Ursprünge des Verbrechens* [Origins of Crime], Leipzig, 1936). In many instances we are fully able to pick out, even in their early years, future incorrigible criminals and candidates for preventive detention; and it is our duty to translate this knowledge into action.

It is noticeable how many of the ineducable pupils among those in welfare institutions belong to the 'travelling' people. This observation brings up a problem which is as important as it is unfamiliar, both to practitioners within institutional education and to the NSV [National Socialist Public Welfare]. We must therefore give a brief account of it here. For most of us, the 'travelling' people, the 'wayfarers' [*Vaganten*], the '*Vagi*' or the '*Jenischen*' are figures of romantic description, figures who have found frequent expression in stories, songs and in the theatre. In reality, the romantic nature of this life is highly debatable. The problem is one of demographic biology and of sociology. In the society of the middle ages, those who were not 'honest folk' – that is, the rabble, 'rogues', '*Gauner*' or '*Jauner*' – were a familiar phenomenon. Such people, forming a strand of the population clearly marked off from society in the proper sense, survive all the way through from the middle ages to the modern era, when they gradually, owing to the dominance of ideas of human equality, disappear from popular consciousness though not from biological fact. They themselves are well aware of their own distinctiveness, and even speak their own language, the '*jenisch*' argot. Attempts to demarcate the '*Jenischen*' on a racial or national [*völkisch*] basis have not so far been successful, nor do they seem likely to be. The origins of the 'rabble' can therefore only be a matter of conjecture. What unifies them is their way of life, language and social inferiority – the latter, perhaps, the result of centuries of cultivation of inferior stock in the sense of socially negative characteristics and of the inbreeding resultant upon their situation. Individual members of the 'honest' community may also have been added to their numbers, after forfeiting their respectability by committing some misdemeanour. The wayfarers lived, and still live, by trading and peddling – which can easily cross the dividing line into begging and swindling – and they engage as individuals and in bands in theft, mountebankery, fortune-telling and all sorts of other 'dishonest' activities. The unsettled existence and the urge to move on are in their blood. They have a dread of settled work. So it was always, and so it remains today.

In all ages the travelling people have been regarded as a nuisance, and each age has tried to combat the nuisance in its own way: through ruthless legal measures or strict segregation, or by attempting to incorporate the people into the national community through settlement. Others dealt with the phenomenon by simply accepting the wayfarers – as even the weeds in a garden are the work of God.

No less than the monasteries and feudal overlords, wayfarers form part of the characteristic picture of the middle ages, and continue thus into the nineteenth century. The significance they retained in Upper Swabia, for example, split as it was into the tiniest sovereign domains, is vividly depicted in the memoirs of the Biberach painter J. B. Pflug (ed. M. Gester, Ulm, Höhnverlag, 1937), to whom we also owe excellent pictorial representations of groups of rogues.

Today only a proportion of the wayfarers are genuine travellers. Many – especially in the eighteenth century – became settled. In Württemberg, and no doubt elsewhere in the Reich, we have a number of compact settlements of so-called 'free folk'. In other places they became immigrants into existing local communities. In their closed communities they have remained astonishingly pure amidst the adjoining peasantry. Farming does not suit them, and the farmers reject them. Even today they live by trading and often by begging. Their social value is in inverse relation to their fertility. Many amongst their excess numbers are forced to migrate – and we encounter them again in the shanty settlements on the outskirts of the industrial cities, where they augment the lowest ranks of the protelariat.

It is a noteworthy fact that the entire travelling population, and the inhabitants of the wayfarers' colonies, are Catholic, and that in our Catholic educational institutions the children of these wayfarers and from the wayfarers' villages account for a sizeable and scarcely gratifying proportion of the numbers. We intend no criticism here of our national comrades of the Catholic faith. The facts are offered merely for their genetic significance.

Ritter (cf. *Ein Menschenschlag* [A Breed of Men], Leipzig, Thieme, 1936), after conducting exhaustive investigations of Swabian travellers' kinship groups, has been able to trace the direct descent of an asocial genealogical group settled in Tübingen for several generations from such 'rogues' from the late middle ages. We should repeatedly stress that such cases are not rarities. Anyone who keeps his eyes open can observe them everywhere, and in all such cases comparable research would yield genealogical proof. For some years, under commission from the Reich Public Health Office, Ritter has been working on a full genetic survey of all the German travellers' kinship groups, and the highest practical importance has been attached to this work.

Ritter has introduced the term 'disguised feeble-mindedness' to characterise the asocial descendants of the rogues he has investigated. He thus includes them among the congenitally feeble-minded, which in my view is to stretch the concept of congenital feeble-mindedness too far. I believe it makes for greater conceptual clarity to call '*Vaganten*' by their right name, i.e. 'wayfarers', and not to over-burden even further the concept of feeble-mindedness, which is already put so such varied use. Not a few wayfarers, in addition to being wayfarers, are also feeble-minded; the great majority of them, however, are not. This is also the view reflected in the sentencing practice of the Genetic Health Courts.

I pass on now to the question of congenital feeble-mindedness in welfare education. The severest instances of congenital feeble-mindedness are placed in the idiot asylums. Their mental capacities are such that welfare education is out of the question. It must be pointed out, as far as these severest cases of feeble-mindedness are concerned, that a not inconsiderable proportion of them (one-third, say) are not hereditary. We must therefore be wary of concluding, on the basis of the incidence of individual instances of feeble-mindedness in a family, that the genealogical group is genetically inferior as a whole. Each individual case here calls for careful and expert examination. Indeed, one specific form of severe congenital feeble-mindedness, mongoloid idiocy, often and typically occurs at the conclusion of a long sequence of otherwise normal children.

In welfare education, on the other hand, there are considerable numbers of cases of the mild and moderate forms of congenital feeble-mindedness, and here the proportion of hereditary cases increases markedly and directly with their mildness, i.e. as we approach the border line with normality. The educable feeble-minded pose special requirements as far as therapeutic pedagogy is concerned. They are therefore placed together in special schools and schools for the feeble-minded, and in this way, to a very respectable degree, they are at least made useful and productive enough to be able to work efficiently and earn their own living. The present shortage of agricultural labour makes it a matter of pressing urgency, within the framework of the Four-Year Plan, that their modest abilities too should be available on the labour market and that, if at all possible, they should not be kept in asylums. As regards the schooling of these categories of feeble-minded, which is conducted in exemplary fashion in the various institutions in Württemberg, the aim is not to burden these children with quantities of book-learning. Rather, they are taught discipline and self-discipline, moderation and the independent performance of such work tasks as are suited to their abilities. By virtue of this approach they are thus also able to assume a modest place within the national community. Proof that this method of education for the feeble-minded is the correct one is given by the readiness of the agricultural labour market to employ them. Many more jobs are available for the educated feeble-minded than there are people to fill them. In the past, of course, departure from the institution also created the possibility of pointless and unregulated further reproduction. It goes without saying that no feeble-minded person leaves an institution today unless sterilisation has been undertaken. Bringing together the deficient feeble-minded in special homes and schools hence also provides a practical way of meeting the provisions of the Genetic Health Laws.

Even after that proportion of institutionalised youth which is severely mentally handicapped has been filtered out, it remains the case that a large number of the remainder must be termed low in aptitude and stunted in character, even though we are not in a position to draw sharp boundaries between them and the average. No feature, however, is so characteristic of the mental make-up of institutionalised youth as their lack of intellectual aspirations and interests.

It remains to mention a relatively small number of defectively developed, psychopathic youths, often straying 'problem children' from the higher social classes. That, in essentials, completes our survey of the categories of those who, in terms both of genetics and of social prospects, represent the most critical and most markedly inferior cases. We should point out that the hereditary groups displaying the major mental illnesses, dementia praecox and cyclic insanity, are virtually absent from this list. These kinship groups, with which the well-known studies of Kretschmer have now made us more closely acquainted, show little tendency to delinquency. The groups displaying hereditary epilepsy loom somewhat larger, and of congenital feeble-mindedness larger again.

We can now turn to the larger number of children in institutions whose hereditary make-up and social prospects are to be adjudged quite differently. These have already been listed. They are children and young people whose disruptive behaviour in school and manifestations of delinquency are reactions to disturbances within the family unit: illegitimate children, orphans and semi-orphans, children of divorced parents or broken marriages, stepchildren. We have also mentioned youth crime in this connection. We should not ignore the fact that the ability to sustain a marriage, for example, also has its hereditary side and can indicate flaws in the structure of the personality which again in turn point to hereditary factors. In the first instance, however, we must proceed on the assumption that the damage transmitted to children's development and education by a broken marriage is an environmental factor. We must not ignore the point, either, that the hereditary quality of illegitimate children is very much lower than that of legitimate children and that we sometimes find among the former the most severe instances of hereditary degeneracy. This in no sense alters the fact that in the great majority of cases illegitimate birth is not a blemish and has nothing, as such, to do with genetic inferiority.

I should also like to say a few words about the defective development of stepchildren, which is very common and shows typical features. It is almost always a misfortune when a child loses one of its parents. Adaptation to a new father, but especially to a new mother, is not easy, particularly when the child has superior endowments of temperament and character. Certainly, many such relationships are completely successful. But frictions and complications can easily arise and can lead inescapably to tragedy. Many of these children then simply suffer a warping of their emotional development which can affect them for the rest of their lives. Those of a more active temperament go into opposition, often in alliance with incomprehending grandparents, aunts and neighbours, and make their step-parents' lives difficult in grotesque ways, the stepmother's in particular. Without a doubt the 'wicked stepmother', pure and simple, also exists; but that is a decidedly rarer occurrence than these specific cases of defective development on the part of stepchildren.

These children find their way into the educational institutions along with children of broken marriages whose characters have become calculating and untruthful out of the necessity of swinging back and forth between their feuding parents. We also find children where all that is involved is the economic fact that both parents need to be in employment. If such children are left to their own devices after school, day after day, and attach themselves to unsuitable or unruly friends, then unwholesome consequences can by no means be ruled out. A child must be unusually dull and lifeless if it does not get up to mischief under these circumstances. We certainly hope that the NSV, HJ and BDM will succeed in their efforts to cause such cases to disappear in future. For the present these children are in our educational institutions and foster homes and are our responsibility.

This kaleidoscopic array of children and young people of every kind is to be found indiscriminately jumbled together in our institutions at the present day, and there are even teachers in these institutions who would make a virtue of necessity and espouse the surprising view that it is possible to mould these highly disparate elements into one institutional family. These so-called 'institutional practitioners' are also wont to say that this comprehensive form of education will cause the lower elements to be pulled up by the better elements. Our response to that is to cite the simple fact that one rotten apple can infect all the sound ones around it. Cases of the inverse relationship are not known. Until any such are found, we shall assume that the same applies to children in institutions.

The way forward for institutional education is thus clear. A decree by the Württemberg Minister of the Interior which is shortly to come into force will reorganise education in welfare homes so as to bring our findings into practical effect.

We shall first seek to gain a clear picture of pupils' physical and mental condition and disposition, using all methods and evidence from present-day psychiatry, theories of character, and pedagogy. Reception homes with requisite facilities will be charged with this task, and institutions and pupils will then be grouped so that compatible and intrinsically related cases are dealt with together. We shall therefore remove certain cases from the 'blanket' system that institutional education in Württemberg still to some extent represents, viz.:

1. Children of normal hereditary disposition who are not delinquent.
2. The severely handicapped and feeble-minded, as well as those severely psychopathic cases which cannot be dealt with by the standard practices of institutional education.
3. Gypsies and other gypsy-like elements.

Special treatment for the feeble-minded and mentally defective has already been attempted and has been partially successful. In future it will become the rule. The provision of the Reich Compulsory Education Law of 6th July 1938 which establishes obligatory special schooling and schooling for backward children comes in very usefully as far as this goal is concerned.

Naturally, we shall not be content merely with an initial examination and shall keep pupils' further development under review. The welfare education system has in its charge a significant proportion of those German young people who are socially at risk, and it has them at a vital age. It has to decide on likely outcomes, but at this age a great number of these young people are still malleable enough not to be lost to the community.

We infer from this fact the clear obligation to neglect nothing that brings us closer to this goal.

Welfare education, however, as befits its dual character, also serves as a genetic filter of these young people. It is likely to collect a good-sized share of the dregs of the youth population, and it is therefore under an obligation to filter out those elements whose behaviour is unacceptable to the community and who are genetically unbeneficial for future generations. The laws are there to enable us to put our knowledge into practice. We should be guilty of irreparable disservice to our nation's future if we were to neglect to apply these laws with care, as and where appropriate. On this point, the files of the youth offices and welfare authorities and, especially the observational material gathered by the educational institutions are of particular importance. Training of teaching staff and careful record-keeping are therefore more pressing obligations then ever. It is not only the terms of the Law for the Prevention of Progeny of the Genetically Unhealthy that are involved here. As is known, the application of this law calls for very considerable restraint and careful checking of criteria. The law also deals only with the absolutely clear and extreme cases of disease. Furthermore, within our genetic legislation the Law for the Prevention of Progeny of the Genetically Unhealthy represents only the final stage of an extensive system of measures ranging from the long-term promotion of high-value groups to sterilisation. There is one particularly important law in this system, the Marital Health Law of 18th October 1935, §1 Para. 1(c) of which forbids marriage, among other circumstances, 'if one of the betrothed is suffering from a mental disorder which renders the marriage detrimental to the national community'. Whereas application of the Law for the Prevention of Progeny of the Genetically Unhealthy requires proof of the presence of one of the nine hereditary diseases, the Marital Health Law employs the immeasurably wider concept of mental disorder. It makes it possible for the great unwelcome host of psychopaths and criminals to be excluded at least from contracting marriages – and thus to a large extent from reproduction as well.

The implementation of these laws is the task of the State Public Health Offices. They are entitled to expect to be kept closely informed about the results of institutional education. The aim must therefore be to provide, upon completion of what may be several years of welfare education, a summary and final assessment of individual cases. In most instances, after several years of welfare education, it is possible to make a precise judgement as to likely outcomes, or at the least to say if prognosis is uncertain. The Health Office must be briefed with regard to these assessments.

In those cases, happily not many, where we are forced to conclude that welfare education will not succeed in its aims and that the pupil will not become an acceptable member of the community, administrative and legislative procedures remain to be devised for coming to terms with the current unsatisfactory situation. Today, when such persons come to the end of their compulsory welfare education, they commonly have to be set free, against our better judgement, despite the fact that liberty is quite unsuitable for them, and despite the clear prospect that they will cause nothing but harm and mischief before being rapidly entangled once again in some other part of the legal network. There is therefore a need for a clear legal basis for transferring people who are incapable of life in the community directly from welfare education into custody. (Cf. Villinger, this vol., above, pp. 1–20.)

The reorganisation of institutional education along these lines is necessary in two senses. In a negative sense, it is desirable that it fulfil what the state is entitled to expect of it; in a positive sense, it must cast off its hybrid character as an agency of poor relief and the police, on the one hand, and an institution of therapeutic pedagogy on the other. It will then become the institution to which every national comrade will as confidently entrust his problem child as we entrust ourselves to the sure care of hospitals and German doctors in times of illness.

This address by Eyrich makes it plain that the National Socialists' project of social selection founded on genetic criteria attributed 'scientifically' to individuals rested on a quite lengthy tradition of psychological and anthropological research. This was the basis of its claim to 'scientific' validity. Certainly, only those who knew how fragmentary are the records of social and family history could see through the impressive historiographical 'proofs' of the genetic determination of 'rogue' kinship groups and point up their arbitrariness and baseless methodology. And by no means all psychologists had a true enough grasp of the limitations of scholarly enquiry to be able to show up the charlatanry of the apparent empirical correlation of data on social behaviour with genotypic assertions.[27] Racialism, however, did not present itself in scientific garb alone; it was also a reflection of welfare workers' everyday experience and problems, to which a racialist solution seemed to be the obvious one. It took the form of concern: concern for the reputation and success of welfare work and for the administration of justice. And it was for the sake of this reputation and success that the racialist scheme proposed the segregation of everyone who put them at risk. In order that the scheme should not be exposed as a betrayal of social welfare and as social and moral bankruptcy – as it would be if the 'incurable' character of those deemed 'inferior' were admitted to be due to environmental factors – it was essential to maintain that nonconformist behaviour had a genetic cause. Only in this way could the segregation of 'successful' and 'unsuccessful' welfare cases be legitimised. This, however, then completed the circle: the 'inferior' were irrefutably circumscribed within the circle, and the pedagogic theorists and welfare authorities could balance their casebooks.

This basic conviction, that pernicious genetic dispositions must exist, because only they could satisfactorily explain the all-too-common failures of social-welfare practices, finally carried racialist biology into the realms of chiliastic fantasy. The application of meticulous scientific research closely backed up by state power would make possible a eugenic process of selection and elimination whereby poverty, misery, illness and crime would finally be abolished. 'All' that was needed was to realise the dream of total scientific knowledge: to wrap human beings (and their ancestors, no less) in an information network which would yield exact forecasts of every individual's future social behaviour. This in turn called for the total state, which would carry out the scientifically planned programme of sorting people according to their genetically determined social value. This racialist utopia broke down for two reasons: it spawned Kafkaesque bureaucratic processes for gathering the racial-biological data and making the racial policy decisions;[28] and it led to the institutionalisation, hitherto unimaginable, of industrialised, multi-millionfold murder, where the nuances of individual cases shrank into statistical 'insignificance' in the face of sheer numbers.

Racial discrimination in the Third Reich has a prehistory; it also has an aftermath. It would be absurd to postulate any sort of unbroken continuity, but, with our senses sharpened by the study of National Socialism, we are forced to pay closer attention to events in contemporary everyday public life that cause disquiet. We must be concerned when Jews are defamed in the GDR and Poland in the name of 'anti-Zionism'; when political dissidents in the Soviet Union are locked up as 'mentally ill'; when intelligence tests in the USA purport to prove the intellectual inferiority of blacks; when a group of well-known professors in the Federal Republic bemoans, in its 'Heidelberg Manifesto',[29] the 'infiltration of the German people by the influx of many millions of foreigners and their families, and the spread of foreign influences into our language, our culture and our national traditions'; or when the Chief Medical Officer in the Braunschweig District, Dr Kahnt, writes about people without settled residence:[30]

> Public health officers and practitioners in industrial medicine have considerable experience of dealing with these people. They know that there are research findings which show beyond dispute that there is gypsy blood in their ancestry. All attempts at socialisation break down for this reason.

And it is precisely because National Socialist racialism was in no sense a sudden, inexplicable irruption of 'medieval barbarism' into a progressive society, but owed its seductive power to the pathologies of 'progress' itself, that vigilance is still required when a fast-food restaurant in the German industrial town of Wattenscheid can put up a sign which says:[31]

> Turks and Arabs are not permitted to stay longer than 20 minutes in the restaurant.

THIRTEEN

The atomisation of everyday life

Many Germans who supported the Nazi regime, or at least accepted it, believed the 'Führer' when he promised that he would deliver them from the 'abnormal' conditions which had been brought about by the upheavals of modernisation and the hardships of the depression. Their vision was hardly the *perpetuum mobile* of a utopian *Volksgemeinschaft* bent on struggle – the stuff of the leading National Socialists' vague dreams. They were looking for a return to normality,[1] to regular work, to secure planning of their lives and certainty about their own place within the social scheme. Much of this seemed, in the second half of the 1930s, to have come about or to be well on the way to coming about. In face of this long-lost sense of private well-being, various other warning signs were thrust to one side, virtually excluded from everyday awareness: the fact that employment was serving the cause of war-readiness, that terror against 'community aliens' was continuing, and that the regime's goals and measures were being increasingly radicalised, not scaled down. People 'didn't talk about' these things. But they dreamed about them at night. Their dreams betrayed the oppressive presence of anxieties which were all too willingly denied in the light of day.[2]

An employer, a committed Social Democrat who ran his firm on highly patrariachal lines, dreamed only three days after Hitler's seizure of power about his own future powerlessness, the compulsion to conform and the destruction of personal relationships:

> Goebbels comes into my factory. He has the staff line up in two rows, on the left and the right. I have to stand between them and raise my arm in the Hitler salute. It takes me half an hour to bring my arm up, a millimetre at a time. Goebbels watches my exertions like a spectator at a play, without signalling either applause or displeasure. But when I have eventually got my arm up, he says five words: 'I don't want your salute.' He turns and goes to the door. So I am left standing in my own factory, between my own people, in the pillory, my arm raised. The only way I am physically able to do it is by

keeping my eyes riveted on his club-foot as he limps out. I keep on standing like this until I wake up.

A 45-year-old doctor dreamed in 1934 about the bureaucratised abolition of private life:

After my surgery, getting on for nine in the evening, I want to stretch out peacefully on the sofa with a book about Matthias Grünwald. But the walls of my room, of my whole flat, suddenly vanish. I look round in horror: all the flats, as far as the eye can see, have lost their walls. I hear the roar of a loudspeaker: 'As per decree abolishing all walls, 17th instant.'

There was not only the sense of the private sphere being exposed to Nazi penetration; the individual's own psychological make-up and personal identity were affected. People who did not wish to be 'co-ordinated' and who wanted at least to continue to think and feel, if not to act, against the current, could sense how they had to harden their inner selves: almost to hide from themselves. This too was articulated in dreams:

I'm going to turn into lead. Tongue already leaden, sealed with lead. Fear will go away if I'm solid lead. Lie motionless, shot into lead. If they come, I'll say, 'Lead people can't stand up.' Oh, no: they want to throw me into the water because I've turned to lead. [. . .]

An SA man is standing in front of the big old-fashioned blue tiled stove in the corner of our living-room, where we always sit and talk in the evenings. He opens the stove door, and the stove begins to speak in a snarling, penetrating voice [note once more the allusion to the shrill loudspeakers of daytime]: it repeats every sentence we have spoken against the government, every joke we have made. O God, I think: now what's going to happen? What about all my little comments on Goebbels? But at the same time I see clearly that one sentence more or less is immaterial, because absolutely everything we have ever said within these four walls is already known. Yet I also realise that I have always pooh-poohed the idea of built-in microphones, and I still don't in fact believe it. Even as the SA man ties a strap round my wrist to take me away – he uses our dog's lead – I think he's doing it in fun. I even say out loud: 'This isn't serious, surely; it can't be.'

I dream that I am speaking Russian, as a precaution. (I can't in fact speak Russian, and I never talk in my sleep.) I am doing it so that I can't understand myself and so that no one can understand me, in case I say anything about the state – because that, of course, is forbidden and has to be reported.

When the national organisational director of the National Socialists, Robert Ley, declared:

The only people who still have a private life in Germany are those who are asleep.

one young man in 1933 already knew in his dreams that this was not true – that an unviolated private life was no longer possible and that the non-political idyll which the majority of Germans tried to live out in the thirties could not bury the knowledge of horror:

> I am dreaming that all I am dreaming about is rectangles, triangles and octagons, which somehow all look like Christmas biscuits, because dreaming is of course forbidden.

The anxiety-dreams of Germans living under the Third Reich show that the retreat from National Socialist pressures into private life and familiar social circles had its price. Tensions and fears could not simply be left outside the front door. Certainly, an undisrupted family life, or the sort of well-established social solidarity that continued to exist in many workers' housing estates, in Catholic circles and quite often in the countryside, did offer a refuge from the demands of National Socialism. These communities could even give rise to the formation of a kind of 'alternative public life' that subsisted below the threshold of Gestapo intervention. But only a minority of Germans lived in such socio-ecological networks, and these networks themselves were not as unaffected as may appear to have been the case.

Retreat into the private sphere and refusal to yield up anything more than the minimum necessary participation in the public stage-management of *Volksgemeinschaft* still entailed, at the least, passive acceptance of the prevailing order. In addition, these social milieux could escape the arm of the Gestapo only if explicit political activity was utterly discontinued. They were in any case no longer the same milieux they had been before 1933, even if the people who composed them were the same and their non-political everyday modes of communication had not altered. A clear indicator of this change is the quantity of denunciations of political misdemeanours that came in to the Gestapo from the general public.[3] An analysis of surviving documents of the Düsseldorf Gestapo dealing with people prosecuted for political reasons (in the widest sense)[4] shows that at least one in every four cases handled by the Gestapo was initiated by denunciatory reports from the general public. The Gestapo and the Special Courts had to deal with a flood of reports directed against neighbours, drinking companions, chance acquaintances met on train journeys, and relatives. The thinly-veiled purpose of many of these denunciations was to invoke the aid of the Gestapo in settling a private grudge. Among the Düsseldorf Gestapo case-files mentioned, 24 per cent of the denunciations can be regarded as having been motivated by loyalty to the system; 37 per cent as serving to resolve private disputes. Of the latter group, three-quarters were concerned with domestic disputes, family rows, quarrels in the workplace, business competition and other economic matters.

Many of the situations in which 'malicious' utterances were made were notable for their very familiarity, openness and ordinariness. The regime's demands for loyalty, the power of its agencies of surveillance and the co-operation of its informers were ever-present facts: on the fringes of the surviving social milieux and the private family circle, and even within them.

Control over everyday social behaviour resulted not only from the potential presence of informers in the individual's immediate surroundings, but also from the loyalty reporting operated by the Party organisations, the so-called 'Political Assessments' recorded in the course of day-to-day matters such as the granting of loans, decisions on promotion and contacts with public officials.[5] A person's style of greeting, the size of his donations to the incessant collections (and the degree of willingness that accompanied them), a style of life in conformity with the petty-bourgeois norms and morals of the Party's functionaries, and the behaviour of one's children – all served as indices of political reliability and were observed by a whole army of lower-grade Party dignitaries, from the *Blockwart* (block warden) to the air-raid warden and NSV collector. It goes without saying that this activity generated little genuine loyalty but, rather, a style of behaviour in public and semi-public places in which the acceptability or otherwise of spoken opinions was constantly kept in mind. Such behavour was inevitably marked by loss of spontaneity, calculation and conformity, and loss of intimacy with, and concern for, others.

The need for self-control, for caution vis-à-vis one's surroundings and for a calculated weighting of simulated loyalty and sincere aversion remained so strong that even in the ultimate refuges of private life a truly autonomous realm, in which one could still be oneself, was not achievable. 'I didn't trust my own backside any more,' was how a Bremen worker summed it up. Could you still be yourself, if you could so little trust yourself? If you conformed and joined in the parade, you became merely one interchangeable figure in the mass decor of the Reich Party rallies; if you held back, all basic everyday relationships still lost their intimate, accustomed character and had to become matters of calculation if they were to survive at all. Either way, the end result was still an individual stripped of social relationships, fighting for himself alone, 'scraping by'.

The 'fellow-traveller' and the non-participant, then, were equally threatened by the atomisation of everyday life, the dissolution of social bonds, the isolation of modes of perception, the shrinking of prospects and hence the loss of the capacity for social action. The draining experience of wartime life, with its daily descents into the air-raid shelter, aggravated these tendencies even further. By the end of the war the German population, apathetic, exhausted by the arduous performances of daily routine, bereft of all ability to act, could look ahead only to one thing: for it all 'somehow' to be over.

It may seem paradoxical that the atomisation created by the National Socialist brand of mass mobilisation and the attempt to sustain resistance within everyday life should both have had the same effect of withdrawal into privacy. This is not, however, mere theorising after the event: the process was early noted by alert observers at the time. An extract from the SOPADE 'Reports on Germany' for November 1935 is a case in point:[6]

> The purpose of all the National Socialist organisations is the same. Whether we are talking of the Labour Front or Strength through Joy, the Hitler Youth or Labour Service, in each case the organisation's purpose is the same: to 'include' or 'look after' the 'national comrades', to make sure that they are not left to their own devices and, as far as possible, to see that they do not come to their senses at all. Just as empty restless activity prevents a person from doing any serious work, so the National Socialists are forever providing excesses of excitement with the express aim of preventing any real communal interests or any form of voluntary association from arising. Ley recently said as much quite openly: 'national comrades' were not to have a private life, and they should certainly give up their private skittles club. The aim of this organisational monopoly is to rob the ordinary man of all independence, to suffocate whatever initiatives he might take to create even the most primitive forms of voluntary association, to keep him at a distance from anyone who is like-minded or merely sympathetic, to isolate him and at the same time to bind him to the state organisation. The effects are inevitable. Occasionally one can hear working men or women express their appreciation of Strength through Joy, and comment: 'Nobody ever bothered about us before.' Sure enough, the state did not previously regard it as its job to send rotas of working men and women off to the theatre in their 'free time'. Previously, it was a point of pride for the workers to 'bother' about such things for themselves. But many people will prefer the state-run forms of pleasure and 'relaxation' because they are less trouble. If that is the way things are, then clearly it cannot be just a side-issue for us to show the workers that one or another particular achievement has come about because they stood firm, 'shoulder to shoulder': this task becomes a central feature of illegal active work.
>
> The essence of fascist control of the masses is compulsory organisation on the one hand and atomisation on the other.

During the war, in November 1942, the Communist resistance newspaper, *Der Friedenskämpfer* [The Peace Fighter], distributed in Berlin and in the Ruhr district, likewise traced the absence of a German resistance to the fragmentation of social relations, modes of perception and forms of behaviour:[7]

> Why have the people not yet been able to give stronger voice to their hatred of the war and against the war-guilt of the Hitler gang? Why can Hitler, who is now faced by the condemnation and animosity of a majority of the people, nevertheless continue to take the people's name in vain, and commit in its name the vilest crimes? The simple answer is that it has not yet found itself as a people again and has not yet united against the enemy within.
>
> Hitler turned the people into a collection of individuals who denounced one another and feared one another. Everyone had a special uniform and everyone ran around with different badges of rank. But it was not only a question of externals. National comrades were undermined intellectually by refined, demagogic propaganda and through force and terror. The people were split up into innumerable castes and tribes, and the Hitler regime was always able to play off one national comrade against another and one social stratum against another.

The Nazis had set out to impose a new order on the disquieting complexities and social upheavals that the modernisation of the twenties had brought with it: as they promised, to bring harmony. The visionary force of their ideas, however, was never sufficient to generate more than some half-baked attempts at reorganisation, attempts which soon came to a standstill or fell foul of jurisdictional wrangles between competing internal power blocs, while the regime's hectic dynamism swept forward, in compensation, to new campaigns. But the Nazis, with their terror apparatus, did succeed in breaking up the complex jigsaw of society into its smallest component parts, and changing much of its traditional coherence almost beyond recognition. By the end of the Third Reich, and of the world war the Reich had staged, the vision of a 'national community' had dissolved. Instead, there lay a society in ruins – ruined not only in a material sense (though the post-war period was to show how astonishingly well it had actually held up) but psychologically, morally and in respect of its social bonds. If the Third Reich could boast any achievement, it was the destruction of public contexts and responsibilities and the dislocation of social forms of life, even in traditional environments which provided some measure of refuge and scope for resistance. Private spheres of behaviour were impoverished and isolated, relapsing into a self-serving individualism devoid of all potentially dangerous social connections and meanings. The *Volksgemeinschaft* that had been so noisily trumpeted and so harshly enforced became, in the end, an atomised society.

In the immediate post-war period there was an attempt on the part of the political culture to fill this vacuum by joining the short-lived but powerful international trend towards an anti-fascist left-wing hegemony.[8] After the onset of the Cold War, however, the traditional patterns of political culture in Germany reasserted themselves. Yet, spurious though the brief anti-fascist hegemony in Germany may have been, the 'restoration' political culture of the 1950s was equally artificial, even if its effects were more pervasive. With an anxiety touching on the grotesque, post-war German society clutched at the values and standards of behaviour of the 'good old days' before 1933 – or, better still, before 1914 – and behaved as though nothing had happened in the interim.

Yet if 'restoration' was a veneer – promising security, normality and continuity, while beneath the surface people's lives remained marked by the uncertainties that had prevailed since the 1920s – the genuinely integrative, and highly modern, dynamism of post-war society was making itself felt none the less, in the shape of economic expansion.[9] The mood of *Wirtschaftswunder* and take-off now profited from the very destruction of tradition and recasting of standards of behaviour brought about by the Third Reich.[10] Part and parcel of the change were the new type of worker, achievement-orientated, individualistic and prepared to trade high productivity for high wages; the modern nuclear family, isolated in its private life, satisfying its social needs in the market place; and the growth of modern mass consumption, leisure and mass media.

The break-up of socio-cultural environments which began under the Third Reich, with the smashing of political and religious clubs and associations and the intrusion of political control into everyday life, and the corresponding destruction of communal social experience, together maintained their dynamic advance even after enforced political loyalty and surveillance had gone. The National Socialists' pervasive intervention in society had meant that it was impossible in 1945 simply to resurrect the conditions of 1932. The disappearance of contexts and traditional forms of life that is characteristic of modern societies in general continued to apply to Germany too. The atomisation of society, however, took on a new connotation as the dynamic, achievement-orientated, high-consumption industrialism of the fifties emerged. For most people, the opportunities for integration which in the thirties had been promised but not always delivered, were now realised. *Volkswagen, Volkseigenheim, Volksempfänger* – a car, a home and a radio (and later television) set of one's own – these symbols shed the ideological overtones of the Nazi era. After many detours, the normality they stood for had been attained.

Nazi Germany and the pathologies and dislocations of modernity: thirteen theses

We have seen that an examination of the Third Reich from the perspective of everyday life yields a number of important insights. It helps to explain how it was possible that the regime came into being; how it was able to function; what was the relationship between the considerable amount of 'popular opposition' to the regime and the simultaneous, appalling amount of unthinking or enthusiastic support; and the extent to which National Socialism had an impact on long-term social structures and trends. Everyday life under Hitler was thus not mere conformity on the one hand – 'National Socialist everyday life', so to speak – and mere 'everyday deprivation', loss of rights and freedoms, on the other: as if there was only a black-and-white division between rulers and ruled, rather than the multiple everyday ambiguities of 'ordinary people' making their choices among the varying greys of active consent, accommodation and nonconformity.

Nevertheless, if we are to understand people's modes of behaviour fully, the appeal to everyday experience is not of itself sufficient. However wide-ranging and careful the documentation of such experience may be, it is always necessary in addition to offer an interpretation of the economic, social, political and cultural aspects of the period in question based on the systematic and analytical elaboration of theory. Those who denounce the effort to systematise concepts, analyses and judgements as the 'rationalistic arrogance of science' (Hannes Heer) are driven to the position that the only kinds of 'authentic' everyday experience that can be cited are those of the '*alte Kämpfer*', Wehrmacht veterans and the man in the corner shop who 'never had a clue what was going on'. This sort of history ends up merely reproducing some of the most influential propaganda formulae of National Socialism itself: introspection instead of intellect; feeling instead of analysis; 'community' instead of social contradictions; ideals instead of interests; homeland instead of civil society.

National Socialism was unable to abolish the reality of industrial society, but it did, through propaganda, impede the clear perception of this reality, and through terror it largely prevented its victims from organising themselves. One of the effects of National Socialism, indeed, was that those sections of the population that were socially and politically subjugated were split into a multiplicity of opposing groups and individuals with competing privileges (or apparent privileges), and could reunite only in meaningless rituals and mass organisations made rigid by bureaucratic inertia. The Nazis' claims and demands on individuals and social groups were such that approval, rejection and acceptance became intertwined within the individual in a host of different ways. Even an uncompromising political resister had to make compromises in daily life, if only to camouflage his illegal work. But each confrontation, even a mere call to donate to the Winter Relief Fund, not only raised the tactical problem of whether to accede or hold out, but posed the fundamental dilemma that consent to the regime *in toto* consisted in any case precisely in taking a large number of similar small steps of compliance. In addition, the Nazi scheme of social order backed up by terror moved into areas which had previously lain on the margins of, or quite outside, the traditional domain of political controversy. This was the case with anti-Semitism, of course, but also applied to the racialist social policies of the Third Reich quite generally.

A study of everyday life under National Socialism, then, provides basic insights into the ambivalence of political activity, and shows how pervasively elements of inadvertent conformity or conscious approval entered into calculations about opposition and compromise. It also shows that Nazi terror posed a moral challenge even to those who shut themselves off from it, and not just to the very limited numbers of people who were part of the political culture or who simply displayed a humanitarian concern for innocent victims.

The Nazi variant of modern industrial society is not the only kind of society to draw a sharp dividing line between accepted norms and unacceptable nonconformity. Nazism merely displayed particular moral insouciance in its attempt to regiment socially and biologically defined groups of individuals by means of a modern society's over-applied norms and misapplied technology, and in its use of procedures of segregation and eradication in order to destroy the unpalatable variety of real life and replace it with system, utility and efficiency. The values we should assert in response to this historical experience are easily stated but hard to practise: reverence for life, pleasure in diversity and contrariety, respect for what is alien, tolerance for what is unpalatable, scepticism about the feasibility and desirability of chiliastic schemes for a global new order, openness towards others and willingness to learn even from those who call into question one's own principles of social virtue.

Everyday experience never tallies exactly with large analytical or systematic hypotheses. At the same time, if such experience is to be understood at all, it cannot do without synoptic interpretation either. Furthermore, as we have tried to show, an analysis of the Third Reich from the perspective of everyday life provides a stimulus for a new and comprehensive historical interpretation. We shall close this study, therefore, by restating, in however provisional and imbalanced a form, some of the ideas and conclusions that have been formulated within it, in the hope that they will serve as a basis for continuing discussion.

1   German National Socialism emerged in the period between the two world wars, when the conjunction of hectic processes of social modernisation, profound economic upheaval and the disintegration of the political system led to a complex sense of crisis, particularly among the disorientated new and old middle classes, the unemployed, the *declassés* and a younger generation deprived of secure prospects for the future. The response to the crisis, however, was no longer couched merely in the conservative or traditionalist plebeian terms that had characterised the critique of modernity up to the middle of the nineteenth century, but took on utopian and reactionary features as well as ideas from the prevailing cultural pessimism and from schemes for reform based on social biology. Eclectic as regards ideas, but up to date in its attitude to technology, Nazism laid claim to offer a 'conclusive' new answer to the challenges and discomforts of the age.

2   The opaque nature of the crisis afflicting the Weimar 'system' was offset, ideologically, by the imputation of guilt to the stereotyped amalgams of 'the Jew', 'the Marxist' and the rapacious 'capitalist'. The positive appeal of Nazism lay less in any details of its programme defining the proposed harmonious 'national community' than in the fact that the individual could feel secure within a disciplined, militarised 'movement' that was forever being whipped up by new campaigns. It was more important to travel hopefully than to arrive.

3   Attempts were made to keep the mass movement going by artificial means after the *Machtergreifung*, but restrictions imposed by the newly established cartel of power elites from industry, the armed forces and the Nazi Party had to be accepted. At the same time, the elites took over and institutionalised the movement's terrorist dynamism in order to retain and extend their own power. Aggression and the pressure

towards annihilation were thus translated on to a highly evolved state apparatus.

4 Since the hollow model of the 'national community' was ill-equipped to lead to lasting and positive integration, stand-by strategies were needed: at first, gestures towards community through mass rituals; then the eliciting of passive consent through social concessions and non-political leisure provisions; and finally the establishment in reverse of the boundaries of the 'national community' through repeated identifications of internal and external enemies.

5 The much-heralded *Volksgemeinschaft* of the National Socialists in no way abolished the real contradictions of a modern industrial society; rather, these were inadvertently aggravated by the use of highly modern industrial and propaganda techniques for achieving war-readiness. The ideal *Volksgemeinschaft* celebrated in speeches at Party rallies thus conflicted with the straitened and oppressive conditions of everyday life, and the population gave plentiful expression to its criticisms, in the form of so-called '*Volksopposition*' [popular opposition]. Nevertheless, these expressions of displeasure made little real impact. They were too much concerned with specific, isolated matters, and those who made them were cut off from one another and were driven back into essentially non-political privacy. In any case, 'grumbling' was not necessarily incompatible with consent to the regime, as the indisputable popularity of the *Führer*, even among those expressing criticism, shows. Something approaching consent on an everyday level thus emerged as far as the majority of the population was concerned, particularly during the phase of rearmament-led boom, this consent attaching itself to what were regarded as non-political indicators of normalisation and prosperity.

6 We must distinguish the many and varied expressions of nonconformist behaviour: the steadfast non-response of traditional environments to National Socialist pressure, and more far-reaching forms of resistance and non-cooperation. Active resistance was only a minority affair. Certainly, as young people's wartime acts of non-compliance illustrate, conflict with the Nazi authorities did not necessarily remain static, and those involved might move from mere assertion of a dissident style to more deliberate acts of protest. In individual cases we can trace an entire 'career', graduating from nonconformist behaviour, via refusal, to protest and resistance. But the cumulative effect of the use of terror against political opponents, proclaimed as enemies, of the fragmentising social processes and of the cross-cutting devices of integration, was to paralyse even the anti-fascist resistance. Although soon robbed of its mechanisms of political expression by Gestapo terror, the resistance mobilised tens of thousands of people into performing acts of courage and sacrifice, but it remained decentralised, disorientated and historically ineffectual. The true historical significance of the resistance was its preservation of non-fascist traditions.

7   The deep-seated social contradictions that ran through the Third Reich cut across the racial frontiers prescribed by the ideology of *Volksgemeinschaft*; but they also failed to correspond to the principal division on which the enemies of fascism wished to insist, namely that between 'authority' and 'society', the Nazi rulers and the people. In fact, the long-term trends characteristic of a modern industrial society, which had been interrupted by the world economic crisis, continued to run their course. Many of these trends were deliberately encouraged by the National Socialists; others were pragmatically accepted; yet others persisted in contradiction of the NSDAP's scheme and, so to speak, behind the Party's back. In this sense we cannot properly speak of Hitler's 'social revolution', even though the resultant effect of this parallelogram of mainly destructive forces was that a more 'modern' society emerged from the ruins of the Third Reich at the end of the war.

8   A central feature of the 'modernisation' that was fostered partly by the regime's policies and partly by resistance to its mobilisation of the population and its stage-management of public life, was the atomisation of traditional forms of social integration and modes of behaviour. From this retreat into isolated, depoliticised privacy the dynamism of the post-war 'economic miracle', with its orientation to consumption and efficiency, was to emerge.

9   The longing of insecure middle-class people for 'normality' played no small part in the spread of National Socialism. But as comparative economic and social normality were restored, by the mid-1930s, so the National Socialist movement lost most of its mass impetus, even though the promised 'national community' was further away than ever. Thenceforward the only way the ideal could serve was to complement 'normalisation' by discovering internal and external enemies.

10   The Nazis' utopian project of a 'national community' envisaged the creation of a society that was ideologically homogeneous, socially conformist, orientated towards efficiency and hierarchical in structure; the means for bringing this society into being were the education of

those of 'good type' (*gut Geartete*) and the 'eradication' of those deficient as to 'type' (*Ungeartete*). This distinction, however, founded on racial biology, was an elastic one. Terrorist punishments were inflicted on all nonconformist social behaviour, and the laws of the concentration-camp state were extended step by step to society as a whole. Terror accordingly bit ever deeper (as external aggression simultaneously increased), from the margins of society into its heart. The regime's escalating radicalism did not come about through detailed advance planning, but was a pattern of ever more brutal responses to the internal contradictions within society and the insuperable constraints imposed upon it from outside.

11 The racialist project of a harmonious society, freed of con-tradictions through the gradual eradication of all actual or potential perpetrators of nonconformist social behaviour, was a radicalised version of schemes of social policy that had been advocated, sometimes on optimistic, progressive grounds, since the turn of the century. The practice of terror by the National Socialists thus made apparent the repressive features that were inherent in the normative and disciplinary methods of these schemes.

Consistent in its rejection of the legacy of 1789, National Socialism envisaged a society with modern technologies and institutions but owing nothing to the ideals of equal rights, emancipation, self-determination and common humanity. It pushed the utopian belief in all-embracing 'scientific' final solutions of social problems to the ultimate logical extreme, encompassing the entire population in a bureaucratic racial-biological design and eradicating all sources of nonconformity and friction. It demonstrated the destructive power of modern technology by waging world war; in everyday life it offered a foretaste of a depressing, atomised form of society abjuring social, political and moral responsibilities and deriving its coherence solely from bureaucratic procedures and institutions of incorporation and from the vapid, specious charms of mass consumption.

12 Nazism arose as an aimless rebellion against the thrust towards modernisation that had been bound up with the crises of the 1920s; once in power, however, it absorbed and came to terms with the technologies and trends of modernity. Both in its use of terror against 'community aliens' and in its creation of an atomised society normalised by force, National Socialism demonstrated, with heightened clarity and murderous consistency, the pathologies and seismic fractures of the modern civilising process.

13 The view that National Socialism was the outcome of the 'special German path of development' or '*Deutscher Sonderweg*' need on no account entail the conclusion that barbarism was founded in the German national character; in the same way, the view that it was one of the pathological developmental forms of modernity does not imply that barbarism is the inevitable logical outcome of modernisation. The point, rather, is that we should not analyse away the tensions between progressive and aberrant features by making a glib opposition between modernity and tradition: we should call attention to the rifts and danger-zones which result from the modern civilising process itself, so that the opportunities for human emancipation which it simultaneously creates can be the more thoroughly charted. The challenge of Nazism shows that the evolution of modernity is not a one-way trip to freedom. The struggle for freedom must always be resumed afresh, both in enquiry and in action.

Notes

Preface, pages 11–13

1 A brief preliminary sketch for this book appeared under the title *Alltag unterm Nationalsozialismus* as Volume 17 in the series *Beiträge zum Thema Widerstand*, published by the Gedenk- und Bildungsstätte Stauffenbergstraße, Berlin, 1981. In addition, various sections have benefited from experience gained in lectures and discussions of source materials in adult education, including the Landeszentralen für politische Bildung in Berlin, Mainz and Lower Saxony, the Gedenk- und Bildungsstätte Stauffenbergstraße in Berlin, the Deutsches Institut für Fernstudien in Tübingen, the Friedrich-Ebert-Stiftung and the Bundeszentrale für politische Bildung. The text of Chapters 2, 8 and 11 includes reworked versions of parts of the following papers: 'Thesen zur Faschismusdiskussion', in *Spaltung der Arbeiterbewegung und Faschismus*, ed. Joachim Bischoff *et al*, Hamburg, 1980, pp. 197–217; 'Edelweißpiraten, Meuten, Swing. Jugendsubkulturen im Dritten Reich', in *Sozialgeschichte der Freizeit*, ed. Gerhard Huck, Wuppertal, 1980, pp. 307–29; 'Heinrich Himmler und der Swing', *Journal für Geschichte*, vol. 2, no. 6 (1980), pp. 53–58.

2 The illustrations are arranged in order of the chapters to which they are thematically linked.

3 The notes provide more than just sources of quotations and statistics, but they do not purport to be a full-fledged system of references. Their purpose is to draw attention to publications which are of central importance for the topic in question or which are particularly suitable for further reading. In general I have avoided explicit discussion of theses from the specialised literature, on matters which would have been obvious to experts while being uninteresting to laymen, and I have also dispensed with tedious repetitions of references to publications that have been of fundamental significance in many of the areas discussed – e.g. David Schoenbaum's searching and stimulating study, to which, as will readily be seen, I am considerably indebted even if the process of coming to terms with his views has led me to different conclusions.

Introductory note: research problems, pages 14–17

1 David Schoenbaum, *Hitler's Social Revolution: Class and Status in Nazi Germany 1933–1939*, Garden City, NY, 1966.

2 On these controversies, see notes to Chapters 1 and 2 below.

3 David Blackbourn and Geoff Eley, *The Peculiarities of German History: Bourgeois Society and Politics in Nineteenth-Century Germany*, Oxford and New York, 1984; Hans-Jürgen Puhle, 'Deutscher Sonderweg. Kontroverse um eine vermeintliche Legende', *Journal für Geschichte*, vol. 3, no. 4 (1981), pp. 44f.

4 Schoenbaum, op. cit.; Ralf Dahrendorf, *Society and Democracy in Germany*, New York, 1967; Horst Matzerath and Heinrich Volkmann, 'Modernisierungstheorie und Nationalsozialismus', in *Theorien in der Praxis des Historikers. Geschichte und Gesellschaft*, ed. Jürgen Kocka, Sonderheft 3, Göttingen, 1977, pp. 86–116; cf. Henry Ashby Turner Jr, 'Faschismus und Antimodernismus', in id., *Faschismus und Kapitalismus in Deutschland*, Göttingen, 1972, pp. 157–82; Tim W. Mason, 'Zur Entstehung des Gesetzes zur Ordnung der nationalen Arbeit vom 20. Januar 1934: Ein Versuch über das Verhältnis "archaischer" und "moderner" Momente in der deutschen Geschichte', in *Industrielles System und politische Entwicklung in der Weimarer Republik*, ed. Hans Mommsen, Dietmar Petzina and Bernd Weisbrod, Düsseldorf, 1974, pp. 322–51; Karl-Dietrich Bracher, 'Tradition und Revolution im Nationalsozialismus', in *Hitler, Deutschland und die Mächte*, ed. Manfred Funke, 2nd edn., Düsseldorf, 1978, pp. 17–29; Martin Broszat, 'Soziale Motivation und Führer-Bindung des Nationalsozialismus', *Vierteljahreshefte für Zeitgeschichte*, 18 (1970), pp. 392–409.

5 See the work of Michel Foucault, especially *Discipline and Punish*; research inspired by the work of Norbert Elias's *The Civilising Process*; and recent discussions of Max Weber's concept of rationalisation. Also: Jürgen Habermas, *Theorie des kommunikativen Handelns* (2 vols.), Frankfurt, 1981. Habermas, in particular, demonstrates that an alert and critical awareness of the pathologies of modernity need not lead to general cultural pessimism but can clear the ground for a proper understanding and extension of the humane and emancipatory aspects of modernity. A stimulating interpretation of National Socialism in terms of the pathologies of modernity, albeit one which is provocative on many points of detail, is: Ernst Nolte, 'Die negative Lebendigkeit des Dritten Reiches', *Frankfurter Allgemeine Zeitung*, no. 169, 24th July 1980.

6 This book treats the phenomenon of National Socialism as the German instantiation of the general phenomenon of inter-war European fascism. Variation in choice of terminology within this book – 'National Socialism', 'Third Reich', 'fascism' – has less to do with any competing global theories of fascism than with the pragmatic question whether the National Socialist movement or the European phenomenon happens to be under discussion. A description and analysis of theories of fascism based on a subtle and expert understanding of the Italian movement is provided by: Renzo de Felice, *Die Deutungen des Faschismus*, Göttingen/Zürich, 1980.

7 The everyday behaviour and attitudes of Germans during the Third Reich

are documented in an extraordinarily wide range of sources. For some detailed references, see the notes to Chapters 3 and 4 below. The description and analysis of everyday experience attempted here keeps to the empirical findings yielded by the sources; there is no attempt to offer generalisations in breach of the constraints of customary typological and interpretative methodology. I do not feel competent to offer the sorts of more ambitious interpretation found in various psychohistorical approaches, especially since these are based on fragmentary data dealing with obscure facets of the individual or even collective psyche, and are methodologically questionable.

1 The history of everyday life – a different perspective, pages 21–25

1 E.g. in 1980 the Kurt A. Körber-Stiftung announced a 'Schools German History Competition for the Federal President's Prize', on the subject 'Everyday Life under National Socialism'; see the accompanying teacher's booklet, obtainable from the Kurt A. Körber-Stiftung; study aids are provided in *Sozialwissenschaftliche Informationen für Unterricht und Studium*, vol. 9, no. 4 (October 1980); see also Falk Pingel, 'Nationalsozialismus im Geschichtsunterricht – Neue Perspektiven seit "Holocaust"?', *Geschichtsdidaktik*, vol. 4 (1979), pp. 306–18. Cf. also Lutz Niethammer, 'Anmerkungen zur Alltagsgeschichte', *Geschichtsdidaktik*, vol. 5 (1980), pp. 131–242; Dieter Galinski, Uli Herbert and Ulla Lachauer (eds.), *Nazis und Nachbarn. Schüler erforschen den Alltag im Nationalsozialismus*, Reinbek, 1982.

2 On the current state of the debate on fascism, see as an excellent guide to the historical problems and literature, Ian Kershaw, *The Nazi Dictatorship: Problems and perspectives of interpretation*, London, 1985. See also: *Theorien über den Faschismus*, ed. Ernst Nolte, NWB-Geschichte, vol. 21, 5th edn., Königstein/Taunus, 1979; Gerhard Hirschfeld and Lothar Kettenacker (eds.), *Der 'Führerstaat'. Mythos und Realität. Studien zur Struktur und Politik des Dritten Reiches*, Stuttgart, 1980; Eike Hennig, *Bürgerliche Gesellschaft und Faschismus in Deutschland. Ein Forschungsbericht*, Frankfurt, 1977; Projekt Ideologie-Theorie, *Faschismus und Ideologie* (2 vols.), Berlin (West), 1980. For the Marxist debate, see: Dietrich Eichholz and Kurt Gossweiler (eds.), *Faschismusforschung. Positionen, Probleme, Polemik*, Berlin (East), 1980. An essential new study is: Renzo de Felice, op. cit.

On the history of everyday life under National Socialism, see: Johannes Beck *et al* (eds.), *Terror und Hoffnung in Deutschland 1933–45. Leben im Faschismus*, Reinbek, 1980; Harald Focke and Uwe Reimer, *Alltag unterm Hakenkreuz*, Reinbek, 1979; idd., *Alltag der Entrechteten*, Reinbek, 1980; Detlev Peukert and Jürgen Reulecke (eds.), *Die Reihen fast geschlossen. Beiträge zur Geschichte des Alltags unterm Nationalsozialismus*, Wuppertal, 1981; George L. Mosse's book *Nazi Culture*, New York, 1966. Since the present book first was published in German, there has appeared a three-volume study of daily life experience in the 1930s and 1940s based on an oral-history project in the Ruhr district: Lutz Niethammer (ed.), *Lebensgeschichte und Sozialkultur im Ruhrgebiet 1930–1960* (3 vols.), Berlin/Bonn, 1983–5.

3 For recent teaching approaches, see: Peter Meyers and Dieter Riesenberger (eds.), *Der Nationalsozialismus in der historisch-politischen Bildung*, Göttingen, 1979; *Der Nationalsozialismus als didaktisches Problem. Beiträge zur Behandlung des NS-Systems und des Widerstands im Unterricht*, published by the Bundeszentrale für politische Bildung, Schriftenreihe vol. 156, Bonn, 1980; Peter Dudek (ed.), *Hakenkreuz und Judenwitz. Antifaschistische Jugendarbeit in der Schule*, Bensheim, 1980; Jürgen Radkau, 'Erfahrungen aus Unterrichtsprojekten "Kriegsalltag am Heimatort 1939–1945"': Lokalhistorische Ansätze zu einer elementaren Friedenserziehung in Unterklassen (4.–7. Schuljahr)', *Geschichte in Wissenschaft und Unterricht*, vol. 29 (1978), pp. 39–60; Gewerkschaft Erziehung und Wissenschaft – Landesverband Niedersachsen (ed.), *Faschismus in Deutschland und Neonazismus*, Hanover, 1979.

4 On methodology, see: Klaus Bergmann *et al* (eds.), *Handbuch der Geschichtsdidaktik* (2 vols.), Düsseldorf, 1979, especially the contributions on everyday life, local history, learning by discovery and project work, and further references to the literature on these topics.

5 There is no single, up-to-date, comprehensive history of the Third Reich. For the power structure, see: Martin Broszat, *The Hitler State: The Foundation and Development of the Internal Structure of the Third Reich*, London, 1981; also the study by the *emigré* German social scientist Franz Neumann, published in the USA in 1944, *Behemoth. Struktur und Praxis des Nationalsozialismus 1933–1944*, edited and with an afterword by Gerd Schäfer, Cologne, 1977. Schäfer's informative afterword enables the reader to make critical allowance for the weaknesses in Neumann's study and for the results of subsequent research into fascism. An interesting interpretative essay on National Socialism is: Peter Hüttenberger, 'Nationalsozialistische Polykratie', *Geschichte und Gesellschaft*, vol. 2 (1976), no. 4, pp. 417–22. The Militärgeschichtliches Forschungsamt in Freiburg has begun publication of a ten-volume series *Das Deutsche Reich und der 2. Weltkrieg*; the first volume to appear has been: *Ursachen und Voraussetzungen der deutschen Kriegspolitik* (by W. Deist, M. Messerschmidt, H.-E. Volkmann and W. Wette), Stuttgart, 1979. This book is a solid and well-balanced survey, based on up-to-date research, of the internal politics, economic situation, military weaponry and foreign policy of the Third Reich up to 1939 and looks likely to become a standard work. By 1985 three more volumes had been published, but these deal only with more traditional political and military history. The most compact general survey has been reprinted in paperback: Karl Dietrich Bracher, *The German Dictatorship: The Origins, Structure and Effects of National Socialism*, Harmondsworth, 1973. On the literature up to about 1978, see: Peter Hüttenberger, *Bibliographie zum Nationalsozialismus*, Arbeitsbücher zur modernen Geschichte, vol. 8, Göttingen, 1980. The more recent attempt at an overall survey by Klaus Hildebrand, *The Third Reich*, London, 1984 deals only marginally with issues of social and everyday history.

6 Schoenbaum, op. cit.; Richard Grunberger, *A Social History of the Third*

Reich, Harmondsworth, 1974. Studies on policy towards the middle class, the position of women, youth, Poles in the Ruhr, social-welfare policy and the German Labour Front may be found in: *Archiv für Sozialgeschichte*, vol. XVII (1977), Bonn-Bad Godesberg.

7 E.g. the life story of Elisabeth Grassmann, in: Jochen Köhler, *Klettern in der Großstadt. Volkstümliche Geschichte vom Überleben in Berlin 1933–1945*, Berlin, 1979.

2 The rise of National Socialism and the crisis of industrial class society, pages 26–46

1 Karl Dietrich Bracher, *Die Auflösung der Weimarer Republik*, 5th edn., Düsseldorf, 1978; Hans Mommsen *et al* (eds.), *Industrielles System und politische Entwicklung in der Weimarer Republik*, Düsseldorf, 1974; Michael Stürmer (ed.), *Die Weimarer Republik. Belagerte Civitas*, NWB Geschichte 112, Königstein, 1980; Jürgen Kocka, 'Ursachen des Nationalsozialismus', in 'Aus Politik und Zeitgeschichte', supplement to *Das Parlament*, no. 25 (1980), pp. 3–15.

2 Bracher, Sauer and Schulz, *Die nationalsozialistische Machtergreifung* (3 vols.), 2nd edn., Frankfurt/Berlin/Vienna, 1971; Erich Matthias and Rudolf Morsey (eds.), *Das Ende der Parteien 1933*, 2nd edn., Königstein, 1979; Wolfgang Luthardt (ed.), *Sozialdemokratische Arbeiterbewegung und Weimarer Republik. Materialien zur gesellschaftlichen Entwicklung 1927–1933* (2 vols.); Wolfgang Schieder (ed.), *Faschismus als soziale Bewegung*, Hamburg, 1976; Gerhard Schulz, *Aufstieg des Nationalsozialismus. Krise und Revolution in Deutschland*, Frankfurt, 1975.

3 T. W. Mason, E. Czichon, D. Eichholtz and K. Gossweiler, *Faschismus-Diskussion*, Argument-Studienhefte 6 (reprint of studies originally produced between 1966–68). See also Tim Mason, 'The Primacy of Politics – Politics and Economics in National Socialist Germany', in Henry A. Turner (ed.), *Nazism and the Third Reich*, New York, 1972, pp. 175–200. The differences between the ultra-left Comintern account of fascism (sc. a 'method' that can be applied by all representatives of capitalist domination, including 'social fascists') and the right-wing variant (sc. a specific system of domination, against which a democratic alliance can be mobilised) are significant for political strategy but of secondary importance as far as the analytical criticism of economism is concerned. Cf.: Barbara Timmermann, *Die Faschismus-Diskussion in der Kommunistischen Internationale (1920–1938)*, doctoral dissertation, Cologne, 1977; Manfred Weißbecker, *Entteufelung der braunen Barbarei*, Berlin (East), 1975; Kurt Goßweiler, 'Über Wesen und Funktion des Faschismus', in id., Kühnl and Opitz, 'Faschismus: Entstehung und Verhinderung von Faschismus', *Das Argument*, no. 37, November 1974, pp. 537–42; Ulrike Hörster-Philipps, 'Großkapital, Weimarer Republik und Faschismus', in Kühnl and Hardach (eds.), *Die Zerstörung der Weimarer Republik*, Cologne, 1977, pp. 38–141.

4 Dirk Stegmann, 'Kapitalismus und Faschismus in Deutschland 1929–1934', *Gesellschaft*, no. 6, Frankfurt, 1976, pp. 19–91; id., 'Zum Verhältnis von Großindustrie und Nationalsozialismus 1930–1933', *Archiv für Sozialgeschichte*, vol. XII (1973), pp. 399–382. Essential reading now are: Reinhard Neebe, *Großindustrie, Staat und NSDAP 1930–1933*, Göttingen, 1981; Henry A. Turner, *German Big Business and the Rise of Hitler*, New York, 1985; Geoff Eley, 'What Produces Fascism: Pre-industrial Tradition or a Crisis of the Capitalist State?' in *Politics and Society*, 12 (1983), pp. 53–82.

5 Elfriede Lewerenz, *Die Analyse des Faschismus durch die Kommunistische Internationale*, Berlin (East), 1975.

6 Niels Kadritzke, *Faschismus und Krise*, Frankfurt/New York, 1976; Stefan Schild, 'Faschismustheorie im Zerrspiegel der Kritik', *Beiträge zum wissentschaftlichen Sozialismus*, no. 16 (March 1978), pp. 92–120, and no. 17 (May 1978), pp. 106–24.

7 Jürgen Kocka, *Facing Total War : German Society 1914–1918*, Leamington Spa, 1984; Gerald D. Feldmann, *Army, Labor and Industry*, Princeton, 1966; Charles P. Kindleberger, *The World in Depression*, London, 1977; Alan S. Milward, *War, Economy and Society 1939–1945*, London, 1977.

8 The extensive documentation in *Europastrategien des deutschen Kapitals 1900–1945*, ed. Reinhard Opitz, Cologne, 1977 and *Weltherrschaft im Visier*, ed. Wolfgang Schumann and Ludwig Nestler, Berlin (East), 1975 certainly illustrates the general thrust of industry's expansionism, but does not show it to have been directly responsible for the military and foreign-policy operations of the Third Reich.

9 A conflicting interpretation is contained in: Richard Overy, *The Nazi Economic Recovery*, London, 1982 and *Goering, the 'Iron Man'*, London, 1984. But see also the contributions in Friedrich Forstmeister and Hans-Erich Volkmann (eds.), *Wirtschaft und Rüstung am Vorabend des Zweiten Weltkriegs*, Düsseldorf, 1975. The diversion of important military and industrial resources to the pursuit of the mass annihilation of real or imagined enemies is also relevant here.

10 On the impoverishment theory, it should be noted that Jürgen Kuczynski, *Geschichte der Lage der Arbeiter unter dem Kapitalismus*, vol. 6, Berlin (East), 1964 distorts the data. His findings have since been cited in numerous publications, e.g.: Reinhard Kühnl, *Der deutsche Faschismus*, Cologne, 1975.

11 Timothy W. Mason, *Arbeiterklasse und Volksgemeinschaft*, Opladen, 1975. A contrasting view is: Ludolf Herbst, 'Die Krise des nationalsozialistischen Regimes am Vorabend des Zweiten Weltkriegs und die forcierte Aufrüstung', *Vierteljahreshefte für Zeitgeschichte*, vol. 26, no. 3, pp. 347–92.

12 Mason, op. cit.; id., 'The Legacy of 1918 for National Socialism' in Eric Matthias and Antony Nicolls (eds.), *German Democracy and the Rise of Hitler*, London, 1971.

13 Reinhard Kühnl, *Faschismustheorien. Ein Leitfaden*, Reinbek, 1979.

14 Schoenbaum, op. cit.

15 Michael Schneider, *Unternehmer und Demokratie*, Bonn-Bad Godesberg, 1975; Bernd Weisbrod, *Schwerindustrie in der Weimarer Republik*, Wuppertal, 1978.

16 Stegmann, op. cit.; Turner, *Big Business*, op. cit.

17 Heinrich August Winkler, *Mittelstand, Demokratie und Nationalsozialismus 1918–1933*, Cologne, 1972; Jürgen Kocka, *Angestellte zwischen Demokratie und Faschismus*, Göttingen, 1977.

18 Cf. the role of the Wirtschaftspartei (Economic Party) or the remoulding of the Deutsche Demokratische Partei (DDP, German Democratic Party) into the Deutsche Staatspartei (German State Party). Larry E. Jones, 'The Dissolution of the Bourgeois Party System in the Weimar Republic', in Richard Bessel and E. J. Feuchtwanger (eds.), *Social Change and Political Development in Weimar Germany*, London, 1981, pp. 268–88.

19 Winkler, op. cit.; Kocka, *Angestellte*, op. cit.; Hennig, op. cit., especially pp. 126–226.

20 Klaus Theweleit, *Männerphantasien* (2 vols.), Frankfurt, 1977.

21 Christoph Schmidt, 'Zu den Motiven "alter Kämpfer" in der NSDAP', in Peukert and Reulecke, op. cit., pp. 21–44; Peter Merkl, *Political Violence under the Swastika: 581 Early Nazis*, Princeton, 1975; id., *The making of a Stormtrooper*, Princeton, 1980; Reinhard Mann (ed.), *Die Nationalsozialisten*, Stuttgart, 1980; Wolfgang Schieder (ed.), *Faschismus als soziale Bewegung*, Hamburg, 1978; Mathilde Jamin, *Zwischen den Klassen*, Wuppertal, 1984; Michael Kater, *The Nazi Party*, Oxford, 1983. See also recent studies about electoral support, e.g. Richard Hamilton, *Who Voted for Hitler?*, Princeton, 1982; Thomas Childer, *The Nazi Voter*, Chapel Hill/London, 1983.

22 Quoted in Schmidt, op. cit. On the function of the continuous propaganda campaigns as occupational therapy for Party supporters, see also: Richard Bessel, 'The Rise of the NSDAP and the Myth of Nazi Propaganda', *Wiener Library Bulletin*, vol. XXXIII (1980), New Series, nos. 51/52, pp. 20–29.

23 Quoted in Helmut Lessing and Manfred Liebel, *Wilde Cliquen*, Bensheim, 1981, pp. 153f.

24 Schmidt, op. cit., p. 37. On the Führer cult, see also: Wolfgang Horn, *Der Marsch zur Machtergreifung. Die NSDAP bis 1933*, 2nd edn., Düsseldorf, 1980. For many sophisticated detailed insights into the National Socialist movement, now see also the work by the GDR historians Kurt Pätzoldt and Manfred Weißbecker, *Geschichte der NSDAP 1920–1945*, Cologne, 1981. Graphic source material is in: Ernst Deuerlein (ed.), *Der Aufstieg der NSDAP in Augenzeugenberichten*, Munich, 1974; Conan Fisher, *Stormtroopers: A Social, Economic and Ideological Analysis 1929–1935*, London, 1983.

25 Cf. Theweleit, op. cit.; Merkl, op. cit.; Jamin, op. cit.; Richard Bessel, 'The Role of Political Terror in the Nazi Seizure of Power', *Acta Universitatis Wratislaviensis*, no. 484, Wroclaw, 1980, pp. 199–216; Eve Rosenhaft, *Beating the Fascists? The German Communists and Political Violence 1929–1933*, Cambridge, 1983.

26 George L. Mosse, *The Nationalisation of the Masses*, New York, 1975; id., *Ein Volk, ein Reich, ein Führer. Die völkischen Ursprünge des Nationalsozialismus*, Königstein, 1979; Schultz, op. cit.; Rainer Lepsius, *Extremer Nationalismus. Strukturbedingungen vor der nationalsozialistischen Machtergreifung*, Stuttgart, 1966; Kurt Sontheimer, *Antidemokratisches Denken in der Weimarer Republik*, Munich, 1962.

27 Kocka, *Angestellte*, op. cit.; id., *Die Angestellten in der deutschen Geschichte 1850–1980*, Göttingen, 1981; Winkler, op. cit.

28 The standard works on fascist ideology are still: Ernst Nolte, *Three Faces of Fascism*, New York, 1966; Eberhard Jäckel, *Hitlers Weltanschauung*, new edn., Stuttgart, 1981. See also: Mosse, *Volk*, op. cit.; Schulz, op. cit. My discussion does not seek to provide an outline of Nazi ideology, but only to trace certain connections between Party ideology and everyday anxieties, experiences and projections on the part of the National Socialist masses.

29 Turner, op. cit.

30 An up-to-date survey is: Hermann Giesecke, *Vom Wandervogel bis zur Hitlerjugend. Jugendarbeit zwischen Politik und Pädagogik*, Munich, 1981. Cf. also the report by Klaus Schönekäs, *Jugend auf dem Weg ins Dritte Reich*, working paper no. 9 of the Institut für historisch-sozialwissenschaftliche Analysen, Frankfurt, 1980.

31 Charles S. Maier, 'Between Taylorism and Technology: European Ideologies and the Vision of Industrial Productivity in the 1920s', in *Journal of Contemporary History*, vol. V, 1970, pp. 27–61; Peter Hinrichs, *Um die Seele des Arbeiters. Arbeitspsychologie, Industrie- und Betriebssoziologie in Deutschland 1871–1945*, Cologne, 1981; cf. also Wilhlem Treue (ed.), *Deutschland in der Weltwirtschaftskrise in Augenzeugenberichten*, 2nd edn., Munich, 1976.

32 Tim Mason, 'Women in Germany, 1925–1940: Family, Welfare and Work', in *History Workshop Journal*, nos. 1 and 2, 1976; Annemarie Tröger, 'Die Frauen im wesensgemäßen Einsatz', in Frauengruppe Faschismusforschung (ed.), *Mutterkreuz und Arbeitsbuch. Zur Geschichte der Frauen in der Weimarer Republik und im Nationalsozialismus*, Frankfurt, 1981, pp. 246–72.

33 Ludwig Preller, *Sozialpolitik in der Weimarer Republik*, 2nd edn., Düsseldorf, 1978.

34 Giesecke, op. cit.; John R. Gillis, *Youth and History: Tradition and Change in European Age Relations, 1770–Present*, London, 1981; Walter Laqueur, *Young Germany: A History of the Youth Movement*, New York, 1975.

35 Walter Laqueur, *Weimar. A Cultural History*, New York, 1975; Peter Gay, *Weimar Culture: The Outsider as Insider*, New York, 1968.

36 On the 'out of phase' relations between social-structural change, value systems and forms of socialisation, see: Talcott Parsons, 'Demokratie und Sozialstruktur in Deutschland vor der Zeit des Nationalsozialismus', in id., *Beiträge zur soziologischen Theorie*, 2nd edn., Neuwied, 1968, pp. 256–81.

37 It is important not to dismiss the sense of crisis felt during the Weimar years as merely the lamentation of social groups left behind by the march of progress. The damage done by the process of modernisation was often very real. But the intellectual and emotional response was such as to make any real solutions unlikely. This gave rise to an every stronger urge to look for 'the enemy' and to cling to the utopian and radical pseudo-solutions that fascist ideology offered. A compact description and interpretation of the European crisis from 1917 onwards is given by Karl Dietrich Bracher, *Europa in der Krise. Innengeschichte und Weltpolitik seit 1917*; for National Socialism, see especially pp. 175f.

38 See the stimulating sketch by Rainer Rothermundt, *Verkehrte Utopie*, Frankfurt, 1980.

39 The classic account is still Bracher, *Auflösung*, op. cit. Cf. also Karl Holl (ed.), *Wirtschaftskrise und liberale Demokratie*, Göttingen, 1978; Werner Conze and H. Raupach (eds.), *Die Staats: und Wirtschaftskrise des deutschen Reiches 1929–1933*, Stuttgart, 1967.

40 Hans Mommsen, 'Zur Verschränkung traditioneller und faschistischer Führungsgruppen in Deutschland beim Übergang von der Bewegungs- zur Systemphase', in Schieder, op. cit., pp. 157–82. See also the contributors in Peter D. Stachura (ed.), *The Nazi Machtergreifung*, London, 1983.

41 Bracher, Sauer and Schulz, op. cit.

42 On the partial coincidence between Hitler's ideas on rearmament and *Lebensraum* and talk of a policy of economic autarky in the early 1930s, see: Peter Krüger, 'Zu Hitlers "nationalsozialistischen Wirtschaftserkenntnissen"', *Geschichte und Gesellschaft*, vol. 6 (1980), no. 2, pp. 263–82; Avraham Barkai, *Das Wirtschaftssystem des Nationalsozialismus. Der historische und ideologische Hintergrund 1933–1936*, Cologne, 1977; Dietmar Petzina, *Autarkiepolitik im Dritten Reich*, Stuttgart, 1968; Hans-Erich Volkmann, 'Die NS-Wirtschaft in Vorbereitung des Krieges', in Deist *et al*, *Das Deutsche Reich und der Zweite Weltkrieg*, vol. 1, Stuttgart, 1979, pp. 177–370.

43 Hüttenberger, 'Polykratie', op. cit.

44 Neumann, op. cit.

45 See 'Introductory note: research problems', notes 3 and 4, above; cf. also Thomas Nipperdey, '1933 und die Kontinuität der deutschen Geschichte', in Stürmer, op. cit., pp. 374–92; Klaus Hildebrandt, 'Hitlers Ort in der

Geschichte des preußisch-deutschen Nationalstaates', *Historische Zeitschrift*, no. 217 (1973), pp. 584–632.

46 Hannah Arendt, *Eichmann in Jerusalem. A Report on the Banality of Evil*, New York, 1965.

3 Contradictions in the mood of the 'little man', pages 49–66

1 *Deutschland-Berichte der Sozialdemokratischen Partei Deutschlands (SOPADE) 1934–1940*, ed. Klaus Behnken (7 vols.), Frankfurt, 1980. See also: Michael Voges, 'Klassenkampf in der "Betriebsgemeinschaft". Die "Deutschland-Berichte" der Sopade (1934–1940) als Quelle zum Widerstand der Industriearbeiter im Dritten Reich', *Archiv für Sozialgeschichte*, no. XXI (1981), pp. 329–84. A concise analysis of popular mood based on regional sources is given by Ian Kershaw, *Popular Opinion and Political Dissent in the Third Reich*, Oxford, 1983.

2 Martin Broszat, Elke Fröhlich and Falk Wiesemann (eds.), *Bayern in der NS-Zeit*, vol. 1, *Soziale Lage und politisches Verhalten der Bevölkerung im Spiegel vertraulicher Berichte*, Munich and Vienna, 1977; Martin Broszat and Elke Fröhlich (eds.), *Bayern in der NS-Zeit*, vols. 2–4, *Herrschaft und Gesellschaft im Konflikt*, Munich and Vienna, 1979–81; Robert Thevoz, Heinz Brannig and Cecilia Lowenthal-Hansel (eds.), *Pommern 1934/35 im Spiegel von Gestapo-Lageberichten und Sachakten* (2 vols.), Cologne and Berlin, 1974; Franz Josef Heyen (ed.), *Nationalsozialismus im Alltag. Quellen zur Geschichte des Nationalsozialismus vornehmlich im Raum Mainz-Koblenz-Trier*, Boppard, 1967; Bernd Vollmer (ed.), *Volksopposition im Polizeistaat*, Stuttgart, 1957; Jörg Schadt (ed.), *Verfolgung und Widerstand unter dem Nationalsozialismus in Baden*, Stuttgart, 1976.

3 The following extracts from secret monthly situation reports by Gestapo stations in Rhine-Westphalia during 1934–35 are taken from: Geheimes Staatsarchiv Preußischer Kulturbesitz, Berlin-Dahlem, Rep. 90P; quoted also in Detlev Peukert, *Die KPD im Widerstand. Verfolgung und Untergrundarbeit an Rhein und Ruhr 1933–1945*, Wuppertal, 1980, pp. 204–18.

4 Heinz Boberach (ed.), *Meldungen aus dem Reich*, Neuwied, 1965, pp. 387–90.

5 Ibid., p. 418.

6 Peukert, *Die KPD im Widerstand*, op. cit., p. 208.

7 Ibid., p. 214.

8 Boberach, op. cit., p. 211.

9 An impressive literary account of this situation is: Hans Fallada, *Jeder stirbt für sich allein*, Reinbek, 1964.

10 Peukert, *Die KPD im Widerstand*, op. cit., p. 215.

11 Ibid., pp. 209f.

12 Fischer, op. cit.; Jumin, op. cit.; Christoph Schmidt, op. cit., pp. 37–43; Ulrich Klein, 'SA-Terror und Bevölkerung in Wuppertal 1933–34', in Peukert and Reulecke, op. cit., pp. 45–61.

13 Ian Kershaw, 'Alltägliches und Außeralltägliches: Ihre Bedeutung für die Volksmeinung', in ibid., pp. 273–92.

14 Heinz Boberach (ed.), *Berichte des SD und der Gestapo über Kirche und Kirchenvolk in Deutschland 1934–1944*, Mainz, 1971; Kershaw, *Popular Opinion*, op. cit., pp. 156–223; Jeremy Noakes, 'The Oldenburg Crucifix Struggle of November 1936: A Case Study of Opposition in the Third Reich', in Peter D. Stachura (ed.), *The Shaping of the Nazi State*, London, 1978, pp. 210–33.

15 Ian Kershaw, 'The Persecution of the Jews and German Popular Opinion in the Third Reich', in *Leo Baeck Year Book*, vol. xxvi, 1981; Falk Wiesemann, 'Juden auf dem Lande: die wirtschaftliche Ausgrenzung des jüdischen Viehhändlers in Bayern', in Peukert and Reulecke, op. cit., pp. 381–96. Cf., however, the account of the village of Rhina in Hesse: Peter O. Chotjewitz and Renate Chotjewitz-Häfner, *Die mit Tränen säen*, Munich, 1980. For the more traditional interpretation see Lucy Davidowicz, *The Holocaust and the Historians*, Cambridge, Mass./London, 1981.

16 William S. Allen, 'Die deutsche Öffentlichkeit und die "Reichskristallnacht" – Konflikte zwischen Werthierarchie und Propaganda im Dritten Reich', in Peukert and Reulecke, op. cit., pp. 397–412.

17 *Deutschland-Berichte der SOPADE*, op. cit., vol. 5, pp. 1205ff.

18 Ibid., pp. 1352ff.

19 Quoted in Kershaw, 'The Persecution of the Jews', op. cit., p. 328.

20 *Bayern in der NS-Zeit*, op. cit., vol. 1, p. 473.

21 Ibid., p. 475.

22 Herbert Obenaus, 'Haben sie wirklich nichts gewußt? Ein Tagebuch zum Alltag von 1933–1945 gibt eine deutliche Antwort', *Journal für Geschichte*, vol. 2 (1980), no. 1, pp. 26–31.

23 *Deutschland-Berichte der SOPADE*, op. cit., vol. 2, p. 10; subsequent quotation from ibid., vol. 5, p. 267.

24 Peukert, *Die KPD im Widerstand*, op. cit., p. 210. On public opinion and Nazi propaganda, see especially: Jutta Sywottek, *Mobilmachung für den totalen Krieg. Die propagandistische Vorbereitung der deutschen Bevölkerung auf den Zweiten Weltkrieg*, Opladen, 1976.

25 Boberach, *Meldungen aus dem Reich*, op. cit., pp. 77f.; subsequent quotation from ibid., p. 79.

26 Cf. also Marlis Steinert, *Hitler's War and the Germans*, Athens, Ohio, 1977; Franz Dröge, *Der zerredete Widerstand*, Düsseldorf, 1970; Hans-Jochen Gamm, *Der Flüsterwitz im Dritten Reich*, Munich, 1978.

27 *Deutschland-Berichte der SOPADE*, op. cit., vol. 2, pp. 1363f.

28 Ibid., vol. 5, p. 138f.

29 National Socialist propaganda also acknowledged this; cf.: Jutta Sywottek, op. cit.; W. S. Allen, 'Die deutsche Öffentlichkeit und die "Reichskristallnacht"', op. cit.

30 Ian Kershaw, *Der Hitler-Mythos. Volksmeinung und Propaganda im Dritten Reich*, Stuttgart, 1980.

31 Peter Hüttenberger, 'Heimtückefälle vor dem Sondergericht München 1933–1939', in *Bayern in der NS-Zeit*, op. cit., vol. 4, pp. 435–526.

4 The Führer myth and consent in everyday life, pages 67–80

1 Kershaw, 'Alltägliches', op. cit.

2 *Deutschland-Berichte der SOPADE*, op. cit., vol. 3, p. 310.

3 Ibid., vol. 5, pp. 280f.

4 Based on calculations by Tim W. Mason, *Arbeiterklasse und Volksgemeinschaft*, op. cit., p. 61. For the subsequent statistics, see also the contributions by Ludwig, Petzina, Volkmann, Fischer, Milward and Mason in: Friedrich Forstmeier and Hans-Erich Volkmann (eds.), *Wirtschaft und Rüstung am Vorabend des Zweiten Weltkrieges*, Düsseldorf, 1975.

5 Hasso Spode, '"Der deutsche Arbeiter reist". Massentourismus im Dritten Reich', in Gerhard Huck (ed.), *Sozialgeschichte der Freizeit*, Wuppertal, 1980, pp. 281–306.

6 Jürgen Reulecke, 'Die Fahne mit dem goldenen Zahnrad: der "Leistungskampf der deutschen Betriebe" 1937–1939', in Peukert and Reulecke, op. cit., pp. 245–70; Chup Friemert, *Produktionästhetik im Faschismus. Das Amt 'Schönheit der Arbeit' von 1933–1939*, Munich, 1980.

7 Hans Dieter Schäfer, *Das gespaltene Bewußtsein*, Munich, 1981, p. 151.

8 *Deutschland-Berichte der SOPADE*, op. cit., vol. 1, pp. 198ff.

9 Kershaw, *Hitler-Mythos*, op. cit.

10 *Deutschland-Berichte*, op. cit., vol. 1, p. 10.

11 Boberach, *Meldungen aus dem Reich*, op. cit., p. 239.

12 The role of the concept of 'normal times' in everyday consciousness and in autobiographical memoirs has been examined by Uli Herbert in the Essen project, 'Lebensgeschichte und Sozialkultur im Ruhrgebiet 1930–1960'.

13 Essential reading here is: Schäfer, *Das gespaltene Bewußtsein*, op. cit., from which the subsequent examples are taken.

14 Quoted in: Erwin Reiss, *'Wir senden Fröhsinn'. Fernsehen unterm Faschismus*, Berlin, 1979, p. 120.

15 Quoted in Schäfer, op. cit., p. 140.

16 Quoted in ibid., p. 160.

5 Areas of conflict in the Third Reich, pages 81–85

1 Hans Mommsen, 'Hitlers Stellung im nationalsozialistischen Herrschaftssystem', in Hirschfeld and Kettenacker (eds.), *Der 'Führerstaat'*, op. cit., pp. 43–72.

2 Cf. Peter Hüttenberger, 'Nationalsozialistische Polykratie', op. cit.; id., 'Vorüberlegungen zum "Widerstandsbegriff"', in *Theorien in der Praxis des Historikers*, ed. Jürgen Kocka, *Geschichte und Gesellschaft*, Sonderheft 3, Göttingen, 1977, pp. 117–34.

3 Klaus Scholder, *Die Kirchen und das Dritte Reich*, vol. 1, Frankfurt, 1977; Klaus Gotto and Konrad Repgen (eds.), *Kirche, Katholiken und Nationalsozialismus*, Mainz, 1980.

4 Klaus-Jürgen Müller, *Armee, Politik und Gesellschaft in Deutschland 1933–1945*, Paderborn, 1979; Klaus-Jürgen Müller, 'The Structure and Nature of the National Conservative Opposition in Germany up to 1940', in H. W. Koch (ed.), *Aspects of the Third Reich*, London, 1985.

5 Cf. the sub-title of *Bayern in der NS-Zeit*, op. cit.: 'Authority and Society in Conflict'. Revealing case studies of the effects of National Socialism on smaller-sized rural communities are in: Wolfgang Kaschuba and Carola Lipp, 'Kein Volk steht auf, kein Sturm bricht los. Stationen dörflichen Lebens auf dem Weg in den Faschismus', in Beck *et al* (eds.), *Terror und Hoffnung*, op. cit., pp. 111–55; Kurt Wagner and Gerhard Wilke, 'Körle – zur Geschichte eines hessischen Dorfes im Dritten Reich', in Peukert and Reulecke, op. cit., pp. 85–105; Falk Wiesemann, 'Juden auf dem Lande: Die Ausschaltung der jüdischen Viehhändler in Bayern', in ibid., pp. 381–96; Peter O. Chotjewitz and Renate Chotjewitz-Häfner, op. cit.

6 Christoph Klessman, 'Gegner des Nationalsozialismus. Zum Widerstand im Dritten Reich', in 'Aus Politik und Zeitgeschichte', supplement to *Das Parlament*, B 46/79, pp. 25–37; id. and Falk Pingel (eds.), *Gegner des Nationalsozialismus. Wissenschaftler und Widerstandskämpfer auf der Suche nach historischer Wirklichkeit*, Frankfurt/New York, 1980; Ger van Roon, *Widerstand im Dritten Reich*, Munich, 1979; Hermann Langbein, . . . *nicht wie Schafe zur Schlachtbank. Widerstand in den nationalsozialistischen Konzentrationslagern 1938–1945*, Frankfurt, 1980; id., *Die Stärkeren. Ein Bericht aus Auschwitz und anderen Konzentrationslagern*, Cologne, 1982; Richard Löwenthal and Patrick von zur Mühlen (eds.), *Widerstand und Verweigerung in*

Deutschland 1933–1945, Bonn, 1982; Gerhard Beier, *Die illegale Reichsleitung der Gewerkschaften 1933–1945*, Cologne, 1981.

6 The middle classes and the Nazi state, pages 86–100

1 My account is based principally on: Adelheid von Saldern, *Mittelstand im 'Dritten Reich'. Handwerker – Einzelhändler – Bauern*, Frankfurt/New York, 1979. Cf. also: Heinrich August Winkler, *Mittelstand, Demokratie und Nationalsozialismus. Die politische Entwicklung von Handwerk und Kleinhandel in der Weimarer Republik*, Cologne/Berlin, 1971; id., 'Der entbehrliche Stand. Zur Mittelstandspolitik im "Dritten Reich"', *Archiv für Sozialgeschichte*, vol. XVII (1977); Peter John, *Handwerkskammern im Zwielicht. 700 Jahre Unternehmerinteressen im Gewande der Zunftidylle*, Cologne, 1979. For the role of the middle classes as Nazi Party members and voters, see Hamilton, Childers, Kater, op. cit. A considerable body of material on middle-class opinion is given by Kershaw, *Popular Opinion*, op. cit.

2 Data based on: Dietmar Petzina *et al*, *Sozialgeschichtliches Arbeitsbuch*, vol. III, *Materialien zur Statistik des Deutschen Reiches 1914–1945*, Munich, 1978, pp. 55ff.

3 Winkler, 'Der entbehrliche Stand', op. cit.

4 For this section, see: Kocka, *Die Angestellten*, op. cit.; Hans Mommsen, *Beamtentum im Dritten Reich*, Stuttgart, 1966; Jane Caplan, 'Civil Service Support for National Socialism: an Evaluation', in Hirschfeld and Kettenacker, op. cit., pp. 167–93; Karl-Heinz Ludwig, *Technik und Ingenieure im Dritten Reich*, 2nd edn., Düsseldorf, 1979; Gunnar C. Boehnert, 'The Jurists in the SS-Führerkorps, 1925–1939', in Hirschfeld and Kettenacker, op. cit., pp. 361–74.

5 William Sheridan Allen, *The Nazi Seizure of Power: The Experience of a Single German Town*, revised edn., London 1984; Zdenek Zofka, 'Dorfeliten und NSDAP. Fallbeispiele der Gleichschaltung aus dem Kreis Günzburg', in *Bayern in der NS-Zeit*, op. cit., vol. IV, pp. 383–434; Evi Kleinöder, 'Verfolgung und Widerstand der Katholischen Jugendvereine. Eine Fallstudie über Eichstätt', in ibid., vol. II, pp. 175–236; Wagner and Wilke, op. cit.; Kaschuba and Lipp, op. cit.; Hannes Heer, 'Das Fischerhuder Totenbuch. Lebensläufe aus einem deutschen Dorf', in Beck *et al*, op. cit., pp. 79–110. Cf. also the contributions by Noakes, Matzerath and Fröhlich in Hirschfeld and Kettenacker, op. cit.; Kershaw, *Popular Opinion*, op. cit.

6 Zofka, op. cit.

7 Kleinöder, op. cit.

8 Franz Sonnenberger, 'Der neue "Kulturkampf". Die Gemeinschaftsschule und ihre Voraussetzungen', in *Bayern in der NS-Zeit*, op. cit., vol. III, pp. 235–328; Noakes, op. cit.

9 Arno Klönne, 'Jugendprotest und Jugendopposition. Von der HJ-Erziehung zum Cliquenwesen der Kriegszeit', in ibid., vol. IV, pp. 527–620.

7 The working class: everyday life and opposition, pages 101–144

1 The literature on the working class and the labour movement before 1933 is vast. For an initial guide, see Arno Klönne, *Die Deutsche Arbeiterbewegung*, Düsseldorf/Cologne, 1980. On self-defence measures by the left, see Rosenhaft, *Beating*, op. cit. Other references are given in the notes to this chapter.

2 Cf. Erich Fromm, *The Working Class in Weimar Germany: A Psychological and Sociological Study*, Leamington Spa, 1984. See also: Tim Mason, 'Injustice and Resistance: Barrington Moore and the Reaction of German Workers to Nazism' in R. J. Bullen, H. Pogge von Strandmann and A. Polonsky (eds.), *Ideas into Politics. Aspects of European History 1880–1950*, London, 1984, pp. 106–18.

3 Cf. various regional studies, including: Kurt Klotzbach, *Gegen den Nationalsozialismus. Widerstand und Verfolgung in Dortmund 1930–1945*, Hanover, 1969; Hans-Josef Steinberg, *Widerstand und Verfolgung in Essen 1933–1945*, 2nd edn., Bonn, 1973; Detlev Peukert, *Die KPD im Widerstand. Verfolgung und Untergrundarbeit an Rhein und Ruhr 1933–1945*, Wuppertal, 1980; Gerhard Hetzer, 'Die Industriestadt Augsburg. Eine Sozialgeschichte der Arbeiteropposition', in *Bayern in der NS-Zeit*, op. cit., vol. III, pp. 1–234; Klaus Tenfelde, 'Proletarische Provinz. Radikalität und Widerstand in Penzberg/Oberbayern 1900–1945', in ibid., vol. IV, pp. 1–382.

4 Heinrich Galm, *Ich war halt immer ein Rebell*, Offenbach, 1981, p. 124.

5 Tim. W. Mason, 'Zur Enstehung des Gesetzes zur Ordnung der nationalen Arbeit vom 20. Januar 1934: Ein Versuch über das Verhältnis "archaischer" und "moderner" Momente in der neuesten deutschen Geschichte', in Mommsen *et al* (eds.), *Industrielles System*, op. cit., pp. 322–52; id., *Arbeiterklasse und Volksgemeinschaft*, op. cit.; Reulecke, op. cit.; Friemert, op. cit.; Maier, op. cit.; Hinrichs, op. cit.; Gustav-Hermann Seebold, *Ein Stahlkonzern im Dritten Reich. Der Bochumer Verein 1927–1945*, Wuppertal, 1981; Voges, op. cit.

6 *Deutschland-Berichte der SOPADE*, op. cit., vol. 1, p. 31; subsequent extract is from ibid., vol. 2, p. 137.

7 Timothy W. Mason, 'The Worker's Opposition in Nazi Germany', in *History Workshop Journal*, no. 11, 1981.

8 This and the following extract are from a collection of confidential reports, 'Lage der Arbeiterschaft, Arbeiteropposition, Aktivität und Verfolgung der illegalen Arbeiterbewegung 1933–1944', in *Bayern in der NS-Zeit*, op. cit., vol. I, pp. 193–326, esp. pp. 261 and 284.

9 *Deutschland-Berichte der SOPADE*, op. cit., vol. 2, p. 1376.

10 These tables are taken from T. W. Mason, *Arbeiterklasse und Volksgemeinschaft*, op. cit., pp. 1262, 1284.

11 On this, see: Michael Zimmermann, '"Ein schwer zu bearbeitendes Pflaster". Der Bergarbeiterort Hochlarmark unter dem Nationalsozialismus', in Peukert and Reulecke, op. cit., pp. 65–84.

12 Facsimile in: Detlev Peukert, *Der deutsche Arbeiterwiderstand gegen das Dritte Reich. Beiträge zum Thema Widerstand*, published by the Gedenk- und Bildungsstätte Stauffenbergstraße, vol. 13, Berlin, 1980, p. 30.

13 According to files in the Wiedergutmachungsamt (Reparations Office) for the city of Dortmund, a total of 1,925 names of people persecuted for political resistance are known for the city of Dortmund alone. Of these, 511 were Socialists and 1,250 Communists (cf. Klotzbach, op. cit., p. 244). In Oberhausen the names of 382 victims of political persecution are known. 20 per cent of these were miners and 16 per cent metal workers; a bare 10 per cent of the victims were not workers (cf. Michael Zimmermann, *Opposition und Widerstand gegen den Nationalsozialismus in Oberhausen*, state examination thesis, Bochum, 1977, p. 288). Naturally, these are industrial cities, and for the Reich as a whole the proportions would need to be scaled down somewhat. The fact remains that workers took part in resistance in disproportionately high numbers.

14 Peter Hüttenberger, 'Vorüberlegungen', op. cit., pp. 117–39.

15 Even in a theory of fascism which assumes 'polycracy' among the National Socialist organs of authority (i.e. a theory which assumes that control in the Third Reich lay not with the 'leader' alone but with a variety of power blocs such as the Party and SS, economic interests and the military), the tendency for control over the population to become total must be recognised. Cf. Hüttenberger, 'Nationalsozialistische Polykratie', op. cit.

16 Adam Wolfram, *Es hat sich gelohnt. Der Lebensweg eines Gewerkschaftlers*, Koblenz, 1977, pp. 57ff.

17 Jacob Zorn, 'Der Parteisoldat', in Dirk Gerhard, *Antifaschisten*, Berlin, 1976, pp. 92–110.

18 Rudi Goguel, *Es war ein langer Weg*, Düsseldorf, 1947, p. 12f.

19 Zorn, op. cit.

20 Galm, op. cit.

21 Detlev Peukert, 'Der deutsche Arbeiterwiderstand gegen das Dritte Reich', in 'Aus Politik und Zeitgeschichte', supplement to *Das Parlament*, B 28–29/79, 14th July 1979, pp. 22–36; id., 'Zur Rolle des Arbeiterwiderstandes im Dritten Reich', in *Gegner des Nationalsozialismus*, ed. Christoph Klessmann and Falk Pingel, Frankfurt/New York, 1980, pp. 73–91; Gerhard Beer, *Die illegale Reichsleitung der Gewerkschaften 1933–1945*, Cologne, 1981; Richard Löwenthal and Patrik von zur Mühlen (eds.), *Widerstand und Verweigerung in Deutschland 1933–1945*, Bonn, 1982;Manfred Geis et al, 'Widerstand und Exil der deutscher Arbeiterbewegung 1933–1945', *Grundlagen und Materialien*, Bonn, 1982.

22 Dietmar Petzina, 'Soziale Lage der deutschen Arbeiter und Probleme des Arbeitseinsatzes während des Zweiten Weltkriegs', in *Zweiter Weltkrieg und sozialer Wandel*, ed. W. Dlugoborski, Göttingen, 1981, pp. 65–86; Edward I. Homze, *Foreign Labor in Nazi Germany*, Princeton, 1967; Hans Pfahlmann, *Fremdarbeiter und Kriegsgefangene in der deutschen Kriegswirtschaft 1939–1945*, Darmstadt, 1968; Eva Seeber, *Zwangsarbeiter in der faschistischen Kriegswirtschaft*, Berlin (East), 1964; Christian Streit, *Keine Kameraden. Die Wehrmacht und die deutschen Kriegsgefangenen 1941–1945*, Stuttgart, 1978; id., 'Sozialpolitische Aspekte der Behandlung der sowjetischen Kriegsgefangenen', in Dlugoborski, op. cit., pp. 184–96; Ingrid Schupetta, 'Jeder das Ihre – Frauenerwerbstätigkeit und Einsatz von Fremdarbeiterinnen/ -arbeitern im Zweiten Weltkrieg', in Frauengruppe Faschismusforschung (ed.), *Mutterkreuz und Arbeitsbuch*, Frankfurt, 1981, pp. 292–317; Ulrich Herbert, *Fremdarbeiter. Politik und Praxis des 'Ausländer-Einsatzes' in der Kriegswirtschaft des Dritten Reichs*, Berlin/Bonn, 1985. See also: Aurel Bilstein, *Fremdarbeiter in unserer Stadt 1939–1945*, Frankfurt, 1980.

23 Quoted in Schupetta, op. cit., p. 303.

24 Herbert, op. cit.

25 Ibid.

26 This passage, including the two quoted extracts, follows Streit, op. cit.

27 Herbert, op. cit.

28 Hauptstaatsarchiv Düsseldorf, Gestapo-Generalia, Stapostelle Köln files, not paginated.

20 For Gestapo reports on these incidents, see: Detlev Peukert, *Die Edelweißpiraten*, Cologne, 1980, pp. 103–15 ('Partisanen in Köln').

30 From 'Meldungen wichtiger staatspolizeilicher Ereignisse', Reichssicherheitshauptamt, Bundesarchiv Koblenz, R 58.

31 Hauptstaatsarchiv Düsseldorf, Gestapo Generalakten, not paginated.

32 Copy made available to the author by Max Mikloweit, Duisburg.

33 *Freiheit*, May 1942, Library of the Institut für Marxismus Leninismus, Central Committee of the Socialist Unity Party, GDR.

8 Young people: mobilisation and refusal, pages 145–174

1 As yet there is no social history of youth or youth policy in the Third Reich. Informative and stimulating partial studies include: Arno Klönne, 'Jugendprotest und Jugendopposition. Von der HJ-Erziehung zum Cliquenwesen der Kriegszeit', in *Bayern in der NS-Zeit*, op. cit., vol. IV, pp. 527–620; id. (ed.), *Jugendkriminalität und Jugendopposition im NS-Staat*, Münster, 1981; id., *Jugend im Dritten Reich. Die Hitler-Jugend und ihre Gegner*, Düsseldorf, 1982; Fritz Petrick, *Zur sozialen Lage der Arbeiterjugend in Deutschland 1933 bis 1939*, Berlin (East), 1974; Hermann Giesecke, *Vom Wandervogel bis zur*

Hitlerjugend. Jugendarbeit zwischen Politik und Pädagogik, Munich, 1981.

2 Rolf Eilers, *Die nationalsozialistische Schulpolitik*, Cologne/Opladen, 1963; Kurt-Ingo Flessau, *Schule der Diktatur. Lehrpläne und Schulbücher des Nationalsozialismus*, Frankfurt, 1979; Manfred Heinemann (ed.), *Erziehung und Schulung im Dritten Reich* (2 parts), Stuttgart, 1980; Elke Nyssen, *Schule im Nationalsozialismus*, Heidelberg, 1979; Wilfried Breyvogel and Thomas Lohmann, 'Schulalltag im Nationalsozialismus', in Peukert and Reulecke, op. cit., pp. 197–221; Michael H. Kater, 'Hitlerjugend und Schule im Dritten Reich', *Historische Zeitschrift*, vol. 228 (1979), no. 3, pp. 572–623.

3 Arno Klönne, *Hitlerjugend. Die Jugend und ihre Organisation im Dritten Reich*, Hanover/Frankfurt, 1955; Hannsjoachim W. Koch, *Geschichte der Hitlerjugend*, Percha, 1975; Hans-Christian Brandenburg, *Die Geschichte der HJ*, Cologne, 1968; Michael H. Kater, 'Bürgerliche Jugendbewegung und Hitlerjugend in Deutschland von 1926 bis 1939', *Archiv für Sozialgeschichte*, vol. XVII (1977), pp. 127–74.

4 The following memoirs are particularly worthy of mention: Hermann Glaser and Axel Silenius (eds.), *Jugend im Dritten Reich*, Frankfurt, 1975; Peter Brückner, *Das Abseits als sicherer Ort. Kindheit und Jugend zwischen 1933 und 1945*, Berlin, 1980; Melita Maschmann, *Fazit. Mein Weg in der Hitler-Jugend*, 2nd edn., Munich, 1979; Renate Finckh, *Mit uns zieht die neue Zeit*, Baden-Baden, 1978; Horst Burger, *Warum warst du in der Hitler-Jugend?*, Reinbek, 1978; Hans Siemsen, *Die Geschichte des Hitlerjungen Adolf Goers*, new edn. by Hellmut Lessing *et al*, Berlin, 1981; cf. also Rolf Schörken, 'Jugendalltag im Dritten Reich – Die "Normalität in der Diktatur. Anmerkungen zu einigen Erinnerungsbüchern', in *Geschichte im Alltag – Alltag in der Geschichte*, ed. Klaus Bergmann and Rolf Schörken, Düsseldorf, 1982, pp. 236–46.

5 Wolfram Siebeck, 'Meine Kindheit unter dem Hakenkreuz', *Die Zeit*, no. 7, February 1982.

6 Wolfdietrich Schnurre, 'Gelernt ist gelernt', part 14 of 'Meine Schulzeit im Dritten Reich', *Frankfurter Allgemeine Zeitung*, no. 31, 6th February 1982.

7 Brückner, op. cit., pp. 56–63.

8 Hans Günter Zmarzlik, 'Einer vom Jahrgang 1922', in Glaser and Silenius, op. cit., pp. 11–14.

9 Klönne, in *Bayern in der NS-Zeit*, op. cit.; id., *Hitlerjugend*, op. cit.

10 Maschmann, op. cit., p. 152.

11 Ibid.; Finckh, op. cit.; Martin Klaus, *Mädchen in der Hitlerjugend*, Cologne, 1980.

12 Klönne, op. cit.; Detlev Peukert, 'Protest und Widerstand von Jugendlichen im Dritten Reich', in Löwenthal and von zur Mühlen, op. cit., pp. 177–201.

13 *Deutschland-Berichte der SOPADE*, op. cit., vol 5, pp. 1390–93.

14 Maschmann, op. cit., p 35

15 Quoted in: Reichsjugendführung – Personalamt – Überwachung, 'Cliquen- und Bandenbildung unter Jugendlichen', MS, Berlin, September 1942; cf. Peukert, *Die Edelweißpiraten*, op. cit., p. 218.

16 Following the issuing of the Youth Service decree of 25th March 1939, the HJ Streifendienst (the HJ disciplinary arm) and the police could compel young people to do their Hitler Youth service. These repressive measures were then substantially reinforced by Himmler's circular of 20th October 1942, 'Enforcement of Youth Service Duty' (Bundesarchiv Koblenz, R 22/1176, Bl. 298).

17 Reichsjugendführung; cf. Peukert, *Die Edelweißpiraten*, op. cit., p. 160.

18 Ibid. See also: Daniel Horn, 'Youth Resistance in the Third Reich', *Journal of Social History*, 7 (1973), pp. 26–50. On gangs before 1933, see: Helmut Lessing and Manfred Liebel (eds.), *Wilde Cliquen*, Bensheim, 1981; Eve Rosenhaft, 'Organising the "Lumpenproletariat": Cliques and Communists in Berlin during the Weimar Republic', in *The German Working Class 1888–1933: the Politics of Everyday Life*, ed. Richard J. Evans, London, 1982, pp. 174–219.

19 Other groups are known to have existed in Wuppertal, Bonn, Bochum, Recklinghausen, Bottrop, Duisberg, Krefeld and even in Frankfurt and Nuremberg.

20 Lothar Gruchmann, 'Jugendopposition und Justiz im Dritten Reich. Die Probleme bei der Verfolgung der "Leipziger Meuten" durch die Gerichte', in *Miscellanea. Festschrift für Helmut Krausnick*, Stuttgart, 1980, pp. 103–30.

21 Hauptstaatsarchiv Düsseldorf, RW 58, Bd. 23599, Bl. 55.

22 Ibid., Bd. 9213, Bl. 21.

23 Ibid., Bl. 31f. See also: Michael Zimmermann, *Opposition und Widerstand gegen den Nationalsozialismus in Oberhausen*, op. cit.

24 See the more level-headed analysis by the Cologne juvenile court judge, Pastor, 7th November 1943 and the memoirs of the Oberhausen Edelweiß Pirate Günter O., in: Peukert, *Edelweißpiraten*, op. cit., pp. 14–27, 40–48. Be this as it may, the freer sexual life of the Edelweiß Pirates did not mean that there was equality between the sexes. Male sexism was dominant, as in the traditional working-class culture generally; the girls were confined to the fringes.

25 Ibid., pp. 50f.

26 Ibid., p. 75.

27 Ibid.

28 This and the subsequent quotations are from: Hauptstaatsarchiv Düsseldorf, RW 58, Bd. 9212, Bl. 40; Bd. 23599, Bl. 24, 155.

29 Matthias von Hellfeld, *Edelweißpiraten in Köln*, Cologne, 1981.

30 In Peukert, *Edelweißpiraten*, op. cit., pp. 123–37.

31 Ibid., pp. 35f., 52.

32 Detlev Peukert and Michael Winter, 'Edelweißpiraten in Duisburg. Eine Fallstudie zum subkulturellen Verhalten von Arbeiterjugendlichen unter dem Nationalsozialismus', *Duisburger Forschungen*, 1982.

33 In Peukert, *Edelweißpiraten*, op. cit., pp. 90–92.

34 Judgement 50, Js 252/39, Oberlandesgericht Dresden, Bundesarchiv Koblenz, R 22, Bd. 1177, Bl. 291–312; Gruchmann, op. cit.; Peukert, *Edelweißpiraten*, op. cit., pp. 188–91.

35 This claim would appear to be valid even taking into account the fact that the Gestapo and the law made efforts to play up the communist aspect in order to underpin charges of 'acts preliminary to high treason'.

36 Differences in social behaviour and political expression within working-class radicalism are explored in: Erhard Lucas, *Zwei Formen von Radikalismus in der deutschen Arbeiterbewegung*, Frankfurt, 1976.

37 Reichsjugendführung report, September 1942; cf. Peukert, *Edelweißpiraten*, op. cit., pp. 187–225.

38 Ibid., pp. 201–18.

39 This and subsequent extracts, ibid.

40 Himmler, letter to Heydrich, 2nd January 1942; see notes to Chapter 11, below.

41 Klaus Theweleit, *Männerphantasien* (2 vols.), Reinbek, 1980.

42 In my remarks on everday culture I follow the approach of the British Centre for Contemporary Cultural Studies: Stuart Hall and Tony Jefferson (eds.), *Resistance through Rituals*, London, 1976.

43 G. H. Elder, *Children of the Great Depression: Social Change in Life Experiences*, Chicago/London, 1974 gives an account of similar processes in the USA.

9 'Brown revolution'?, pages 175–183

1 On continuity, see: Nipperdey, in Stürmer, op. cit.; Nolte, *Three Faces of Fascism*, op. cit.

2 Manfred Heinemann (ed.), *Erziehung und Schulung im Dritten Reich* (2 parts), Stuttgart, 1980; Kurt-Ingo Flessau, *Schule der Diktatur*, Frankfurt, 1979; Elke Nyssen, *Schule im Nationalsozialismus*, Heidelberg, 1979; Michael

Kater, 'Hitlerjugend und Schule', *Historische Zeitschrift*, vol. 227 (1979), pp. 572–623; O. Ottweiler, *Die Volksschule im Nationalsozialismus*, Weinheim, 1979; Ulrich Popplow, 'Schulalltag im Dritten Reich. Fallstudie über ein Göttinger Gymnasium', in 'Aus Politik und Zeitgeschichte', supplement to *Das Parlament*, B 18/80, pp. 33–69; Karl-Christoph Lingelbach, *Erziehung und Erziehungstheorien im nationalsozialistischen Deutschland*, Weinheim, 1970; Theo Wolsing, *Untersuchungen zur Berufsausbildung im Dritten Reich*, Kastellaun, 1977; Manfred Höck, *Die Hilfsschule im Dritten Reich*, Berlin, 1979; Wilfried Breyvogel and Thomas Lohmann, 'Schulalltag im National-sozialismus', in Peukert and Reulecke, op. cit., pp. 199ff.

3 Wilfried Breyvogel, *Die soziale Lage und das politische Bewußtsein der Volksschullehrer 1927–1933*, Königstein/Taunus, 1979.

4 Horst Ueberhost (ed.) *Elite für die Diktatur. Die nationalpolitischen Erziehungsanstalten 1933–1945. Eine Dokumentation*, Düsseldorf, 1969. It is arguable that 'non-ideological' technocrats did in fact function fairly smoothly even within the Nazi system of authority: cf. Karl-Heinz Ludwig, *Technik und Ingenieure im Dritten Reich*, Düsseldorf, 1979.

5 Tim. W. Mason, 'Women in Germany', op. cit.; Dörte Winkler, *Frauenarbeit im Dritten Reich*, Hamburg, 1977; Jill Stephenson, *The Nazi Organisation of Women*, London, 1981; id., *Women in Nazi Germany*, London, 1975. See also: Annemarie Tröger, 'Die Frau im wesensgemäßen Einsatz', in Frauengruppe Faschismusforschung (ed.), *Mutterkreuz und Arbeitsbuch*, Frankfurt, 1981, pp. 246–72, on which the following remarks are particularly based.

6 Quoted in ibid., p. 258.

7 Quoted in ibid., p. 256.

8 Quoted in ibid., p. 269.

9 Dahrendorf, op. cit.; Schoenbaum, op. cit.

10 Joachim Petsch, *Baukunst und Stadtplanung im Dritten Reich*, Munich, 1976; id., 'Architektur und Städtebau im Dritten Reich – Anspruch und Wirklichkeit', in Peukert and Reulecke, op. cit., pp. 175–97; Manfred Walz, *Wohnungsbau und Industrieansiedlungspolitik in Deutschland 1933–1939*, Frankfurt/New York, 1979.

11 Wolfgang Schäfer (ed.), *Eure Bänder rollen, nur wenn wir es wollen! Arbeiterleben und Gewerkschaftsbewegung in Südniedersachsen*, IG Chemie-Verwaltungsstelle Hann. Münden, 1979, especially pp. 113ff. and 163ff.; cf. Jürgen Reulecke, 'Die Fahne mit dem goldenen Zahnrad, der "Leistungs-kampf" der deutschen Betriebe 1937–1939', in Peukert and Reulecke, op. cit., pp. 245–72.

12 References to continuities with the pre-1933 and post-1945 periods are in, e.g.: Wolfgang Strohmeyer, 'Der "Arbeitskreis für Arbeitsstudien'. Ein

Beitrag zur Strategie der Gewerkschaften nach 1945', *Jahrbuch Arbeiterbewegung*, vol. 6, Frankfurt, 1978, pp. 44–77; Peter Hinrichs and Lothar Peter, *Industrieller Friede? Arbeitswissenschaft, Rationalisierung und Arbeiterbewegung in der Weimarer Republik*, Cologne, 1976; Peter Hinrichs, *Um die Seele des Arbeiters*, Cologne, 1981. Waltraut Bergmann *et al*, *Soziologie im Faschismus 1933–1945*, Cologne, 1986. Cf. also: Ludolf Herbst, 'Die Mobilmachung der Wirtschaft 1938/39 als Problem des nationalsozialistischen Herrschaftssystems', in Wolfgang Benz and Hermann Graml (eds.), *Sommer 1939*, Stuttgart, 1979, pp. 62–106.

13 See notes to Chapter 12, below.

14 Cf. references to the relevant literature in notes to 'Introductory note: research problems', above.

10 Public show and private perceptions, pages 187–196

1 Rainer Stommer, '"Da oben versinkt einem der Alltag . . .". Thingstätten im Dritten Reich als Demonstration der Volksgemeinschaftsideologie', in Peukert and Reulecke, op. cit., pp. 149–74.

2 See Chapter 4 above. Essential reading is: Hans Dieter Schäfer, *Das gespaltene Bewußtsein. Deutsche Kultur und Lebenswirklichkeit 1933–1945*, Munich, 1981, especially pp. 114–62.

3 Rainer Stollmann, 'Nazi-Weihnacht', in Beck *et al*, *Terror und Hoffnung*, op. cit., pp. 300–14.

4 Joachim Petsch, 'Architektur und Städtebau', op. cit.; id., *Baukunst und Stadtplanung*, op. cit.

5 Cf. the materials collected by Joseph Wulf, *Presse und Funk im Dritten Reich*, Gütersloh, 1964; id., *Die bildenden Künste im Dritten Reich*, Gütersloh, 1963; id., *Literatur und Dichtung im Dritten Reich*, Gütersloh, 1963; Hildegard Brenner, *Die Kunstpolitik des Nationalsozialismus*, Reinbek, 1963.

6 Cf. Ralf Schnell, 'Innere Emigration und kulturelle Dissidenz', in Löwenthal and von zu Mühlen, op. cit., pp. 211–25; Hans Dieter Schäfer, 'Die nichtnationalsozialistische Literatur der jungen Generation im Dritten Reich', in id., *Das gespaltene Bewußtsein*, op. cit., pp. 7–54.

7 A classic instance is the 1944 film of Spoerl's *Feuerzangenbowle* with Heinz Rühmann, which uses modern fashions but seeks to depict a 'normal' school atmosphere shorn of all contemporary references to the Nazi era (no Hitler Youth or pictures of the Führer). See the stimulating study by Erwin Reiss, *'Wir senden Frohsinn'. Fernsehen unterm Faschismus*, Berlin, 1980.

8 *Berliner Illustrirte*, no. 15, 13th April 1939. (See also the front cover of this book.) Subsequent extracts quoted are from this issue. On the connection between military aggression and the new opportunities for exploring foreign countries through 'tourism', see: Johannes Beck, 'Die Feldzüge des alten Fiete.

"Jetzt sag mal ehrlich, kann Dir Neckermann das bieten?', in Beck *et al*, *Terror und Hoffnung*, op. cit., pp. 276–80.

9 Bertholdt Hinz, *Die Malerei im deutschen Faschismus. Kunst und Konterrevolution*, Frankfurt, 1977; Frankfurter Kunstverein (ed.), *Kunst im Dritten Reich. Dokumente der Unterwerfung*, catalogue, Frankfurt, 1975; Hermann Hinkel, *Zur Funktion des Bildes im deutschen Faschismus*, Gießen, 1974; Akademie der Künste (ed.), *Zwischen Widerstand und Anpassung. Kunst in Deutschland 1933–1945*, catalogue, Berlin, 1978.

10 Hinz *et al* (eds.), *Die Dekoration der Gewalt. Kunst und Medien im Faschismus*, Gießen, 1979.

11 Dieter Hoffman-Axthelm, 'Das Kind und der Kohlenklau. Erinnerungsfunde 1943–45', in Beck *et al*, *Terror und Hoffnung*, op. cit., pp. 315–21.

12 Adelheid Gräfin zu Castell-Rüdenhausen, '"Nicht mitzuleiden, mitzukämpfen sind wir da!" Nationalsozialistische Volkswohlfahrt im Gau Westfalen-Nord', in Peukert and Reulecke, op. cit., pp. 223–44.

13 Hasso Spode, '"Der deutsche Arbeiter reist". Massentourismus im Dritten Reich', in Gerhard Huck (ed.), *Sozialgeschichte der Freizeit*, Wuppertal, 1980, pp. 281–306.

14 *Deutschland-Berichte der SOPADE*, op. cit., vol. 2, p. 1375.

15 Ibid., vol. 3, pp. 881ff.

11 Order and terror, pages 197–207

1 The public nature of the use of terror in the immediate aftermath of the Nazis' seizure of power is demonstrated, particularly, in local studies, e.g.: William S. Allen, *Nazi Seizure*, op. cit.; Bernd Burkhardt, *Eine Stadt wird braun. Die nationalsozialistische Machtergreifung in der schwäbischen Provinz*, Hamburg, 1980; Heinz-Dieter Schmidt, *Die nationalsozialistische Machtergreifung in einer Kleinstadt. Ein Lokalmodell zur Zeitgeschichte*, Frankfurt, 1979; Ulrich Klein, 'SA-Terror und Bevölkerung in Wuppertal 1933/34', in Peukert and Reulecke, op. cit., pp. 45–64; cf. also Kurt Pätzoldt, *Faschismus. Rassenwahn, Judenverfolgung. Eine Studie zur politischen Strategie und Taktik des faschistischen deutschen Imperialismus (1933–1935)*, Berlin (East), 1975. On public knowledge about the concentration-camp system during the war, see: Elmer Luchterhand, 'Das KZ in der Kleinstadt. Erinnerungen einer Gemeinde an den unsystematischen Völkermord', in Peukert and Reulecke, op. cit., pp. 435–55.

2 Kershaw, *Hitler-Mythos*, op. cit.

3 Quoted in: Günter Brakelmann, 'Hoffnungen und Illusionen evangelischer Prediger zu Beginn des Dritten Reiches: Gottesdienstliche Feiern aus politischen Anlässen', in Peukert and Reulecke, op. cit., pp. 129–48, specifically p. 143.

4 Peter Hüttenberger, 'Heimtückefälle vor dem Sondergericht München 1933–1939', in *Bayern in der NS-Zeit*, op. cit., vol. IV, pp. 435–527, especially pp. 511ff.

5 On the use of force in education, see, *inter alia*, Alfred Andersch's memoirs of his teacher, Heinrich Himmler's father, in: *Der Vater eines Mörders. Eine Schulgeschichte*, Zürich, 1980. More general: Katharina Rutschky (ed.), *Schwarze Pädagogik*, Berlin, 1978; Philippe Meyer, *Das Kind und die Staatsräson*, Reinbek, 1981; Michel Foucault, *Discipline and Punish*, London 1977.

6 Cf. the comment – made in 1980 – by the Marxist-Leninist author Heinz Kühnrich on the committal of 'asocials' to concentration camps: 'The fascists wanted to demonstrate that they saw criminal and political prisoners as being on a par. The political prisoners were to be morally humiliated.' (*Der KZ-Staat 1933–1945*, Berlin (East), 1980, p. 58.)

7 Facsimile in: Peukert, *Edelweißpiraten*, op. cit., pp. 156f.

8 Quoted in: Denkschrift der Reichsjugendführung, September 1942; cf. Peukert, *Edelweißpiraten*, op. cit., pp. 160ff., and also for the subsequent extracts.

9 The quotations from Himmler are taken from: Bradley F. Smith, *Heinrich Himmler 1900–1926. Sein Weg in den deutschen Faschismus*, Munich, 1979.

10 Theweleit, *Männerphantasien*, op. cit.; Merkl, *Political Violence*, op. cit.

11 Detlev Peukert, 'Arbeitslager und Jugend-KZ: Die "Behandlung Gemeinschaftsfremder" im Dritten Reich', in Peukert and Reulecke, op. cit., pp. 413–33.

12 Quoted in id., *Edelweißpiraten*, op. cit., pp. 137–45. The German public was given some information about Moringen, and its division into 'blocks' ranging from 'Persistent Failures' to the 'Educable', by a police colonel from the headquarters of the Reich Security Service, Paul Werner, writing in the semi-official publication *Zum neuen Jugendstrafrecht*: 'Die Einweisung in die polizeilichen Jugendschutzlager', Berlin, 1944, pp. 95–106.

12 Racialism as social policy, pages 208–235

1 Gisela Bock, 'Frauen und ihre Arbeit im Nationalsozialismus', in *Frauen in der Geschichte*, ed. Annette Kuhn and Gerhard Schneider, Düsseldorf, 1979, pp. 113–49. Bock also gives the subsequent quotations and introduces the concept of 'social racialism'. Cf. also id., '"Zum Wohle des Volkskörpers . . ." Abtreibung und Sterilisation im Nationalsozialismus', *Journal für Geschichte*, vol. 2 (1980), no. 6, pp. 58–65. In addition, see Bock's essential work, *Zwangssterilisation im Nationalsozialismus. Studien zur Frauen- und Rassenpolitik*, Opladen 1985. See also Jeremy Noakes, 'Nazism and Eugenics: The Background to the Nazi Sterilization Law of 14 July 1933', in R. J. Bullen, H. Pogge von Strandmann and A. Polonsky (eds.), *Ideas into Politics. Aspects of European History 1880–1950*, London, 1984, pp. 75–94.

2 Wolfgang Scheffler, *Judenverfolgung im Dritten Reich*, Berlin, 1964; Raul Hilberg, *The Destruction of the European Jews*, Chicago, 1961; Gerhard Schoenberner, *Der gelbe Stern. Die Judenverfolgung in Europa 1933–1945*, Munich, 1978; Gerald Reitlinger, *The Final Solution: The Attempt to Exterminate the Jews of Europe*, New York, 1961. From the wealth of memoirs, see especially: Joel König, *David*, Frankfurt, 1980; Inge Deutschkron, *Ich trug den gelben Stern*, Cologne, 1978; Dieter Bednarz and Michael Lüders (eds.), *Blick zurück ohne Haß. Juden aus Israel erinnern sich an Deutschland*, Cologne, 1981.

3 Tilman Zülch (ed.) *In Auschwitz vergast, bis heute verfolgt. Zur Situation der Roma (Zigeuner) in Deutschland und Europa*, Reinbek, 1979; Donald Kenrick and Grattan Puxon, *Sinti und Roma – die Vernichtung eines Volkes im NS-Staat*, Göttingen, 1981.

4 Robert Ritter, 'Die Artung jugendlicher Rechtsbrecher', in *Zum neuen Jugendstrafrecht*, Berlin 1944, pp. 33–60; id., *Ein Menschenschlag. Erbärztliche und erbgeschichtliche Untersuchung über die – durch zehn Geschlechterfolgen erforschten – Nachkommen von 'Vagabunden, Jaunern und Räubern'*, Leipzig, 1937; cf. also Martin Riedl, 'Studie über Verbrecherstämmlinge, Spätkriminelle und Frühkriminelle und deren sozialprognostische und rassehygienische Bedeutung', *Archiv für Kriminologie*, vol. 93 (1933), pp. 7–13, 125–35, 238–57.

5 Quoted in Kenrick and Puxon, op. cit., p. 57.

6 Quoted in Bernhard Streck, 'Die "Bekämpfung des Zigeunerwesens"', in Zülch, op. cit., p. 76.

7 My discussion follows Wolfgang Ayass, *'Es darf in Deutschland keine Landstreicher mehr geben'. Die Verfolgung von Bettlern und Vagabunden im Faschismus*, diploma thesis, Fachbereich Sozialwesen, Gesamthochschule Kassel, December 1980 (MS).

8 Hermann Althaus, *Nationalsozialistische Volkswohlfahrt*, 4th edn., Berlin, 1939, p. 38; quoted in Ayass, op. cit., p. 53.

9 Wuermling, 'Wandererfürsorge', *Der Gemeindetag*, 1934, no. 3, p. 75; quoted in Ayass, op. cit., p. 34. Wuermling was Federal Minister for Family and Youth Affairs, 1953–62. Cf. the intensive publicity campaign for a 'travellers' law' by Wilhelm Polligkeit, until 1935 chairman of the German Association for Public and Private Welfare.

10 Hilde Eisenhardt, 'Die brachliegende Arbeitskraft der Wanderer: Schwierigkeiten und Möglichkeiten ihrer Verwertung', in *Der nichtseßhafte Mensch. Ein Beitrag zur Neugestaltung der Raum- und Menschenordnung im Großdeutschen Reich*, published by the Bayerischer Landesverband für Wandererdienst, Munich, 1938, pp. 315–70, especially p. 359; quoted in Ayass, op. cit., p. 61.

11 Address by Greifelt, January 1939, Nuremberg Documents NO-5591; quoted in H. Buchheim, 'Die Aktion "Arbeitsscheu Reich"', *Gutachten des*

Instituts für Zeitgeschichte, vol. 2, Stuttgart, 1966, pp. 194f.; cf. Ayass, op. cit., p. 85.

12 Quoted in: Detlev Peukert, 'Arbeitslager und Jugend-KZ. Die "Behandlung Gemeinschaftsfremder" im Dritten Reich', in Peukert and Reulecke, op. cit., pp. 413–34, especially p. 427. See also: Wolfgang Franz Werner, 'Die Arbeitserziehungslager als Mittel nationalsozialistischer "Sozialpolitik" gegen deutsche Arbeiter', in Dlugoborski, op. cit., pp. 138–50; Falk Pingel, 'Die Konzentrationslagerhäftlinge im nationalsozialistischen Arbeitseinsatz', in ibid., pp. 151–63; Stefan Karner, 'Arbeitsvertragsbrüche als Verletzung der Arbeitspflicht im "Dritten Reich"', *Archiv für Sozialgeschichte*, vol. XXI (1981), pp. 269–328.

13 Ulrich Herbert, *Fremdarbeiter*, op. cit.

14 Quoted in Zülch, op. cit., pp. 189–91.

15 See also Chapter 11, above.

16 For this and the subsequent discussion, see: Gisela Bock 'Frauen', op. cit.

17 Quoted in ibid., p.126.

18 For this and the subsequent discussion, see: Dirk Blasius, *Der verwaltete Wahnsinn. Eine Sozialgeschichte des Irrenhauses*, Frankfurt, 1980, pp. 155–72; Gerhard Baader and Ulrich Schultz (eds.), *Medizin und Nationalsozialismus*, Berlin, 1980; Lothar Gruchmann, '"Euthanasie" und Justiz im "Dritten Reich"', *Vierteljahreshefte für Zeitgeschichte*, 20 (1972), pp. 235–79; Walter Wuttke-Groneberg, *Medizin im Nationalsozialismus*, Tübingen, 1980.

19 Quoted in Blasius, op. cit., p. 163; the subsequent quotation, ibid.

20 Ibid., pp. 165f.

21 Rüdiger Lautmann, '"Hauptdevise: bloß nicht anecken". Das Leben homosexueller Männer unter dem Nationalsozialismus', in Beck *et al*, *Terror und Hoffnung*, op. cit., pp. 366–90; Hans-Georg Stümke and Rudi Finkler, *Rosa Winkel, Rosa Listen. Homosexuelle und 'Gesundes Volksempfinden' von Auschwitz bis heute*, Reinbek, 1981.

22 Peukert, 'Arbeitslager', op. cit.; the subsequent quotation ibid., p. 416.

23 Detlev J. K. Peukert, *Grenzen der Sozialdisziplinierung. Aufstieg und Krise der deutschen Jugendfürsonge von 1878 bis 1932*, Cologne, 1986.

24 Hans-Günter Zmarzlik, 'Der Sozialdarwinismus in Deutschland', *Vierteljahreshefte für Zeitgeschichte*, 11 (1963), pp. 246–73; Gerhard Baader, 'Zur Ideologie des Sozialdarwinismus', in Baader and Schultz, op. cit., pp. 39–54; see also other contributions to that volume. Cf. also: Till Bastian, *Von der Eugenik zur Euthanasie*, Bad Wörishofen, 1981; Michael Billig, *Psychology, Racism and Fascism*, Birmingham, 1979; George L. Mosse, *Toward the Final Solution: A History of European Racism*, London, 1979; Noakes, 'Eugenics', op. cit.

25 Quoted in Billig, op. cit., p. 13. See also: Daniel Gasman, *The Scientific Origins of National Socialism: Social Darwinism in Ernst Haeckel and the German Monist League,* London/New York, 1971.

26 M. Eyrich, 'Fürsorgezöglinge, erbbiologisch gesehen', *Zeitschrift für Kinderforschung,* vol. 47 (1938), pp. 250–61; more generally see Peukert, *Grenzen,* op. cit.

27 In recent times the American researcher Arthur Jensen has attempted to prove the genetic intellectual inferiority of blacks by using correlations of intelligence-test data with the 'race' (black or white) of the candidates tested. See Billig, op. cit.; see also Brian Evans and Bernard Waites, *IQ and Mental Testing: An Unnatural Science and its Social History,* London, 1981.

28 Hans Mommsen, 'Die Geschichte des Chemnitzer Kanzleigehilfen K.B.', in Peukert and Reulecke, op. cit., pp. 337–66.

29 *Die Zeit,* no. 6, 5th February 1982.

30 Ernst Klee, 'Opfer oder Täter? Ein Medizinaldirektor und das "Zigeunerblut"', *Die Zeit,* no. 4, 22nd January 1982.

31 Quoted in *Der Spiegel,* vol. 35, no. 3, 12th January 1981.

13 The atomisation of everyday life, pages 236–242
1 Ulrich Herbert has pointed out to me, in the context of the Essen project 'Lebensgeschichte und Sozialkultur im Ruhrgebiet 1930–1960', that interviews show how powerfully people's memories are structured according to alternations between 'normal' and non-normal times. In these interviews the years between the mid-1930s and the irruption of war into everyday life – the latter date varying from individual to individual (1939–c. 1941) – are seen as 'normal times'. See Ulrich Herbert, 'Good Times, Bad Times', in *History Today,* vol. xxxvi, February 1986, pp. 42–8.

2 A contemporary collection of dreams of Germans from the 1930s, with retrospective commentary, is: Charlotte Beradt, *Das Dritte Reich des Traums,* Frankfurt, 1981: subsequent quotations, ibid., pp. 7, 19, 25, 37, 41, 5, 42. For a penetrating interpretation of the material, see the afterword by Reinhard Kosellek, ibid., pp. 117–32. Cf. also: Mario Erdheim, 'Die tyrannische Instanz im Innern. Wie totalitäre Herrschaft die Psyche beschädigt', *Journal für Geschichte,* vol. 4 (1982), no. 2, pp. 16–21.

3 See Peter Hüttenberger, 'Heimtückefälle vor dem Sondergericht München 1933–1939', in *Bayern in der NS-Zeit,* op. cit., vol. 4, pp. 435–525; Martin Broszat, 'Politische Denunziationen in der NS-Zeit', *Archivarische Zeitschrift,* 1977, pp. 221ff.

4 Reinhard Mann, 'Politische Penetration und gesellschaftliche Reaktion – Anzeigen zur Gestapo im nationalsozialistischen Deutschland', in *Soziologische Analysen beim 19. Deutschen Soziologentag,* ed. Rainer Mackensen and Felizitas Sagebiel, Technische Universität, Berlin, 1979, pp. 965–85.

5 Dieter Rebentisch, 'Die "politische Beurteilung" als Herrschaftsinstrument der NSDAP', in Peukert and Reulecke, op. cit., pp. 107–25.

6 *Deutschland-Berichte der SOPADE*, op. cit., vol. 2, pp. 1375f.

7 Quoted in Peukert, *Die KPD im Widerstand*, op. cit., p. 435.

8 Lutz Niethammer, 'Rekonstruktion und Desintegration: Zum Verständnis der deutschen Arbeiterbewegung zwischen Krieg und Kaltem Krieg', in *Politische Weichenstellungen im Nachkriegsdeutschland 1945–1953*, ed. Heinrich August Winkler, *Geschichte und Gesellschaft*, Sonderheft 5, Göttingen, 1979, pp. 26–43.

9 Hans-Peter Schwarz, *Die Ära Adenauer 1949–1957. Geschichte der Bundesrepublik Deutschland*, vol. 2, Stuttgart/Wiesbaden, 1981, especially pp. 375–452.

10 Helmut Schelsky, *Die skeptische Generation. Eine Soziologie der deutschen Jugend*, Düsseldorf/Cologne, 1957; id., *Wandlungen der deutschen Familie der Gegenwart*, Stuttgart, 1955; Ralf Dahrendorf, *Society and Democracy in Germany*, op. cit.

Suggestions for further reading

WILLIAM SHERIDAN ALLEN, *The Nazi Seizure of Power. The Experience of a Single German Town*, revised edition, London, 1984.

PIERRE AYCOBERRY, *The Nazi Question*, London, 1983.

RICHARD BESSEL and E. J. FEUCHTWANGER (eds.), *Social Change and Political Development in Weimar Germany*, London, 1981.

RICHARD BESSEL, *Political Violence and the Rise of Nazism*, New Haven and London, 1984.

RENATE BRIDENTHAL et al. (eds.), *When Biology Became Destiny: Women in Weimar and Nazi Germany*, New York, 1984.

KARL DIETRICH BRACHER, *The German Dictatorship. The Origins, Structure and Effects of National Socialism*, Harmondsworth, 1973.

MARTIN BROSZAT, *The Hitler State. The Foundation and Development of the Internal Structure of the Third Reich*, London, 1981.

WILLIAM CARR, *Arms, Autarky and Aggression. A Study in German Foreign Policy*, London, 1973.

WILLIAM CARR, *Hitler. A Study in Personality and Politics*, London, 1978.

THOMAS CHILDERS, *The Nazi Voter. The Social Foundations of Fascism in Germany, 1919–1933*, Chapel Hill and London, 1983.

RALF DAHRENDORF, *Society and Democracy in Germany*, New York, 1967.

WILHELM DEIST, *The Wehrmacht and German Rearmament*, London, 1982.

GEOFF ELEY, 'What Produces Fascism: Preindustrial Traditions or a Crisis of the Capitalist State', in *Politics and Society*, vol. xii (1983), pp. 53–82.

J. E. FARQUHARSON, *The Plough and the Swastika. The NSDAP and Agriculture in Germany 1928–45*, London and Beverly Hills, 1976.

RICHARD GRUNBERGER, *A Social History of the Third Reich*, Harmondsworth, 1974.

JOHN HIDEN and JOHN FARQUHARSON, *Explaining Hitler's Germany. Historians and the Third Reich*, London, 1983.

KLAUS HILDEBRAND, *The Third Reich*, London, 1984.

GERHARD HIRSCHFELD and LOTHAR KETTENACKER (eds.), *Der 'Führerstaat':
Mythos und Realität*, Stuttgart, 1981 (important articles in English).

MICHAEL KATER, *The Nazi Party. A Social Profile of Members and Leaders,
1919–1945*, Oxford, 1983.

IAN KERSHAW, 'The Persecution of the Jews and German Popular Opinion
in the Third Reich', in *Leo Baeck Year Book*, vol. xxvi (1981).

IAN KERSHAW, *Popular Opinion and Political Dissent in the Third Reich.
Bavaria 1933–1945*, Oxford, 1983.

IAN KERSHAW, *The Nazi Dictatorship. Problems and Perspectives of
Interpretation*, London, 1985.

H. W. KOCH (ed.), *Aspects of the Third Reich*, London, 1985.

HELMUT KRAUSNICH et al., *Anatomy of the SS State*, London, 1968.

WALTER LAQUEUR (ed.), *Fascism. A Reader's Guide*, Harmondsworth, 1979.

TIM MASON, 'Women in Germany, 1925–1940: Family, Welfare and Work',
in *History Workshop Journal*, nos. 1 and 2, 1976.

TIM MASON, 'The Worker's Opposition in Nazi Germany', in *History
Workshop Journal*, no. 11, 1981.

ERICH MATTHIAS and ANTHONY NICHOLLS (eds.), *German Democracy and the
Triumph of Hitler*, London, 1971.

ALLAN MERSON, *Communist Resistance in Nazi Germany*, London, 1985.

FRANZ NEUMANN, *Behemoth. The Structure and Practice of National
Socialism 1933–1944*, New York, 1944.

JEREMY NOAKES (ed.), *Government, Party and People in Nazi Germany*,
Exeter, 1980.

JEREMY NOAKES and GEOFFREY PRIDHAM (eds.), *Nazism, 1919–1945. A
Documentary Reader*, Exeter, 1984.

R. J. OVERY, *The Nazi Economic Recovery 1932–1938*, London, 1982.

KARL A. SCHLEUNES, *The Twisted Road to Auschwitz. Nazi Policy towards
German Jews 1933–1939*, Chicago, 1970.

DAVID SCHOENBAUM, *Hitler's Social Revolution*, Garden City, N.Y., 1966.

PETER D. STACHURA, 'Who were the Nazis? A Socio-Political Analysis of the
National Socialist *Machtübernahme*', in *European Studies Review*, vol. xi,
1981.

PETER D. STACHURA (ed.), *The Shaping of the Nazi State*, London, 1978.

PETER D. STACHURA (ed.), *The Nazi Machtergreifung*, London, 1983.

MARLIS STEINERT, *Hitler's War and the Germans*, Athens, Ohio, 1977.

JILL STEPHENSON, *Women in Nazi Germany*, London, 1975.

HENRY A. TURNER (ed.), *Nazism and the Third Reich*, New York, 1972, pp.
175–200.

HENRY A. TURNER, *German Big Business and the Rise of Hitler*, New York
and Oxford, 1985.

Index